DIFFICULT HERITAGE

How do a city and a nation deal with a legacy of perpetrating atrocity? How are contemporary identities negotiated and shaped in the face of concrete reminders of a past that most wish they did not have?

Difficult Heritage focuses on the case of Nuremberg – a city whose name is indelibly linked with Nazism – to explore these questions and their implications. Using original archival, interview and ethnographic sources, it provides not only fascinating new material and perspectives, but also more general innovative theorizing of the relationship between heritage, identity and material culture.

The book looks at how Nuremberg has dealt with its Nazi past post-1945. It focuses especially, but not exclusively, on the city's architectural heritage, in particular, the former Nazi party rally grounds, on which the Nuremberg rallies were staged. The book draws on original sources, such as city council debates and interviews, to chart a lively picture of debate, action and inaction in relation to this site and significant others, in Nuremberg and elsewhere. In doing so, *Difficult Heritage* seeks to highlight changes over time in the ways in which the Nazi past has been dealt with in Germany, and the underlying cultural assumptions, motivations and sources of friction involved.

Whilst referencing wider debates and giving examples of what was happening elsewhere in Germany and beyond, *Difficult Heritage* provides a rich in-depth account of this most fascinating of cases. It also engages in comparative reflection on developments underway elsewhere in order to contextualize what was happening in Nuremberg and to show similarities to and differences from the ways in which other 'difficult heritages' have been dealt with elsewhere. By doing so, the author offers an informed perspective on ways of dealing with difficult heritage, today and in the future, discussing innovative museological, educational and artistic practice.

Sharon Macdonald is Professor of Social Anthropology at the University of Manchester. She has held Alexander von Humboldt Fellowships at the University Erlangen-Nürnberg and the Humboldt University, Berlin. Her publications include *The Politics of Display* (ed. 1998, Routledge).

DIFFICULT HERITAGE

Negotiating the Nazi Past in
Nuremberg and Beyond

Sharon Macdonald

Routledge
Taylor & Francis Group

LONDON AND NEW YORK

For my mother

Because not all heritage is difficult

First published 2009
by Routledge
2 Park Square, Milton Park, Abingdon, Oxon OX14 4RN

Simultaneously published in the USA and Canada
by Routledge
270 Madison Ave, New York, NY 10016

Routledge is an imprint of the Taylor & Francis Group, an informa business

© 2009 Sharon Macdonald

Typeset in Garamond by
HWA Text and Data Management, London
Printed and bound in Great Britain by
TJ International, Padstow, Cornwall

British Library Cataloguing in Publication Data
A catalogue record for this book is available from the British Library

Library of Congress Cataloging-in-Publication Data
Macdonald, Sharon.
Difficult heritage : negotiating the Nazi past in Nuremberg and beyond / Sharon Macdonald.
p. cm.
Includes bibliographical references and index.
1. Postwar reconstruction – Germany – Nuremberg.
2. Nuremberg (Germany) – Buildings, structures, etc. 3. National socialism – Psychological aspects. 4. Collective memory – Germany – Nuremberg.
5. Cultural property – Germany – Nuremberg. 6. Nuremberg (Germany) – History – 20th century. I. Title.
DD901.N92M34 2008
943'.324086 – dc22   2008018739

ISBN10: 0–415–41991–3 (hbk)
ISBN10: 0–415–41992–1 (pbk)
ISBN10: 0–203–88866–9 (ebk)

ISBN13: 978–0–415–41991–8 (hbk)
ISBN13: 978–0–415–41992–5 (pbk)
ISBN13: 978–0–203–88866–7 (ebk)

CONTENTS

ACKNOWLEDGEMENTS

I am grateful to the Alexander von Humboldt Foundation and the Arts and Humanities Research Council for financial support for this research; and to colleagues in Sociological Studies at the University of Sheffield and Social Anthropology at the University of Manchester for the research leave that made the work possible and for discussion that enriched it. In Germany, I was fortunate to be hosted as a guest researcher at the Institut für Soziologie at the Friedrich Alexander University of Erlangen-Nürnberg and the Institut für Europäische Ethnologie at the Humboldt University, Berlin, and I thank staff and students in these institutes for references, reminiscences, insights and companionship. Professor Elisabeth Beck-Gernsheim and Professor Wolfgang Kashuba deserve particular thanks for completing the necessary bureaucratic requirements to make the visits possible, as well as for making them so enjoyable and intellectually rewarding.

In Nuremberg I have received extensive assistance, as evident in the pages that follow; and I thank all of those who gave me time for interviews, many of whom are named in the pages that follow. I offer particular thanks to staff at Nuremberg City Archive, the archive of the *Nürnberger Nachrichten* (especially Roland Schulik), Geschichte für Alle, the City Council, including the Tourism service (especially Michael Weber), the Nuremberg Museums' Service (especially Franz Sonnenberger), and especially the Documentation Centre of the former Nazi Party Rally Grounds. At the latter, Martina Christmeier and especially Hans Christian Täubrich and Eckart Dietzfelbinger provided invaluable assistance and extensive materials. Hermann Glaser's insight and experience were inspirational; and Siegfried Zelnhefer also shared extensive knowledge. Eckart Dietzfelbinger, Hermann Glaser, Franz Sonnenberger and Michael Weber were also kind enough to read parts of the manuscript and to offer comments that have helped to improve it. Formal thanks are due to the poet Fitzgerald Kusz for permission to quote his poem *Bewältigung*; as well as more informal thanks for his friendly discussion.

Running alongside this research, I participated in a research project on European Historical Consciousness at the Kulturwissenschaftliches Institut, Essen, run by Professor Jörn Rüsen. This fed into my understanding of German historical culture and consciousness and I thank Professor Rüsen for inviting me to participate as well as for his support of my research, and for illuminating discussions with him and other members of the project. As this research has been underway, I have published a number of papers on it, listed in the bibliography; and I thank the various editors and (often anonymous) reviewers who pushed me to improve my work. I have also profited from opportunities to present parts of the ongoing research at the universities of Cardiff, Durham, Edinburgh, Erlangen-Nürnberg, Frankfurt, Hull, the Humboldt University in Berlin, Lancaster, Melbourne, Oxford, Sheffield, Stirling, the Technical University of Lisbon, and University College London; at the European Association of Social Anthropology conference in Cracow, at the Goethe Institute, London, at a conference organised by the Centre for Tourism and Cultural Change, Sheffield, at the Piet Zwart Institute, Rotterdam, at the German Historical Museum and at the International Committee on Museums conference in Vienna. I am grateful to the organisers of these events, as well as to the many people who left me with more questions to try to answer and helpful suggestions to follow up. In addition, I have benefited from many friends and colleagues who have talked and sometimes walked difficult heritage with me. Among all of these various interlocutors, I offer particular thanks to the following: Simone Abram, Marta Anico, Stefan Beck, Rosmarie Beier, Tony Bennett, Peter Blundell-Jones, Mary Bouquet, Jeanette Edwards, Gordon Fyfe, Gottfried Gabriel, Michaela Giebelhausen, Neil Gregor, Nicky Gregson, Chris Healy, Michael Herzfeld, Richard Jenkins, Gunther Kress, Fiona MacLean, Morgan Meyer, Danny Miller, Clive Norris, Elsa Peralta, Nuno Porto, Regina Römhild, Alexander Schmidt, John Urry, Gisela Welz, members of the Erlangen Runde; and students at the universities of Sheffield, Manchester, the Humboldt University in Berlin and, especially, at the Sociology Institute in Erlangen-Nürnberg. I also thank Juliane Günther and Anita Littmann for research assistance. At Routledge, Matt Gibbons and Lalle Pursglove have provided the right mix of support, patience and pressure.

Mike, Tara, Thomas and Harriet Beaney have lived Nuremberg, Germany and difficult heritages with me over these years. Thomas helped me with some technical tasks as well as reading and commenting on parts of the manuscript. Only Mike knows just how difficult I have found completing this book. I thank him for helping me to do so, for reading the whole manuscript with his philosopher's attention to detail and argument, and for his reminders of the pleasures of the present and promise of the future.

Picture credits

Figure 1.3: © Anselm Kiefer. The Eli and Edythe L. Broad Collection, Los Angeles (photograph: Douglas M. Parker Studio, Los Angeles).

Figure 3.1 courtesy of Robert Capa/Magnum Photos.

Figure: 3.4 courtesy of Congress und Tourismus-Zentrale Nürnberg.

Figures 2.1, 2.5, 2.6, 2.7, 2.8, 2.10, 3.3, 3.7 courtesy of Nuremberg City Archive.

Figure 5.4. courtesy of Nuremberg Museums Service.

Figures 2.3 (photographer: Herbert Voll), 3.2 (photographer: Thema), 3.5 (photographer: Kurt Schmidtpeter), 3.6 (photographer: Roland Fengler), 3.8 (photographer: Hans Kammler), 3.9 (photographer: Hans Kammler), 4.1 (upper photograph, photographer: Peter Vrbata), 4.2 (photographer Günther Distler), 4.3, 8.1 (photographer Hagen Gerullis) courtesy of the Picture Archive of the *Nürnberger Nachrichten*.

Figures 1.1, 1.2, 2.2, 2.4, 2.9, 2.11, 4.1 (lower photograph), 4.4, 5.1, 5.2, 5.3, 6.1, 6.2, 6.3, 6.4, 7.1, 7.2, 7.3 are photographs by Sharon Macdonald.

1

INTRODUCTION

During the second half of the twentieth century and into the twenty-first, visible markers of the past – plaques, information boards, museums, monuments – have come to populate more and more land- and cityscapes. History has been gathered up and presented as heritage – as meaningful pasts that should be remembered; and more and more buildings and other sites have been called on to act as witnesses of the past. Many kinds of groups have sought to ensure that they are publicly recognised through identifying and displaying 'their' heritage. At the same time, museums and heritage sites have become key components of 'place-marketing' and 'image-management'; and cultural tourism has massively expanded, often bringing visitors from across the world to places that can claim a heritage worth seeing.

This book explores a particular dimension of this public concern with the past. It looks at what I call 'difficult heritage' – that is, a past that is recognised as meaningful in the present but that is also contested and awkward for public reconciliation with a positive, self-affirming contemporary identity. 'Difficult heritage' may also be troublesome because it threatens to break through into the present in disruptive ways, opening up social divisions, perhaps by playing into imagined, even nightmarish, futures. By looking at heritage that is unsettling and awkward, rather than at that which can be celebrated or at least comfortably acknowledged as part of a nation's or city's valued history, my aim is to throw into relief some of the dilemmas about its public representation and reception. Doing so highlights and unsettles cultural assumptions about and entanglements between identity and memory, and past, present and future. It also raises questions about practices of selection, preservation, cultural comparison and witnessing – practices which are at least partly shared by anthropologists and other researchers of culture and social life.

At its core, this book tells a story about one particular especially difficult heritage.[1] This is the struggle with Nazi heritage – especially remaining architectural heritage – in the city of Nuremberg, Germany; a city which has, perhaps more than any other, found its name linked to the perpetration of the appalling and iconic atrocity of modernity – the Holocaust. To give an account of how Nuremberg has negotiated its difficult heritage, and how visitors to the city experience it today, I draw on a combination of historical and anthropological perspectives in order to explore changes over time as well as to try to see how different players, practices and knowledges – local and from further afield – interact, and are brought into being, to shape the ways

1

in which the city's past is variously approached and ignored. By telling this detailed and sometimes untidy story, my intention is also to provide a located position from which to think further about – and to some extent complicate – accounts of how Germany has faced its Nazi past and what this might mean to people today. More generally still, it is to provide some coordinates for understanding difficult heritage – wherever it is found – and its implications.

Difficult heritage

Wars, conflict, triumph over foreigners, the plunder of riches from overseas – these are the stuff of most national histories. Yet whether they are perceived as troubling for contemporary identity may vary considerably; and what was once seen as a sign of a country's achievement may later come to be understood as a reason for regret. Colonialism, for example, once a source of great national pride for colonising countries has increasingly – though not unequivocally – come to be regarded as a more problematic and even shameful heritage; and many explicit depictions of colonial might now languish in museum basements. Wartime episodes that were regarded as military triumphs can also become sources of embarrassment. In Japan, for instance, the 1937 Rape of Nanking, in which the Japanese Imperial Army brutally slaughtered or tortured tens of thousands of Chinese, remains a national achievement for some, and is repeated as such in school textbooks, but has become a mortifying memory for many other Japanese who know about it.[2] The allied bombing of Japanese cities during World War II, and of German cities, especially Dresden, have likewise become increasingly controversial over the years, and the subject of continued memorial and museological dispute.[3]

While what counts as 'difficult heritage' – or indeed worthy heritage – may change, however, the idea that places should seek to inscribe what is significant in their histories, and especially their past achievements, on the cityscape is longstanding and widespread. In a pattern consolidated by European nation-making, identifying a distinctive and preferably long history, and substantiating it through material culture, has become the dominant mode of performing identity-legitimacy. 'Having a heritage' – that is, a body of selected history and its material traces – is, in other words, an integral part of 'having an identity', and it affirms the right to exist in the present and continue into the future. This model of identity as rooted in the past, as distinctively individuated, and as expressed through 'evidence', especially material culture, is mobilised not only by nations but by minorities, cities or other localities.[4] Because of the selective and predominantly identity-affirmative nature of heritage-making, it typically focuses on triumphs and achievements, or sacrifices involved in the struggle for realisation and recognition. Events and material remains which do not fit into such narratives are, thus, likely to be publicly ignored or removed from public space, as have numerous monuments erected by socialist regimes or former colonisers. Or, as Ian Buruma writes of the lack of information about Nanking in Japanese school history texts, they may be 'officially killed by silence'.[5] More dramatically, silencing may involve the physical destruction of material heritage, such as the destruction of mosques as part of 'ethnic cleansing' and the obliteration of the Oriental Institute

2

and Bosnian National Library in Sarajevo – both home to vast archival evidence of Bosnian history – by Serb extremists during the Bosnian War.[6]

Yet ignoring, silencing or destroying are not always options – and the awkward past may break through in some form. This may be because the events are too recent and their effects still being felt, though recency is not a guarantee of public acknowledgment, as we will see below. It may be because some groups or individuals – 'memorial entrepreneurs' – try to propel public remembrance, perhaps of events of which they were victims or which they feel morally driven to commemorate, perhaps because they fear that forgetting risks atrocity being repeated in the future.[7] In some cases, groups or individuals outside the locality, and even beyond the nation, demand that past perpetrations are publicly recalled and exposed. In others, material remains of past events or regimes may defy easy obliteration and thus act as mnemonic intrusions. Archaeological finds or historical scholarship may embarrass accepted narratives. Or public recognition may be prompted by the fact that, while a troubling history may be uncomfortable, it is also of heritage-interest, attracting tourists and bringing revenue. In all such cases – which in reality are likely to be combinations of motives and actors – heritage-management is fraught with multiple dilemmas.

In the field of heritage and tourism management, Tunbridge and Ashworth have devised the term 'dissonant heritage' to express what they see as the inherently contested nature of heritage – stemming from the fact that heritage always 'belongs to someone and logically, therefore, not to someone else'[8] – though which may be relatively 'active or latent'. They chart numerous kinds of dissonance, including where tourist authorities promote a range of differing images of a place and what they call 'the heritage of atrocity',[9] in which, they argue, 'dissonance' may provoke intense emotions and be bound up with memories that have 'profound long-term effects upon [a people's] self-conscious identity'.[10]

Like others, Tunbridge and Ashworth distinguish between atrocity heritage that is primarily concerned with victims – for example, Nazi concentration camps or Khmer Rouge torture buildings – and that which is principally of perpetration.[11] In many cases, of course, it is hard to maintain a clear distinction between sites of victims' suffering and those of perpetration – concentration camps and torture chambers were clearly both. Nevertheless, there are places – such as, say, the Wannsee villa in Berlin or Hitler's complex of buildings on the Obersalzburg in Bavaria – which are part of the apparatus of perpetration but not locations in which suffering was directly inflicted. These might be seen as sites of 'perpetration at a distance', to adapt some language from actor network theory.[12] While all sites of atrocity raise difficulties of public presentation – including the question of how graphically suffering is depicted – there are some specific dilemmas raised by sites of perpetration at a distance. In particular, precisely because heritage-presentation and museumification are typically regarded as markers of worthwhile history – of heritage that deserves admiration or commemoration – their preservation and public display might be interpreted as conferring legitimacy of a sort.[13] This is part of a 'heritage effect' – a sensibility grounded in particular visual and embodied practices prompted by certain kinds of spaces and modes of display.[14] Moreover, there is also the risk that such sites might become pilgrimage destinations for perpetrator admirers. This argument surfaced in the debates over the legitimacy of later public uses of the sites just mentioned, both of which incorporate educational displays (though Hitler's Eagle's Nest on the Obersalzburg also, controversially, opened as a luxury hotel in 2005). In other instances, as with the site of Hitler's bunker in Berlin, this argument has been used to prevent any kind of public marking.[15]

In this book, my aim is neither to try to classify different types of heritage, nor to present a general survey, as do Tunbridge and Ashworth, useful though these may be. 'Difficult heritage', as I use it here, is more tightly specified than their notion of 'dissonance' insofar as it threatens to trouble collective identities and open up social differences. But beyond that, my approach here is to explore 'difficult heritage' as a historical and ethnographic phenomenon – and as a particular kind of 'assemblage' – rather than to establish it as an analytical category.[16] This means looking at how heritage is assembled both discursively and materially, at the various players involved, at what they may experience as awkward and problematic, and at the ways in which they negotiate this. My interest here includes the kinds of assumptions that are made about the nature of heritage, identity and temporality, the terms in which debates about 'difficult heritage' are conducted, what is ignored or overlooked, and how agency is accorded – all of which can be seen as constituents of what is sometimes called 'historical consciousness' (which is a recognised field of historiography within Germany).[17] As Jeffrey Olick has noted, the idea of 'historical consciousness' usefully avoids reifying a sometimes spurious distinction between 'history' and 'memory';[18] and it directs attention not just to the *content* of history or memory but also to questions of the media and patterns through which these are structured, as well as where lines between, say, history and memory might be drawn in particular contexts.

In some historical consciousness theorising, especially in the German tradition, there is an emphasis upon identifying universal 'orientations', in, for example, how people understand the relationship between past, present and future. Rather than revealing universally shared patterns, my own more modest aim is to highlight elements of a repertoire of possible approaches to difficult heritage and to chart some of their implications. That is, I seek to identify a non-exhaustive range of negotiating frames and tactics through which some kinds of past are evoked and engaged within public culture. Unlike the universalist approach to historical consciousness, mine here is not concerned with presumed shared mental patterns but addresses the social and cultural situations and frames in which heritage – and difficult heritage – is assembled and negotiated. These situations and frames are simultaneously local and beyond local. That is, they involve specific local conditions and actors but these never act in a vacuum, even when they are actively producing 'locality'. Instead, as we see below, local actions are frequently negotiated through comparisons with other places, through concepts and ideas produced elsewhere and that may even have global circulation, and through the sense of being judged by others. They are also negotiated in relation to legislation, political structures and economic considerations which are rarely exclusively local.

As I am interested in heritage making and historical consciousness as social and cultural practices, I am concerned to look not just at 'history products' (e.g. a heritage site) but at the practical activities and sometimes rather banal events involved in their production and consumption. I am also concerned with the sometimes messy – and sometimes strikingly consistent, rhythmic and predictable – course of negotiations, and the social alignments and identifications that such negotiations may produce. For these reasons, my focus is on a specific, in-depth case – that of Nuremberg – and my hope is that this can enable me to illuminate better some of the assumptions, oversights, silences and complexities of negotiating difficult heritage than might a wider survey.

As the section below briefly indicates, however, struggles with difficult heritage are extremely widespread, and increasingly likely to result in public display. Moreover, as the Nuremberg study shows too, what goes on in any particular country or city is never culturally isolated – even if it may sometimes feel like it to those involved. Rather, the local is negotiated into being in relation – sometimes through cultural analogy, sometimes via shared concepts and practices, sometimes through the intervention of actors from outside, and sometimes through explicit opposition – to 'elsewhere', be that other cities nearby or other parts of the world.

Other struggles

In many countries the predominant state-supported memorial and museum culture pays little attention to difficult histories, preferring to ignore these and to tell more comfortable or self-affirming narratives. Even in recent years, for example, the destruction of Ottoman heritage in Serbia has paved the way for a nationalist representation of the past that ignores this period of history.[19] More widely, however, it is noticeable that since the 1990s in particular there have been increasing attempts to publicly address problematic heritage and 'difficult pasts'.[20] In many cases, this is in societies that have emerged from previously repressive regimes, where publicly recognising atrocities committed may signal difference from the former regime, as well as a commitment to political openness. Thus in Cambodia, for example, there has been a wave of activity – including building museums at sites of massacre – to mark, commemorate and inform about the atrocities suffered under the Khmer Rouge.[21] Similarly, in post-apartheid South Africa there is a massive ongoing movement to create new heritage sites and memorials and to alter, and sometimes dismantle, earlier ones that legitimated the apartheid regime. Opening up places such as Robben Island, the prison in which Nelson Mandela and others were held for so many years, creating an Apartheid Museum (opened in 2001) and the Slave Lodge, a museum of slavery (currently in preparation), are all part of public cultural strategy to keep alive the memory of the suffering that was endured en route to the new South Africa.[22]

Many former socialist countries have also swept away monuments and exhibitions of socialist periods and instead created museums that turn the spotlight onto the horrors of the recent past, as, for example, in the turning of the former secret police headquarters in Budapest into a museum,[23] or of the maximum-security labour camp, Perm-36, into the Gulag Museum in Russia.[24] While in much of South America, there has been little official commemoration of the victims of twentieth-century dictatorial regimes or civil war, this is showing signs of change. In Argentina, for example, there has been a long and continuing campaign by the mothers and grandmothers of the disappeared (those who were kidnapped and mostly killed by the dictatorial regime of 1976–83) who every Thursday meet in Buenos Aires' Plaza de Mayo to display pictures of their vanished relatives.[25] An initiative to create a lasting material commemoration, the Parque de la Memoria, on the site of a torture camp run by the military, was begun in 1996 and is ongoing. The first sculptural memorial erected there – Monument to the Victims of State Terrorism – has been judged by Andreas Huyssen to be 'persuasive and moving',[26] though the location of the park in the city's outskirts and the fact that it is not yet listed on tourist itineraries or most city information suggests that it may at the same time be being marginalised in public space.

Even the United States of America, which is often at the forefront of museological developments and which has opened up many, and often impressive, Holocaust museums, especially since the 1980s, has been much more nervous of directly addressing its own difficult history of slavery. In 2007 a National Museum of Slavery finally opened in Fredericksburg, Virginia, though this is private rather than federally funded initiative, and was reported to have had difficulty in attracting business sponsors willing to support this socially awkward topic.[27] A new National Museum of African History and Culture has also been approved as part of the Smithsonian complex, its broader scope perhaps making any content on slavery more palatable.[28] The failure to create a museum to slavery is all the more striking given the flourishing of museums to an atrocity that did not take place in the US – the Holocaust of Jews in Europe. While there are various factors involved here, including the political power of Jewish lobby groups in the US, it has been suggested that one reason for the emphasis on Holocaust may be that it helps to relativise the potentially more socially divisive history of slavery.[29]

Within Europe, colonial nations have only recently, if at all, begun any significant public addressing of the colonial past in their museums. In Belgium, for example, the Royal Museum of Central Africa has been revising its displays in recent years in order to address aspects of Belgium's colonial history of terror alongside the display of its plunder. This has, however, been judged fairly limited by Adam Hochschild, whose critical account of the Museum's silences was one impetus for the revision.[30] Likewise, in the Netherlands, where according to James Horton and Johanna Kardux,[31] 'the Netherlands' role in slaveholding and slave trading was so irreconcilable with their sense of national identity that it was long erased from public consciousness'. Museums such as Amsterdam's Tropenmuseum have increasingly come to include at least some appraisal of colonialism in their displays. In Britain, a British Empire and Commonwealth Museum opened in Bristol in 2002, which includes attention to slavery, with a dedicated gallery on the subject opened in 2007, as part of the two hundredth anniversary of the abolition of slavery, at which time an International Slavery Museum – the first museum dedicated to this subject – also opened in Liverpool.[32]

Giving public recognition to suffering endured by minorities within a country – especially where that suffering was inflicted by the majority or another minority – risks igniting social tensions. In the US, exhibitions such as The West as America (National Museum of American Art, Washington DC, 1991), which highlighted 'the displacement of native peoples [and] the suppression of their cultures',[33] have caused fury among self-labelled 'patriots'; and there have been threats against the holders of collections of items relating to slavery that might be included in a museum. Yet, not giving public recognition carries its own risks too – both internally and in the eyes of the outside world. Minorities' resentments may be fuelled by the lack of acknowledgment of wrongs perpetrated, something which has been recognised by the trend for governments to make public apologies. This began in the wake of World War II and has in many cases been bound up with claims for financial reparation but since the 1990s has become a more globally-widespread public performance.[34]

The motivations and implications of this move in many parts of the world to acknowledge and publicly display 'difficult heritage' are discussed later in this book. As the brief discussion here indicates, struggles with difficult heritage are widespread, approaches varied, and social, political and economic implications often considerable. Despite the variety of approaches and the fact that any heritage example is singular in the particular mix that informs its realisation and reworking, there are nevertheless many parallels and connections between even disparate parts of the world. While displaying difficult heritage may be prompted by activist groups within a particular nation-state or locality, they are likely to be acting in awareness of what is done elsewhere, and conduct their campaigns at least partially through concepts and practices – such as, the 'politics of recognition', 'commemoration of victims' and 'heritage' itself – that have widespread global currency, if not necessarily identical local interpretations.[35] More specifically, as Andreas Huyssen has pointed out, local struggles over the public materialisation of memory – as memorials or museums – are frequently performed with reference to debates about the Holocaust, which, he suggests, acts as 'a powerful prism through which we may look at other instances'.[36] Furthermore, not only are local actions refracted through concepts and debates from elsewhere, they are often undertaken in awareness of a potential international – and judgemental – gaze, whether that of tourists or politicians. In dealing with 'their heritage', then, governments and heritage managers of countries or cities enter into imagined or actual negotiations not only with their own populations but often also those of other governments, potential business partners and visitors. Equally, and perhaps increasingly, places may find themselves being interpreted and evaluated – not always as they might wish – in relation to how they present their pasts.

Grass on stone

It is early afternoon on a fine September day in 2003. A man in his early twenties is sitting on the Zeppelin Building just in front of the Hitler podium. He is writing in a notebook. I approach him tentatively, not wanting to disturb him from his concentrated activity, yet also intrigued as to what he might be writing there. When he looks puzzled by my question in German about whether I might speak to him, I try English. He is from Spain and although he apologises for his English, it is very good, though with an engagingly thoughtful hunting for the right word. A student, he is travelling alone through Germany and Austria and had wanted to come to Nuremberg because he had seen the Nazi rallies in film documentaries and had read much about the period. 'I wanted to see the place itself'. He was about to go up onto the Hitler podium but then 'I felt so sickened that I had to stop'. He is writing down his thoughts about this. We sit silently for some moments looking out across the former marching fields, now turned into football pitches, while he sorts some of those thoughts and finds words to express them to me. 'Imagine it', he says, gesturing across the field, 'full of all those people. And all that a madman can do, with just words.' The Nazi ideology makes him feel physically sick, he says, especially in a place like this. These buildings 'have hatred in the basement'.

But he is also surprised at the site. 'Why is so little information about it provided?' Pointing to the weeds flourishing in the cracks of the Zeppelin Building steps he asks rhetorically why the place is so neglected and replies that it must be 'because the Germans do not want to remember it': 'Grass growing is like forgetting'. Pointing to the football pitches he explains that he thinks that buildings can be put to new uses but that these football pitches 'are not really necessary'. He compares with Spain where, he says, you have places of Fascism which are used in new ways but their history is also told. He thinks that such buildings with 'hatred in their basements' should be reused rather than protected – and that this is different from, say, using the results of Nazi experiments on Jews – but that this should be accompanied by information. I ask whether he has visited the exhibition in the new Documentation Centre. He has. But although he found it very informative, his comparisons with Spain again leave him surprised that the exhibition is not 'harder', that is: 'they just explain it [Nazi madness] and do not attack it. I think it is not critical enough'. And he poetically repeats again, 'grass growing is like forgetting', as though the exhibition too has let a layer of grass creep over it.

Germany's difficult heritage

The country that has struggled most and longest over its twentieth-century difficult heritage – with the eyes of the world relentlessly upon it – is Germany. This is especially so in relation to its Holocaust history, though more recently, since German unification in 1990, the country has also faced the question of how to publicly represent the socialist dictatorship of the former German Democratic Republic (GDR) and how to commemorate its victims. The ongoing debates are saturated with analogies between the Nazi and GDR periods. How the Nazi past was publicly represented in East and West has been a focus of moral judgements of each by the other. Although both Germanys have accused each other, and have been accused by outsiders, of not having 'properly faced' the Nazi past, the country has nevertheless generated more texts and debates, and, especially more recently, more museums, monuments and art works, about its difficult heritage than has any other. Not only has Germany been at the

Figure 1.1 Grass on stone: weeds on the Zeppelin Building

heart of debates about Holocaust commemoration – though positioned differently from other key players such as the US and Israel[37] – the fact that there have been significant changes in dominant memorial practices over time, as well as variations between and within the two Germanys, means that the country can illustrate many struggles that may be involved in negotiating difficult heritage.

The idea that the past is difficult and needs to be tackled, and even overcome, is summoned up in the German term *Vergangenheitsbewältigung*. Much used in debates about public memory since the 1960s, it is sometimes glossed as 'coming to terms with the past' or, more often, as 'mastering the past'.[38] Andreas Glaeser suggests translating it as 'processing the past' in order to grasp it as 'a conscious working-through of the past with the intention to free oneself from its negative, potentially destructive influence';[39] and Klaus Neumann explains that it 'presupposes a difficulty that can be overcome'.[40] While the word for 'heritage' in many languages has an overwhelmingly positive public connotation, the German words for 'heritage', *das Erbe* and *die Erbschaft* (which also mean inheritance or legacy, as in several other languages) have a more patriotic connotation than in some languages.[41] Partly for that very patriotism, they are simultaneously regarded with some ambivalence. They can readily be used to denote what my German-English dictionary calls 'unerwünschtes' – un-wished-for – heritage, and for which it provides as example: '*das Erbe des Faschismus* the legacy of fascism'.[42] There are also other associated and telling German compound nouns. *Vergangenheitsbelästigung* means 'burdening by the past'. More compact, but also incorporating the idea of 'burden', this time coupled with that for heritage is – *die Erblast* – the inherited burden. All of these convey the sense of the past as potentially troublesome for the present. Indeed, even the term 'the past' (*die Vergangenheit*) often acts as a shorthand for the period, sometimes also known by its Nazi name of the Third Reich, between 1933 and 1945, when the NSDAP (National Socialist German Workers Party) – National Socialists or Nazis for short – was in power.[43] While none of this is to say that all heritage is regarded in a negative light in Germany – far from it – it does suggest that the idea that heritage can be difficult has pervaded public culture and popular consciousness.

It should be noted here that much of what would be talked about in terms of 'heritage' in English-language debates and policy would be referred to by other terms in Germany. In particular, built heritage is usually discussed in terms of *Denkmäler* – a word that is etymologically related to 'denken', 'to think', and is usually translated as 'monuments' or 'memorials'. Thus the field of 'heritage conservation' is *Denkmalpflege*, or 'heritage protection laws' are *Denkmalschutzgesetze*. As in Britain, the US and elsewhere, this is a field that has grown enormously during the twentieth century, especially since World War II, and has come to widespread prominence since the 1970s, though its roots are often said to lie in industrialisation and an associated tendency to see the past as in attrition.[44] Its formalisation and professionalisation, however, is largely twentieth century; and in drawing up their laws and devising their policy and practice, countries have been informed by those of others, and have also participated in cross-national initiatives such as European Cultural Heritage Year, first held in 1975, or the World Heritage Convention, first held in 1979, though they also have particular inflections.[45] In Britain, while there has been legislation covering prehistoric sites since the 1880s, the listing of buildings only began in 1947; and in Germany, there have been conservation organisations since the late nineteenth century but concerted development of legislation in the Federal Republic was not until the 1970s, where it was still predominantly at the level of federal states (*Länder*) (see Chapter 4).

Since their introduction, most countries have seen heritage policy and law increasingly broadly applied, moving from a predominant emphasis on aesthetically distinguished high culture or ancient history to the inclusion of sites of wider and more recent 'historical significance'. This has accorded more attention to the heritage of everyday life and also to difficult heritage. In the German case, this includes the formal identification of at least some Nazi buildings as *Denkmäler* (see Chapter 4). Partly because of this broadening definition, the number of sites listed increased massively in both Britain and Germany during the 1980s.[46] So too did controversies over heritage. In Britain, in what are known as the heritage debates, controversies centred around questions of the commercialisation of heritage and the Thatcher government's emphasis upon it.[47] In Germany in the same period, heritage debates were equally politicised and contentious, though here they mainly concerned questions of the commemoration and representation of World War II. In what became known as the historians' debate (*Historikerstreit*) they centred especially on the question of whether comparing Germany's crimes with other atrocities constituted an unacceptable moral relativisation or not, a question which had implications for how the Holocaust was represented in public culture as well as for the kinds of 'processing' of history that were deemed – variously – possible, permissible or necessary.[48]

While the Nazi past is widely recognised as an unavoidable, if contested, aspect of the German 'inheritance', there are significant variations between Germans – as the historian's debate also highlighted – over the extent to which they feel that they should feel responsible for 'their' 'Holocaust heritage'. Not least, there have been important differences (as well as perhaps more overlaps than is usually recognised) between the East and West, though again with shifts (as well as continuities) over time.

Postwar, in the East 'an official ideology of "anti-fascism" defined the [...] perspective on both the Nazi past and the contemporary Federal Republic where, East Germans charged, one form of fascism had simply succeeded another'.[49] This effectively cast Nazism largely as a feature of the West, disinheriting the Socialist state from it. Instead, the East was understood as the location of those who had opposed it. This account was evident in how some of the material remains of the Nazi period, particularly concentration camps, were publicly represented.[50] Opened up for visitors and used as pedagogical sites, the emphasis in the display of concentration camps was on political prisoners, especially communists, all of whom were seen as victims of the 'fascism' that the Socialist state was continuing to oppose. The West, by implication, was the not yet fully repentant offspring of the Fascist perpetrators. In the West itself, where such a comfortable fiction of complete rupture was more difficult to maintain, the relationship with the Nazi past has been more troubled and more complex. It was in the *Bundesrepublik* that terms such as *Vergangenheitsbewältigung* were coined and gained currency, and it was here that an academic sub-specialty of research mentioned above on *Geschichtsbewußtsein* – 'historical consciousness' – has grown up. Concerned with questions of the necessity for human beings of finding 'temporal orientation', this focus is undoubtedly itself shaped by the experience of dealing with Germany's own difficult history; though as noted above it also makes important analytical contributions to debates about memory.

Many of those writing on West Germany's postwar memory cultures suggest that a major shift occurred around the late 1960s, when an earlier period of 'historical silence and willing forgetfulness' was superseded by 'an explosion of critical self-examination'.[51] In recent years there has been a wave of important historical scholarship showing that the depiction of the 1950s as a time of repression of trauma and forgetting of victims is overstated.[52] In part, that depiction was itself produced as part of the moral project of those propelling remembrance from the late 1960s onwards. Nevertheless, even those who challenge the forgetful fifties thesis acknowledge that there have been changes of emphasis and form over the years, and that, as Robert Moeller, who has highlighted multiple ways in which the Nazi past *was* addressed in the 1950s, explains, remembering was selective.[53]

In particular, the main, though by no means exclusive, emphasis in the 1950s was on Germans as victims; and what emerged in the 1960s and 1970s was 'a much more critical understanding of National Socialism'.[54] This has been characterised by Jörn Rüsen as 'a new moralistic approach'.[55] Often cast as a generational conflict, what he calls the 'second stage' involved calls for active and visible public commemoration especially of Jewish victims of the Nazis, and at least some acknowledgement of Germany as perpetrator.[56] But this 'new' period was by no means homogeneous. On the contrary, as noted above, it has been characterised by major public conflicts over the nature of German history and its commemoration. There have been heated controversies over the 'uniqueness' or otherwise of Germany's Nazi crimes,[57] huge disputes generated by an exhibition about the role of 'ordinary' German soldiers – the Wehrmacht – during the War,[58] and years of arguments about whether and then how to create a national Holocaust memorial.[59] Ambivalence and what I call 'oscillation', and also fragmentation, complexity and continuities with the earlier period, are as much part of the reality as are changes, as can be seen in the localised study that follows.

Paying attention to some of the complexities over time also adds a cautionary note to the compelling temptation – to which those involved in the work of public commemoration sometimes succumb – to depict Germany as on a neat linear trajectory to ever more complete or satisfactory 'facing up to' its past, in a kind of 'allegory of redemption'.[60] Without denying the important developments that there have been, locally as well as nationally, it is important to understand the redemptive story of progressive improvement as part of a process of cultural accounting rather than as a straightforward description of fact. In other words, its significance lies just as much in its status as 'a story people tell themselves about themselves'.[61]

Within the broad shift since the late 1960s, many authors suggest further periods or stages.[62] In particular, the unification of the two Germanys in 1990 clearly poses new dilemmas for public commemoration and self-presentation.[63] These include revision of the GDR's strong emphasis on resistance to fascism, noted above, and finding ways to persuade the world that the 'new' single-nation Germany is very different from the 'old' single-nation Germany, that immediately preceded 1945. The explosion of commemoration and museum representations of the Holocaust in the 1990s might even be seen as a further new more open period of self-reflection and 'facing-up' underway. Jörn Rüsen suggests that we may be at the beginning of a 'third stage', which he calls 'historisation',[64] in which Germans may be beginning to self-identify as perpetrators rather than as victims. Others have suggested the opposite, that publications about traumatic German experiences of war – especially W.G. Sebald's essay 'Air war and literature' (published in 1999 in Germany), Jörg Friedrich's *Der Brand. Deutschland im Bombenkrieg 1940–1945* (2002; *The Fire: Germany during the Bombing 1940–1945*) and Günther Grass's *Im Krebsgang* (2002; *Crabwalk*) – are indications that Germans are at last able to identify themselves more openly as victims.[65] Taking a somewhat different tack, Daniel Levy and Natan Sznaider argue that in the 1990s in many parts of the world, including Germany, we are witnessing the development of what they call 'cosmopolitan memory'.[66] Instead of public memory being largely framed within what they call the 'container' of the nation-state, it is increasingly decontextualised from its historical time and space, consumed by people with no direct connection to it, and turned into more universal stories, especially those of 'good against evil'.[67]

These arguments and debates are ones to which I return in the chapters that follow. I do so, however, not through the more usual routes of looking at the literature and events through which they are usually discussed but in what might be seen, borrowing Grass's metaphor, as a more crab-like sideways approach, through a story of a particular city's politics and remembrance in relation to a striking and historically significant material heritage.

Now and then, *ab und zu*

A woman in her thirties has been leafing through the visitor book in the Documentation Centre. I approach her and ask if I might interview her about her experience of the exhibition. She agrees and tells me that she is here for the second day running, having spent several hours here the day before but 'you can't do it all in one day' and she is so impressed ('*beeindruckt*') with it. '*Beeindruckend*', 'impressive', is the most common word that visitors use to describe the exhibition here – both in interviews with me and in the visitor books. Born in 1950 and from Berlin, she tells me, her parents were '*Zeitzeugen*' – 'witnesses of that time', and she has a strong interest in German history, especially that of the '*NS-Zeit*' – the National Socialist time, about which she first learnt in school. This interest means that she feels that she has seen many of the images (the *Bildmaterial*) in the exhibition before but she still feels that it is a very good exhibition, 'very intensive' – 'you can't get out at all, you can't even go to the toilet unless you go the whole way through'. Despite her own interest, she has some ambivalence about whether people should keep occupying themselves with this history but thinks that it is important to go back to it now and then (*ab und zu*), and here she searches carefully to find words to explain why, before going on to say of her experience in the exhibition: 'I became clearer about what a person, what an individual, really is. I only went to the GDR eight years ago, and there was there this whole collectivisation, that here [i.e. in the Nazi period] was called "Community" [*Volksgemeinschaft*]. There it was called, I don't know, "Collective" [*Betriebskollektiv*] or something. It is very hard to know how to deal with such uniformity. But what I really learnt from this is that it is really important to remember that every person is an individual, and that you shouldn't see them as merged together'.

She talks too about how she is especially impressed with the architecture of the Documentation Centre, the way that, she thinks, the architect has managed to 'break with the monumentality' ['*dieses Monumental*'] of the building. At the same time, the fact that this is one of the places 'where the history actually took place' is especially impressive, as is also the case, she notes, in the *Topographie des Terrors* in Berlin. She describes this as 'direct' and compares it favourably with a memorial site (*Gedänkstätte*) that she visited in Israel, where the floor was from the concentration camp Theresienstadt.

It is important, she says, that the traces ('*die Spuren*') are not allowed to become covered over – as she says has partly happened with the Berlin Wall. Although it is difficult, she emphasises, the site must be retained – and here she hesitates, searching again for the right word – '*als Denkmal*', as a memorial.

Nuremberg

While Germany forms the broad socio-political frame within which I look at questions of identity, heritage and the Nazi past, this book also has a more specific focus on the city of Nuremberg. Still more specifically, it examines the fate since 1945 of the Nazi Party Rally Grounds (the *Reichsparteitagsgelände*) – an area of former marching grounds and monumental fascist buildings – which lie just a short distance away from Nuremberg's scenic old town (*Altstadt*).

The fact that Nuremberg has such strong Nazi associations as well as such a large area of identifiable Nazi buildings makes it a compelling case through which to explore the post-1945 struggle with difficult heritage. The city was given the name 'City of the Nazi Party Rallies' by Hitler in 1933 (though it had held such rallies already, in 1927 and 1929), and its name was engraved with Nazi crimes by being the place where the 'Nuremberg Laws' – those defining 'racial crimes' and denying Jews citizenship – were declared in 1933 and where, postwar, the trials of Nazi criminals were held. As Nuremberg's Head of Tourism and Marketing, Michael Weber, rather ruefully told me, it is those three linkages – laws, rallies and trials – that define the city for many foreigners in particular: 'They always want to know, show me the place of the trials, where the laws were announced and where Hitler used to stand.'[68]

As he was also keen to point out, however, these were not the only Nurembergs. Long dubbed 'Germany's treasure chest' (*Deutschlands Schatzkästlein*), the city has been a significant tourist destination since the mid-nineteenth century, visitors coming to see its beautiful churches, fountains, walled Old Town, medieval castle and the important collections in the Germanic National Museum. Although much of the Old Town was destroyed during the War, many of the notable buildings have since been painstakingly reconstructed as part of Germany's postwar heritage movement. Nuremberg is also famous for its Christmas market, its toy-making, gingerbread, and sausages. Indeed, a visitor survey from the 1980s that Michael Weber gave to me showed clearly that for most German visitors these were more significant associations than the Nazi heritage. In response to the question 'What comes into your mind when you hear the name Nuremberg?', while foreign tourists (of whom the majority were Americans) almost all mentioned trials, laws and rallies as the primary associations, fewer than 5 per cent of German visitors mentioned anything to do with the Nazi period. Instead, their associations were *Butzenscheiben* (little bull's eye glass window-panes), *Bratwürste* (sausages), *Lebkuchen* (gingerbread) and the *Christkindlesmarkt* (Christmas market). In other words, all things which Michael Weber described as 'small and cute' (*klein und niedlich*), an image that he also thought problematic for a modern dynamic city.

The kind of image that Michael Weber was keen to convey was well set out in a recently produced brochure – entitled *Nürnberg. Ein Erlebnis* (*Nuremberg: An Experience*) – that he gave to me. Beginning 'Be honest: what comes to mind when you think of Nuremberg?' and suggesting that it was likely to be the small and cute responses that the visitor survey had produced, and acknowledging the richness of the city's history and material heritage, the text went on to recommend a correction:

> For that is only one aspect. Today, 950 years after it was founded, Nuremberg is also a modern vibrant city with half a million inhabitants. Not a dusty old museum, but rather a city with a comfortable feel to it, a place that has its own special atmosphere, enticing the visitor to stroll about, take a closer look

at things, discover something new. You get a sense of this special flair when you amble through the town centre with its many attractions for the sightseer and its reasonably priced shops. Street musicians from all over the world play their music in the shadow of the Church of St. Lawrence and on warm summer evenings you'll find next to the house of the artist Albrecht Dürer all those who today are also engaged in an art form, namely the art of living. That is what makes Nuremberg especially charming: the harmonious coexistence of new and old, of now and then, of live and let live. Nuremberg is full of surprises.

The brochure continues through energetically illustrated pages to reveal some of those 'surprises', including the city's cultural and artistic scene, the sporting offer, its cuisine and hotels, and its strengths in technology. In doing so, it represents important aspects of Nuremberg as a lively and multi-cultural city,[69] which successfully couples the traditional and modern. Nuremberg is presented as the leading city in northern Bavaria, or, as local people prefer to put it, of *Franken* (Franconia), or more specifically *Mittelfranken* (Middle Franconia, which unlike Franconia constitutes an administrative district). Historically, Franken was a duchy of the Holy Roman Empire and after various splits and revisions of territory, eastern Franken, including Nuremberg, was incorporated into the State of Bavaria by Napoleon at the beginning of the nineteenth century. It thus became 'Bavaria's second city' to the state capital of Munich, about a hundred and sixty kilometres to the south, a relationship that sometimes rankles. Administratively, Nuremberg has its own city council and city administration, which are responsible for most matters directly to do with the city's environment and day-to-day running, though within a framework mainly established by the state capital. Here, it is worth noting another important image of Nuremberg – as a relatively 'red' city within the predominantly Christian Socialist Union (CSU) Bavarian state. Postwar, the city has had a Social Democrat (SPD) mayor – a position directly elected by the population – continuously except for between 1996 and 2002 when the incumbent was CSU.[70] This identity as left-of-centre also extends to the prewar period, and is reasonably well-known in Germany, even though the wider Franken region is regarded as culturally and politically conservative. As will be evident in the chapters that follow, this political context, and the various possible historical images that Nuremberg can seek to project, are an important part of its telling – and sometimes not telling – its Nazi past.

As I leafed through the brochure that the tourism minister had handed me, I noted to him – no doubt disappointingly confirming his fears about foreigners' preoccupations – that the Nazi Party Rally Grounds seemed not to be mentioned. '*Doch!*' ('On the contrary'), he exclaimed, and turned to a page busy with a collage of pictures of people having a boating joust, a Rastafarian giving a victory sign, a smartly-dressed waiter, a view of the historic *Altstadt* and children on a fairground ride. In the background of the latter he pointed out the Congress Hall on the Rally Grounds (though no label identified it as such). '*Profanierung!*' ('profanation') he announced, and went on to explain to me a 'strategy' for dealing with the Nazi heritage by 'profaning' it with banal or everyday activities. Articulated by the city's culture minister (*Kulturreferent*), the renowned social historian Dr Hermann Glaser, in the 1980s, I discuss it further in Chapter 4. As Michael Weber also observed, this was not the only approach to the city's past. In particular, as the brochure also noted, in 1995 Nuremberg established a biennial Human Rights award. This was part of a raft of Human Rights activities, discussed further in Chapter 5, which are part of Nuremberg's late twentieth-century self-presentation as 'City of Human Rights' rather than 'City of the Nazi Party Rallies'. Also significant here, as he also noted, was the fact that the city was then (2000) in the process of building a new documentation centre and exhibition about, and in, the Rally Grounds, due to open the following year.

These various developments, the historical complexities and layerings, and processes of coupling history and the present – as in the production of tourist literature – were all features that made Nuremberg an interesting, and telling, place to explore negotiations over the Nazi past. Although Nuremberg has been called 'the most German of cities' (including by National Socialist mayor – following a long tradition – in 1938), and although it has been suggested that the various ways in which the Rally Grounds have been treated over the years could act as 'a seismograph of German *Vergangenheitsbewältigung*',[71] my argument here is not that the city is somehow 'typical' of Germany, or even West Germany. Instead, Nuremberg and the Rally Grounds can act as a focus for telling at least part of a wider story about German *Vergangenheitsbewältigung*, not because they constitute the bigger frame writ small, but because those acting locally often do so in awareness of debates ongoing elsewhere, because of shared institutional factors, such as available funding and sometimes because of common assumptions or ways of acting. What the more detailed focus that I provide here also reveals, however, is a story of locally ignoring or rejecting aspects of wider discourses and movements; of local reconfigurations of apparently more broadly (sometimes internationally) shared knowledge and practice; of new initiatives; and of the more specific local concerns and politics in which decisions are made.

Arrival story

The 'Writing Culture' debates of the 1980s drew attention to the rhetorical and sometimes self-legitimating role of anthropologists' 'arrival stories' – perhaps tales of their overcoming of obstacles to get to their chosen location. Nevertheless, arrivals at a place for the first time have a powerful capacity to generate impressions and questions, or to challenge preconceptions, and not only for anthropologists. In my case, in September 1999, when I was still working out what my research focus might be, I found myself at a tramstop uncertain which tram I should take to get to 'Luitpoldhain', the name of the stop at the former Nazi Party Rally Grounds. I asked a woman for direction and, as she was going that way too, she invited me to come with her. We talked a little as we went along, about the lovely fresh vegetables that she had bought in the market, the fine weather, about where I was from and where I had learnt German, but not about where I was heading. Tram 9 trundled through stops that were later to become engrained in my memory: ... Wodanstraße, Holzgartenstraße, Platz der Opfer des Faschismus, Meistersingerhalle, Luitpoldhain. When we alighted she must have registered surprise in my face for she asked 'You're here to see the Reich Party Rally Grounds?', and when I nodded, she laughed and said 'Hitler certainly knew how to choose a beautiful place'. She was right that the peaceful parkland and greenery was what first struck me and that I hadn't expected this. My imagination was filled with black-and-white images of vast marching grounds and monstrous buildings.

She then led me over the busy Bayernstraße further into the grounds, telling me as she did so that her father had been an engineer responsible for some of the electrical work connected with the party rallies, though he had not been a party member. She lived in a house nearby, there being some very nice houses around here, she observed, still enjoying the conflict between my expectation and what I was encountering.

As I wandered further around the Rally Grounds area that day I became fascinated by what seemed to me to be contradictions between the terrible history with which the site was imbued – and which it had been designed to glorify – and its current appearance and uses. The overall impression of the place was of a public park or even nature reserve, leafy and green, with mature trees and woodland walks, and lakes with ducks, moorhens and pleasure boats. There was a yacht club, a beer garden and, in the side of one of the Nazi buildings, something called a 'Serenadenhof' which I later learnt was an area for holding classical concerts. Next to information stands about the history of the site were kiosks selling hot dogs and fizzy drinks. Fairground rides of the annual Volksfest were still in place. My eye could travel from the Ferris wheel and roller coasters of the fair to the Congress Hall – the enormous Colosseum-like building begun by the Nazis but never completed. I could survey the length of the Great Road, the granite-clad marching road along which so many soldiers would have goose-stepped, and see children learning to ride their bikes or people parking their cars to take their dogs for a walk. Everywhere were people roller-blading, hurtling around clad in helmets and knee- and elbow-pads. On benches looking out onto the lake and across to the Congress Hall elderly people sat chatting or simply gazing at the view of the Nazi building romantically reflected in the water. At the Zeppelin Building, which film footage of Hitler ranting to the troops has made the most instantly recognisable Nazi building, groups of youths were perfecting their skate-boarding jumps next to the 'Führer podium', and, against another wall, beside a pair of sculptures made from pieces of spent ammunition (Jan Breuste's 'Overkill I & II'), a man was practising his tennis strokes.

I had been expecting a bleak empty place – a space neglected by the present, a space in which the 'feel' of the past would be overwhelming. Instead I found myself struggling to reconcile past and present, and with my sense of contradiction between what I knew about the site and what I could see today. I could, and did, find some of the buildings and marching grounds chilling – especially the cavernous raw inside of the Congress Hall, belying its classical exterior, and the cool, long, angular lines of the Zeppelin Building. But I also found the Congress Hall, with its allusions to the Roman Colosseum and artful positioning on the edge of the lake, elegantly attractive; and I found the Zeppelin Building, with its side wings now gone (removed in the late 1960s and 1970s) and with weeds growing up among the crumbling steps, rather pitiful. On that day I became compelled to know just when, how and why the site had become what it was. Why had some parts of the site been left intact since the war and others – such as some of the marching grounds – grassed-over? Why had parts of the Zeppelin Building been destroyed, in a peculiar amputation, but not all of it? Who made such decisions and were they the subject of public debate? I also wanted to know more about what the site might mean to the numerous people who used it. Were they aware of its history? And, if so, did it matter to them? Did they feel a sense of conflicting meanings as I was doing myself? These 'arrival questions' – which tapped into more longstanding theoretical interests in identity formation, historical consciousness and material culture – motivated my Nuremberg research.

Figure 1.2   Scenic Nazi Party Rally Grounds. Congress Hall and Lake

18

Negotiating material heritage

In this book I focus primarily on the ways in which Nuremberg's most striking physical heritage of Nazism – the former Nazi (or 'Reich') Party Rally Grounds, the *Reichsparteitagsgelände* – has been variously used, debated and neglected, and partly blown up, grassed-over, restored and exhibited. Built by the Nazis in the 1930s to stage the Nazi Party rallies (or the Nuremberg rallies as they are often known), the grounds today consist of a large area of former marching grounds and buildings in monumental fascist style. Lying a few miles outside Nuremberg's historic walled old town, about three miles from the city's main railway station, this largest existing area of Fascist architecture has remained a material presence and reminder of Nuremberg's Nazi past. Not only an area listed under monument protection laws, the site is also one of Nuremberg's largest green spaces and acts as an important leisure area, especially for those who live in the surrounding suburbs.

The struggle over the Nazi past in Nuremberg has taken place in many civic and private spaces, including the trials, immediate postwar 'denazification' and continuing wrangling over compensation for forced labour, in the content of school education and in family memories. In looking at how a material, physical presence is dealt with, my aim is to bring debates about the public representation and consumption of the past together with those on material culture and the media of remembering and forgetting. Put crudely, Nuremberg's Nazi Party Rally Grounds raise questions of how far forgetting is possible in the face of an enormous physical presence, and how far meaning and historical understanding are constrained or shaped by materiality. On laying a foundation stone at the Rally Grounds Hitler expressed the wish that the buildings would 'speak as eternal witnesses' ('*rede als ewiger Zeuge*') and architect Albert Speer, who was responsible for the overall design of the site, referred to them as 'Words in stone' ('*Worte aus Stein*') (see Chapter 2). But how far do architectural styles inscribe meanings? Are these fixed by the architect or are they available for reinterpretation later? Can buildings and crafted landscapes continue to speak across the decades? This book looks at some of the debates about these as they have occurred in Nuremberg's negotiations of the Party Rally Grounds and in academia.

In using the term 'negotiating' I seek to draw attention to debates and arguments, and to the fact that dealings with difficult heritage typically involve ongoing conflicts of interest and differences of view. A negotiated social practice is differentiated, mobile and emergent rather than homogeneous, fixed or the product of underlying laws. Additionally, I use 'negotiating' because it can also refer to physical movement in relation to objects – negotiation can be an embodied or material as well as a discursive practice. The physical dealings with the site – the destruction, partial destruction or restoration of parts of it and the movement and sensations of individuals encountering it – are part of its negotiation. This is not, however, simply movement between or around fixed positions. Rather, negotiating is a more active process in which spaces, identifications, alignments and even objects are positioned and given recognition. Guided tours, for example, negotiate the Rally Grounds into being as an educational and tourist space. Debates about what should be done with the Nazi buildings consolidate or instigate groupings and alignments.

In using the term negotiating, I am also purposefully choosing a less evocative or discourse-specific term than some of those that have been used by others – often to interesting effect – in discussion of Germany's landscapes. Several commentators, for example, have talked of 'ghosts' – of being 'haunted by' the Nazi and other pasts; and many have used psychoanalytical terms such as 'repression' and 'trauma'.[72] As we will see in the account that follows, these are tropes that are sometimes employed locally too. Because I am interested in exploring such uses ethnographically and historically – that is, looking at their deployment and implications – I avoid using them as tools in my own analysis of what is involved in Nuremberg's heritage negotiations. Moreover, rather than trying to infer transcendent psychological mechanisms – which risks blurring differentiations and ignoring historically located social processes – I am concerned to try to identify the particular cultural assumptions and understandings, and the players and tensions, involved in negotiations and particular courses of action. These, no less than supposedly universal processes, can give insight into other cases, though they do so more modestly, by calling for attention to the possible specificities and complexities alongside an attempt to identify possibly shared concepts, practices and contexts.

Layered history: *Schichte/Geschichte*

Anselm Kiefer is one of Germany's most controversial postwar artists, especially on account of his series of paintings and photographs (with titles such as 'Heroic Symbols' and 'Occupations')in which he poses as Hitler in front of various monuments in Europe. Long intrigued by Kiefer, I was fascinated to discover that he has made several paintings entitled 'Nuremberg'. Like many of his other works, these have dense textured surfaces, thick with layers of paint and other materials. Scenes of Nuremberg's historic old town and vast fields (references to the Nazi marching grounds) are overlaid with layers of straw and dark paint, and words such as '*Festspielwiese*' (festival ground') and '*Meistersinger*' ('Mastersingers' – from Wagner's famous opera, much loved by Hitler, about Nuremberg) are scratched into the surface. In these paintings, it seems to me, Kiefer is playing with the fact that the German word for history – *Geschichte* – also contains the idea of layers (*Schichte*). He suggests that the past is substantially obscured by later layers and only ever partially glimpsed. Simultaneously, the past is depicted as intruding, as finding its way, again partially, through the accumulated layers into the present.[73]

Approach

In order to provide an account of negotiating difficult heritage at the Rally Grounds in Nuremberg, I combine historical and ethnographic research. This has involved work in archives – looking primarily at matters such as city council debates, tourist brochures and city image policies, newspaper reports and visitor books – as well as secondary historical research. It includes interviews with people who I call 'history workers' – those who are involved in presenting the past in the public realm, such

Figure 1.3   Anselm Kiefer: *1945 Nürnberg* (1982) (© Anselm Kiefer. Oil, straw, and mixed media on canvas; 110 3/8 × 149 7/8 inches. The Eli and Edythe L. Broad Collection, Los Angeles. Photograph: Douglas M. Parker Studio, Los Angeles)

as Michael Weber of the tourism office as well as those involved in the making of exhibitions (past as well as present) at and of the Rally Grounds; those involved in establishing and running guided tours; and a range of others whose activities also impinge on the uses and interpretations of the site, such as the city's building minister, people in the historical preservation office (the *Denkmalschutzbehörde*) and journalists who have made it their task to write about the site in the local newspaper, the *Nürnberger Nachrichten*. As part of the gloriously unavoidable nature of human interaction, it also includes all sorts of casual conversations with individuals from Nuremberg and elsewhere who have expressed interest in my work and who have volunteered memories and insights.

In addition, I carried out participant-observation fieldwork, primarily on the Rally Grounds site, including on guided tours and in the Documentation Centre, and have undergone some of the training provided for guides and taken some friends and relatives, as well as a group of university sociology students, on tours myself. As well as discussions with the students and with friends and acquaintances, I conducted interviews with visitors – either singly or in groups – to the Rally Grounds, including, but not only, to the Documentation Centre (see Chapter 8). Those who I interviewed included local people who live nearby and people who work in the grounds, some of whom I met and chatted with on other occasions too; as well as visitors from other parts of Germany and abroad. My interviews were with people sitting on benches, roller-bladers, families having barbecues, and those trying to learn more

21

about the Nazi past. They included pensioners who lived through the Nazi period, schoolchildren who learn about it in school, older people who never learnt about it in school, members of the Bundeswehr (the German army) who are expected to learn about it as part of their training, and people from many parts of the world who have somehow felt compelled to visit the site.

Any study is inevitably selective. Even though this account has a fairly tight central focus – the Rally Grounds – it is only able to relate some of the events and debates, and some of the commentaries and actions, from the rich material available. In making my selections, I have picked those actions and inactions, commentaries and silences, events and debates, which seem to me – on the basis of the materials in which I became immersed – to best give insights into what may be at issue in negotiating and experiencing difficult heritage.

By bringing together historical and contemporary material, it is possible to understand better the specificities of what was going on at certain time periods by comparing and contrasting them with others. This is not just a one-way process. Providing a primarily chronological account seems the best way to show how those coming later have to deal with the material heritage that has resulted from earlier decisions or neglect. But my own thinking and research process has been 'multi-temporal' insofar as my interrogation of earlier times has been at least partly shaped by my conversations with people in Nuremberg today, as well as my own experiences of the site and commentaries by others. To try to reflect this, as well as to emphasise the multiple and not easily contained readings and uses of the Rally Grounds site, my main narrative is also interspersed with 'interventions', that is, with perspectives on or related to the Rally Grounds or linked themes, that are intended to supplement, and sometimes disrupt or complicate, the main account, and sometimes to lay clues and traces for later arguments.

I write as an interested outsider. I have no direct family connections with Germany, and no relatives who were victims of the Holocaust. My husband works on German philosophy and we have long enjoyed German literature, film and music, and, as part of a longstanding interest in nationhood, history and identity that I have explored in other places, I have been fascinated by the case of Germany. Unlike so many German commentators, I didn't begin with a sense of motivating emotional investment in the subject matter, nor with a feeling of compulsion to make normative statements on how the past should or should not be 'dealt with'. While doing so is not my aim, I do nevertheless attempt to map out what I see as some of the implications of particular approaches to the past for the ways in which they are understood as shaped primarily by my understanding of what I have observed and heard in the course of my research. My project is thus conceived as a democratic anthropology in that it is not just 'about' a group of people but is also engaged in many of the same negotiations, and takes its cues from arguments and ideas presented by those 'studied', as well as offering contributions for future negotiation.

On learning of the subject of my research, the immediate response of many of my German acquaintances was to say that they thought it good that I, as a non-German, should be tackling this subject. 'It will be good to have somebody from outside looking at our peculiar German obsessions', joked one German professor. Such comments reflect part of a deeper uncertainty over whether, given the emotional and historical baggage involved, Germans can really trust themselves to know themselves and deal with their own history – even if, at the same time, there is a massive outpouring of attempts to craft such stories. Contrary to, say, the Japanese, who anthropologists have reported as believing that only the Japanese can properly understand Japan,[74] many Germans fear lurking repressions and unconscious drives that undermine their confidence in their own views of themselves. There is consequently a feeling that an outsider's account might be more 'objective', though often accompanied by the suspicion that outsiders will not grasp the difficulty of what is involved. Equally, the fact that an outsider is also interested in these matters is itself a validation that they are worth obsessing over.

If some thought it good that I should be doing this research, others were disappointed in my choice of focus. That my husband and I had learnt German (something always commented upon as unusual, if not astonishing, for *Engländer*), participated in local events, made friends, visited all the places that people said we should visit, and sent our children to German schools, was regarded by many as a welcome affirmation that not everybody from England held the crude negative stereotypes of Germans that are peddled in some parts of the British media. While I find such stereotypes, and constant references to the War, offensively reductive and morally complacent, the fact that I too was spending much of my time engaged with Nazi heritage implied that this figured large in my own understanding of Germany and Germanness. I had no way of really resolving this, for the topic seemed to me not only valid but indeed an unavoidable aspect of understanding contemporary German identity, even if, as I also want to strongly emphasise, it is only part of it.

Is this how they see us?

A man in his late twenties with a large camera slung around his neck is walking on the Zeppelin Building. He tells me that he has come not to see the buildings themselves but because he is interested in sites of car crashes. A few days previously there had been a fatal crash in front of the Zeppelin Building, when a 'joy-ride' went wrong. We talk a bit about how attractive this stretch of road – sometimes officially used as part of a race track – is for speeding; but also how dangerous it is without the crash barriers that are erected for races. I ask him my usual questions – and he tells me, among other things, that he is a salesman who has lived in Nuremberg for many years (though he emphasises that he is not 'from here'), that he has read much about the city's history, has visited the older and new Dokuzentrum exhibition ('excellent, very good'), and that he thinks that there should be even more information available on the site 'though there is a danger of turning it into a temple or something'. Then, as I switch off my tape-recorder, he turns the tables. Is it true, he asks, that there are newspapers in England that refer to Germans as Krauts and even as Nazis?

What are these newspapers? Are they like the *Bild* (the most popular German tabloid newspaper)? Do many people read them? And does it mean that lots of people see Germans in this way? He expresses astonishment that people would label people today through such references to something that happened so long ago and to the fact that this can be 'allowed'. I find myself apologising for newspapers like the *Sun* and trying to emphasise that many English people, myself included, find them deeply embarrassing and offensive. But he still looks hurt and baffled. I go away not only reminded of this unpleasant use of the past but also aware that my questions to him prompted the voicing of his concerns.

* * * * *

The following chapter, 'Building heritage: Words in stone'?, addresses some of the particular issues raised by material, especially architectural, heritage. It does so by examining Nazi architectural practice – including ideas about the agency and 'impact' of certain scales, forms and staging – especially in relation to the building and uses of the Nazi Party Rally Grounds. The remaining chapters discuss the negotiations of what was left of this material heritage after the War. In doing so, they explore a wide range of different possible approaches to difficult heritage. Chapters 3 to 6 are partially chronological. Chapter 3, 'Demolition, cleansing and moving on', discusses some of the most predominant approaches the immediate postwar period – though ones that also continue since and are also widely found elsewhere. Official heritage preservation, beginning in the 1970s, and various attempts to work with or against this, is the subject of Chapter 4, 'Preservation, profanation and image-management'. Chapter 5, 'Accompanied witnessing: education, art and alibis', considers education, and especially exhibitions, about difficult heritage, and other artistic reflections on it. Much of this began in earnest in Nuremberg the 1980s. Chapter 6, 'Cosmopolitan memory in the City of Human Rights', sets out the most recent developments in Nuremberg to create a documentation centre about the Nazi past and to present the city as one of freedom and human rights. This discusses the development of more 'cosmopolitan' approaches to public representation of the past; and highlights some of the particular dilemmas that those directly involved in presenting difficult heritage to the public may face as they try to do so. This theme is continued in Chapter 7, 'Negotiating on the ground(s): guided tours of Nazi heritage', which looks at the work of tour guides at the Rally Grounds – and the challenges involved in dealing with the materiality as well as meaning of difficult heritage. Chapter 8, 'Visiting difficult heritage', turns to those many people who come to the site – either as tourists or as local people – in order to explore how they, variously, negotiate it, both physically and verbally. The final chapter, 'Unsettling difficult heritage', concludes the book by considering the implications of the Nuremberg case for others beyond – and for the future.

2

BUILDING HERITAGE

'Words in stone'?

Buildings are one of the most pronounced forms of heritage in most countries – a phenomenon that has become globally institutionalised through organisations such as UNESCO, with its World Heritage lists, and the spread of heritage-preservation legislation.[1] As one of the biggest forms of material culture and usually durable over considerable periods of time, they are especially likely to be used as evidence of presence or claimed continuities of peoples and identities. Moreover, they are also widely seen as somehow conveying meanings or effects directly and across time – or as acting as 'words in stone', as we have already noted that Albert Speer, architect of many Nazi buildings, hoped. Whether this is so and how it might work is much debated.

What or how buildings and environments mean or do are questions of considerable importance for heritage and public memory.[2] Heritage workers – those who are professionally involved in the public presentation of the past – inevitably make assumptions or formulate ideas about the effects that they think certain material forms might have on those who encounter them. For example, they may be concerned that a confined space will make people feel claustrophobic and thus uncomfortable 'in' a particular history, that some kinds of materials might be perceived as less 'authentic' or 'old' than others or that buildings will somehow 'speak' messages that go against the grain of what they think appropriate or significant. In response, they design strategies intended to heighten or downplay certain physical suggestions. As Jo Littler has written, '[a] heritage practice is in itself a type of theory with its own epistemology'.[3] Exploring any heritage practice, therefore, provides an opportunity to examine its epistemological suppositions about such matters as conceptions of time, value, animacy and materiality.

Subsequent chapters engage in such examination, primarily in relation to how the remains of Nuremberg's Nazi Party Rally Grounds have been variously dealt with or ignored over the years. This chapter, however, does so in relation to what might be seen as the 'heritage practice' of the National Socialists: their ideas about the power of architecture and ritual, their attempt to shape bodily comportments and ways of seeing, and their deployment of historical resonance. The chapter also provides a background to the Nazi Party rallies and Rally Grounds; and describes what was left – for subsequent negotiation – by the end of the war. First, however, I turn briefly to some theoretical debates about materiality in order to set out my

25

own approach, and to act as a basis from which to look at debates about Nazi architecture.

Materiality

Heritage is a material as well as a symbolic practice. (Even what is sometimes called 'intangible heritage' – e.g. dances, songs or ideas – typically takes a material form, if only in its recording, of a sort.) This materiality matters. For example, a building that only exists as a faint trace needs interpretative work to make it visible; or a large solid structure may be harder to remove from a landscape. Despite the claims of some of those involved in preservation debates, it is only rarely the case that material factors alone fully govern the fate of material culture. Rather, human decisions about what to do with a building, including whether to neglect it entirely or fail to secure its foundations against subsidence, are co-determinant in shaping the land- or city-scape.

In recent years there has been a growing critique in material culture studies of approaches to material forms (including landscapes and art) 'primarily as systems of signs, or as texts or discourses which encode meaning and reflect social identities in various ways'.[4] Proposed instead are perspectives that consider them as actors or agents, capable of shaping social action and even producing identities.[5] In my view, what is most interesting is not the rather peculiar question of whether or not material culture 'has agency' but that of how, when and why agency is variously *attributed* and how this interacts with what I call *material relativities* and *material suggestions*. In other words, I accept the idea that there are material features – or 'affordances' – that make a difference to the amount of effort that people need to make to relate to them in particular ways, as well as the fairly obvious point that the physical world can spring surprises or 'kick back'. Furthermore, I accept that certain material characteristics or relativities may prompt, or suggest, particular ways of understanding or relating to them. Robert Hertz's famous classical anthropological argument about the tendency in many cultures to make divisions between right and left which are then invested with symbolic and moral significance, and in which the right side is generally associated with more positive qualities (e.g. with correctness or justice), is a good example of a material suggestion based on a material relativity. Hertz accounts for this cross-cultural tendency in terms of the statistical predominance of right-handedness in populations. The physiological-statistical tendency does not in any sense determine its interpretation but nevertheless acts as a strong material hint.[6] In the course of the discussion below, I note further such examples, linked to relative qualities such as size and durability. I do so, however, in relation to particular contexts or local interpretations and mindful of Hertz's point that such material prompting remains open to reinterpretation and also processes such as inversion (in which symbolic significance is accorded specifically against the grain of the material suggestion). Moreover, rather than see material prompting as an alternative to symbolic interpretation, I see it existing as part of a matrix that also includes, for example, the attribution of significance or the projection of historical allusion.

Here, then, I am not concerned to try to identify how materials or buildings work 'in themselves' but take a more enmeshed approach which includes attention to physical form but also to how buildings and spaces are *attributed* with certain qualities and the implications in practice that flow from this. As will become evident in relation to the case discussed, whether and how people or things are attributed with agency can itself be very significant to the course of events – and the fate of both things and people – that follows. Moreover, as such attributions entail an allocation of responsibility (e.g. blaming 'natural processes' and thus denying human responsibility) they are inherently political; and we may thus talk of the *politics of attributions*. This book is in large part an historico-ethnography of the politics of attributions. While here this is traced through the negotiating of one particular 'difficult heritage', the implications of different attributional positions have, I suggest, significance for other cases too.

Architecture's 'magic'

That architecture was important to the National Socialists, and attributed with agency by them, is in no doubt. Albert Speer writes in his memoirs that 'architecture' was a 'magic word' to Hitler.[7] It was so because it offered the potential to both shape the present population and to leave a lasting legacy that would endure into the future. As Speer recounts, Hitler would muse on the way in which, say, a 'small farmer' from the provinces might feel on encountering particular buildings and how buildings could influence people by their 'impact on the eye' (*Menschenbeinflussung im Auge*).[8] In this, he seems to have been influenced by popular psychological ideas of the day as well as by architectural ideas, derived partly from a fascination with ancient Greece and Rome.[9]

The importance of architecture to the National Socialists was also demonstrated by the massive building programme on which they embarked, with major plans especially for the five cities singled out as *Führerstädte* (Führer cities), among which Nuremberg numbered. Berlin, the Reich capital, was to have been redesigned on a particularly grandiose scale and re-named Germania. The plans, however, were only partially realised, being brought to a halt by the war, during which some of the buildings that had been created were damaged or destroyed.

As part of its National Socialist 'improvement', Nuremberg saw considerable architectural redesign, in various styles. In the Old Town, buildings considered 'out of keeping' – such as the synagogue – were destroyed and many others were given a more medieval look.[10] This 'medievalisation' included timbering being exposed, smaller multiple-paned windows replacing larger single-paned ones, and modern shop fronts being replaced with archways. (Much of this Nazi 'heritagisation' has been retained in the postwar reconstruction of the destroyed Old Town.) Surrounding areas of the city saw the construction of new buildings, often on pared-down functionalist lines, in the so-called *sachliche Baustil* (the functional building style), employed especially for industrial buildings such as factories.[11] There was also building in the *Heimatschutzstil* (literally, the homeland-protection style) – a folksy look, usually of wooden buildings with artisanal craft motifs, that was particularly in evidence in the Strength-through-Joy village that was part of the greater Rally Grounds area.[12]

It was, however, the style of most of the other buildings at the Rally Grounds that is usually seen as 'Nazi' or 'Fascist'. These buildings, especially the Zeppelin Building, and the accompanying marching grounds, were constructed on a massive or *überdimensional* scale in what has been dubbed 'stripped classicism' or 'squared-off pseudo-classicism'.[13] This is characterised by the curving lines of classical architecture being replaced by hard edges and sharp angles, and by rigid symmetry, strong axiality, and extensive flat surfaces – all evident in the Zeppelin Building.[14] Even though the building project at the Rally Grounds was never completed, it nevertheless constitutes 'the largest single complex of monumental buildings ever constructed in National Socialist Germany'.[15] It also constitutes a complex in which architecture was intended to work a particular magic, and to do so not only on those who directly encountered the buildings but also those who encountered them, through visual images, at a distance. As Susan Sontag points out, the fact that Albert Speer is credited on Leni Riefenstahl's *Triumph of the Will* as architect of the film is entirely appropriate for the grounds were also created as a film set and those who participated became actors in an immense propaganda effort whose effects stretched well beyond the Rally Grounds themselves.[16] Photographs (especially Heinrich Hoffmann's artful constructions) were produced for newspapers and commemorative albums, and postcards were produced in their thousands. Films of the rallies were shown not only in cinemas but also on televisions that were produced as a national industry and that were 'frequently viewed collectively in public spaces'.[17]

Despite the description of architecture as 'words in stone', it would be wrong to imply it was conceived by Nazis such as Speer as working in the same way as words in language. Indeed, key to architecture's value to the Nazi project was that it was understood as operating primarily directly on the sensory organs and emotions, unmediated by language, and by-passing reasoning, as the concept of 'eye-impact' suggests. This understanding of the workings of architecture was set out by Speer in his publications after the war.[18] What he argues is that architecture is incapable of inscribing *specific* meanings – it is not language-like in this sense; and this means, therefore, that it cannot be seen as 'ideological'.[19] Architecture can operate, he maintains, as an important tool in the aestheticisation of politics but that process of aestheticisation is itself universal and ideologically neutral. Aestheticisation, that is, is a mere enhancement – a sort of monosodium glutamate flavour enhancer – working to bring out whatever meaning the politics happen to have. Of course, this is a convenient argument for a man seeking to play down his active role in the Nazi regime and to recover a significance for his work as 'art'. As such, it also illustrates well the political implications of claims of material agency and capacity. And it is worth noting that Speer's understanding of 'art' as an apolitical enterprise is one that was largely shared by allied prosecutors at the Nuremberg trails, and that this shared perspective contributed to Speer being spared execution.

It contrast to Speer's tidy understanding of aestheticisation, Walter Benjamin argues that the aestheticisation of politics should itself be seen as a political, rather than neutral, process. Such aestheticisation, he maintains, is 'the logical result of

Figure 2.1   Zeppelin Building during a Nazi Party rally

Fascism' because Fascism turns politics into spectacle and, in so doing, appears to give expression to the masses, while failing to address underlying social relations.[20] In other words, it is a kind of 'mask', working not so much to bring out the real political flavour as to disguise it.[21]

Despite Speer's attempt to depict his work as apolitical, it is also clear from his own writings, as well as other sources, that what was involved at the Rally Grounds was not just some generalised process of enhancement. Rather, specific architectural features were designed in order to try to create particular emotions, bodily responses, actions and associations in ways that were tightly linked to specific aspects of National Socialist politics.[22] Moreover, the implementation of the architectural project itself had massive political, economic and social implications, not least for the thousands of forced labourers (including those interned in concentration camps) who lost their lives quarrying stone for it.

Architectural politics

At an event in London I meet Professor Gunther Kress, who was born in Nuremberg but now works at the Institute of Education, London University. We talk about my work and he recommends that I go to visit Senate House, the university's main administration building. After the meeting, as the winter evening is closing in, I do so. He had correctly anticipated the effect that the building would have upon me: it could be at a Nazi building. In the open walkways at the base of the building, with their atmospheric uplifter lighting, I might be inside the Zeppelin Building.

Senate House, designed by Charles Holden, was begun in 1932 and completed in 1937. The architect had no known fascist or totalitarian leanings and his other designs, including several London underground stations, are not at all like this. Perhaps this was just part of a monumental style with international currency at the time. Nevertheless, it certainly appealed to fascists: Oswald Mosley wanted it to become Parliament if he took over and it is said that Hitler wanted it to become his London headquarters.

Why is it, though, that such architecture seems to appeal to those with similar politics? Why do we find such similar designs used by different totalitarian regimes, those of, say, both Hitler and Stalin? Certainly, there was an international traffic in architectural ideas. In 1937, for example, at the International Exposition in Paris, Speer's German pavilion and the Russian pavilion – the only pavilions completed by the opening date – faced each other; two highly similar, massive, stripped-classical monstrosities, the German topped with an eagle, the Russian with two workers holding a hammer and sickle. Both were awarded gold medals. (Also winning a major prize at the event was a model of the rally buildings.)[23] But is there more to the architectural effect than the fact that we have come to know these as totalitarian and that dictators around the world have adopted similar styles to perform their mastery? Does the combination of massive size, hard lines, axiality, and symmetry necessarily 'speak' totalitarian politics – perhaps even against an architect's intentions? These are questions that I puzzle over again and again as I encounter buildings, Nazi and not Nazi. Material relativity and suggestivity, historical allusion and known symbolism, are surely all part, though perhaps only part, of what is going on.[24]

Architecture as material ideology

Before looking at some of the architectural features that were intended to have effects, I should note two other areas of debate about Nazi architecture. One concerns how far this style of architecture is specific to the National Socialists and whether it should be seen as inherently 'fascist.' The other, of which Speer's arguments above are part, relates to how far architecture can be seen as 'material ideology.'

Although the monumental style of buildings such as those at the Rally Grounds and others elsewhere, such as the Reich Air Ministry in Berlin, the Gauforum in Weimar or Munich's House of German Art, is typically regarded as *the* fascist architectural aesthetic, commentators have pointed out that there was no single unified style of building under the National Socialists, never mind under all fascist regimes.[25] As noted above, the National Socialists built in a mix of styles, in Nuremberg and elsewhere. Even the monumental or heroic-fascist style, according to Petsch, was not the expression of a unified architectural theory, despite the National Socialists' own

Figure 2.2 Senate House interior, 2008

claims, but was 'a conglomeration of diverse architectural influences, partly expressing different positions, that were appropriated according to their intended political-propagandistic effectiveness'.[26] This makes it untenable, he maintains, to claim a particular style as National Socialist, and he is particularly keen to 'rescue' Neo-Classicism from this accusation, pointing out that it had been used in the Weimar period and earlier, and that it could be deployed with the intention of expressing other kinds of ideologies than the fascist.[27] This point can certainly help to explain why a First World War memorial on the Nazi Party Rally Grounds – a building commissioned by the democratic Lord Mayor Hermann Luppe and completed in 1929, before the area became part of the Rally Grounds – could once have been seen as a beautiful example of Weimar architecture, expressive of liberal ideals, but could later seem so in keeping with the Nazi buildings that came to surround it. But does this mean that we cannot associate styles of architecture with particular political ideas and ambitions?

Petsch's argument is that while the same styles in their generality (e.g. Neo-Classicism) can be deployed in relation to a range of ideas and no single style can

31

Figure 2.3   Zeppelin Building interior, 1987

be seen as expressive of a specific political ideology, there are nevertheless certain physical strategies (e.g. the use of massive dimensions and sharp symmetry) and architectural references that are especially likely to be deployed within particular political frameworks. Thus, while we might not see any specific architectural styles deployed by the National Socialists as inherently fascist or exclusive to them, we can nevertheless see certain architectural techniques as appropriate to performing National Socialist ambitions; and we can understand them, *contra* Speer, not just as a kind of universally-sought decorative surface but, more in the manner of Benjamin, as a constitutive part of the fascist project.[28]

The other argument against seeing National Socialist architecture as an expression of ideology has been an approach that puts emphasis on buildings as outcomes of 'the functional implementation of policy'.[29] Rather than attempting to correlate the appearance of buildings with known aspects of ideology, this approach entails detailed attention to the political contexts of the production of buildings, the policies that they were involved in implementing, and the negotiations involved. What is central to such accounts are not individual architects or leaders (with buildings largely understood as the material embodiment of their ideas) but matters such as the financing of the building programmes, and the negotiations and compromises between various players, including various ministries, as well as the way in which 'architectural production … influences other state and Party policies'.[30] Such research has been undertaken on

Figure 2.4 War memorial at former Nazi Party Rally Grounds, 2006

the Nazi Party Rally Grounds by Paul Jaskot and Yasmin Doosry and is invaluable in providing a more rounded and in-depth picture. Doosry's attention to the negotiations between various players highlights the fact that accounts of Hitler being substantially involved in driving the overall projects and paying attention to their details contain a good deal of 'propagandistic legend', and that Nuremberg's city authorities played a considerable role in shaping the outcome of the grounds.[31] Likewise, Jaskot shows, for example, how the choice of stone for the Congress Hall, typically interpreted as a matter of using a building material that would last and convey immortality (see below), was also a result of an attempt to cut down on the use of iron and steel in order to conserve them for the armaments industry.[32] Furthermore, he details the political consequences of this, including the increasing use, and increasing death rates, of forced labourers in quarries, as at the Flossenbürg concentration camp from which much of the stone for the Congress Hall came, and the expanding power of the SS which administered the quarrying operations.

While both Jaskot and Doosry are critical of the notion of reading architecture simply as the expression of ideology, however, both simultaneously fully acknowledge and document ideological intent in the design of buildings such as those at the Rally Grounds. The issue for both is that what was involved was never *just* ideology. As Doosry explains, in the construction of the Rally Grounds site there was almost always a struggle between two goals: (1) providing favourable conditions for the practical use of the grounds and its buildings, and (2) fulfilling the function of the architecture acting as a symbolic carrier of the National Socialist system and its ideology.[33] According to Jaskot too, buildings were designed with symbolic, ideological intent and this could be not only compromised or reshaped by the processes of production but, more importantly, was also a means of actually implementing policy with far-reaching political-economic effects. Before looking at some of the features of the buildings' design, however, it is time to take a brief tour of the Rally Grounds.[34]

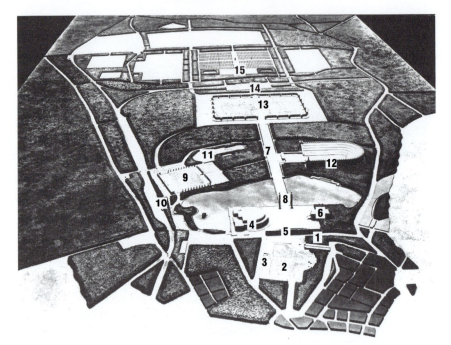

Figure 2.5   Map of Nazi Party Rally Grounds as planned. This is oriented with the south at the top of the map, the north at the lower side

Key to Nazi Party Rally Grounds structures corresponding to numbers on the map:

1 Luitpold Hall – already present when the Nazis began to use the area, this former exhibition machine hall was expanded and given a new monumental limestone façade in building work directed by Albert Speer between 1933 and 1935. Also referred to as the 'Old Congress Hall', it was used for holding party congresses while the new one was being built, and was, as in the image, and as were many of the other buildings, bedecked in swastika-bearing banners during the rallies. It was completely destroyed in the War.

2 Luitpold Arena – this parade ground of 84,000m² could accommodate up to 150,000 participants, and was flanked by tiered seating for an additional 50,000 spectators. At one end was the First World War memorial by architect Fritz Mayer that was unveiled in 1930 (Figure 2.4) – number **3** on the map. From this, an 18 metre wide Straße des Führers (street of the Führer) led to a vast tiered stage, the Ehrentribüne (stage of honour) with its scaffolding for three banners in the centre. At each end of the Ehrentribüne were towers with six metre-high bronze eagles.

4 Congress Hall – (Figure 1.2) begun in 1935, and with work continuing until 1943, by which time the building was still incomplete, the Congress Hall was designed by architects Ludwig and Franz Ruff. Designed to seat 50,000, it covers an area of about 270m² and was intended to be over 60 metres tall, though the planned top layer and glass roof were not built.

5 and **6** Building for cultural events and exhibition building – both planned as monumental structures but not even begun.

7 The Great Road with towers (**8**) at its north end.

9 Zeppelin Field – a marching field of about 300m², with tiered seating on three sides for 150,000 people, and 34 tower structures, containing toilets. On the remaining side was **10** the Zeppelin Building (Figure 2.7), 13 metres high, 50 metres wide, capable of seating 50,000 people. Designed by Albert Speer, building work began in 1934 and was completed in 1937.

11 The old stadium or, as it is also sometimes called, the City Stadium. Constructed before the Nazis came to power, this was partly reconstructed between 1933 and 1937.

12 The German Stadium – designed by Speer, was to have been about 80 metres high, covering a ground area of over 240,000m²; and with seating for 400,000 (Figure 2.8). Only the foundations were dug.

13 The Mars Field – named after the Roman God of War. Planned to be the largest parade ground of all (nearly 600,000 m²), this was to be especially used for military displays and to have seating for 250,000 spectators. Begun in 1935, it was to be surrounded by 24 substantial towers, of which 11 were completed.

14 Mars Field railway station.

15 Accommodation barracks.

Figure 2.6 Luitpold stage and arena, 1934

Figure 2.7 Zeppelin Building and Field, 1939

Figure 2.8   Model of Great German Stadium

A tour of the Nazi Party Rally Grounds

The Rally Grounds were constructed in the 1930s in an area of Nuremberg that had previously mainly been a large public park – with lakes popular for boating and swimming – and in which the city's zoo was also located.[35] Why they were constructed in Nuremberg is itself an interesting and contested matter to which I turn below. But there were a number of features of the particular site that made it attractive to the National Socialists, even though creating the Rally Grounds entailed moving the zoo and also a lighthouse and beach café.

In addition to the fact that a fairly large flat area could be acquired, with good road and rail links, there were several buildings that were used for Nazi gatherings even before site was selected for development. Most important of these was an unusually large and striking memorial – in the form of a hall of honour (*Ehrenhalle*) to victims of the First World War which had been constructed in the 1920s (Figure 2.4). Praised for its beauty by Nuremberg's liberal mayor who had played a part in commissioning it,[36] the memorial's design harmonises well with the monumental architecture that was to be constructed in its vicinity over the following years despite its different political background. Certainly, it was attractive to the National Socialists who held their first rally nearby in 1927 and who later made it the focal point of a vast marching field, the Luitpold arena (Figure 2.6), which among other things was used during the rallies to stage the 'Blood flag' ritual, in which new Nazi regiments were symbolically initiated into the movement by their flags being touched by a special flag (the so-called 'blood flag') that had been carried in the Nazis' failed attempt

36

to gain power in 1923. By drawing on the iconography of World War I, the Nazis equated those who had died in the failed putsch as having, like soldiers during the War, been sacrificed fighting to try to uphold Germany's honour. In so doing, they also depicted themselves as avengers of what was widely seen in Germany as the shame of the Treaty of Versailles.[37]

Also at the north end of the Rally Grounds site, flanking the other end of the Luitpold arena from the war memorial, was a machine hall left from the a major exhibition of Bavarian trade and industry that had been held there in 1906 to mark the centenary of Franken becoming part of Bavaria. It had also been used for National Socialist congresses and meetings prior to the development of the area, but as part of the Rally Grounds project it was given a new façade, with angular lines and flat surfaces, covered in whitish limestone, specially designed for mounting banners and flags in a style that became one of the hallmarks of Nazi display (as in Figure 2.6).

The other building that was retained on the site was the municipal sports stadium that had been opened in 1928 as part of the previously planned extension of the area as a leisure space. This was incorporated by the Nazis into their plans, and used, among other things, for ceremonies involving young people during the Hitler Youth Day of the rallies. It was, however, to have been accompanied by a considerably larger stadium – the so-called 'German stadium' (*Deutsche Stadion*) that was planned to be largest stadium in the world, with seating for 400,000 spectators (Figure 2.8). However, construction work only got as far as the digging out the foundations. As these had a tendency to fill with water, an enormous diesel pump was installed to keep them dry.[38] After the war, however, this was disconnected and the hole filled with water, making it into a lake, which came to be called the Silbersee (Silver Lake) by local people, most probably after Karl May's novel *Der Schatz im Silbersee* (*The Treasure in the Silver Lake*) and linked with local rumours that Nazi treasure might have been left there (see Chapter 7).

In addition to the Luitpold arena, two other vast marching grounds were constructed. One of these was the Zeppelin Field, named after Count Zeppelin, who had landed there in one of his airships in 1909. On one side of this was the Zeppelin Building, consisting of an external podium, tiered seating and galleries and grand internal rooms. South of this lay the even bigger Mars Field (*Märzfeld*, sometimes translated March Field), which was only partially built and was also to have been given a similar, though even larger, building with stage similar to that of the Zeppelin Building.[39]

The other main building on the Party Rally Grounds site is the Congress Hall (*Kongreßhalle*), often referred to colloquially as the 'Colosseum' (*Kolosseum*), its allusion to the Roman precursor (visited by Hitler) being unmistakable (Figure 1.3). A massive horseshoe-shaped building, the Congress Hall was never fully completed, and what is now a raw red-brick interior courtyard was to have been an interior chamber with a glass roof. In 2001 a Documentation Centre, in striking glass and steel architecture, was opened in this building. Between the north and south ends of the site, a wide granite-clad road was built – the 'Great Road' (*Große Straße*) – that also survives today; though the two towers that appear on the map were never built.

Figure 2.9   Interior of Congress Hall, 2006

Figure 2.10   Planned interior of Congress Hall

The structures described so far constituted the main part of the Rally Grounds and covered an area of approximately eleven square kilometres. This is the area which today is usually defined as the Nazi Party Rally Grounds. The complex, as planned and partly realised, was even larger, including a number of other buildings and areas too. The map shows an area called 'Lager', which was an accommodation area, mainly for tents but also including some basic wooden structures. Here too was a railway station, Bahnhof Märzfeld (opened in 1938), which not only served to bring participants to the rallies but also for the deportation of many of Nuremberg's Jews.[40] Built in monumental style, it provided an image of Nazi power from the moment of arrival, and departure. At the eastern side of the site was the Strength-through-Joy village (*Kraft-durch-Freude Stadt*), built to provide rally participants with leisure activities, such as dances and films – the half-hourly tannoy instructions to 'Enjoy yourselves' showing the extension of (possibly counterproductive) discipline even into leisure-time.[41] At the north-west of the site, also in monumental style, were the barracks of the SS (the military elite *Schutzstaffel* – protective guard), the *SS-Kaserne*.[42] This building-complex also survived the war and since 1996 has been a government office dealing with claims for asylum and naturalisation by foreign refugees and migrants (*das Bundesamt für Migration and Flüchtlinge*, renamed in 2005 as *das Bundesamt für die Anerkennung ausländische Flüchtlinge*).

Figure 2.11 SS Barracks, now used as government office for processing asylum and immigration claims, 2007

Number sickness and superlatives

Training to be a tour guide of the Rally Grounds entails mastering numerous numbers – dates, dimensions of buildings and marching grounds, seating capacities, numbers of participants and spectators, quantities of stone and metal, numbers deported and dead. Like many guides, I found it hard to get my head round them when I prepared to take people on tours, and sometimes felt like I was suffering from number sickness. Like others, I was both suspicious of the dizzying numbers – it seemed like subscribing to Nazi bureaucracy to relate them – and yet could also see their use in trying to convey size, especially of buildings that were not built. One feature of numbers is that they can make concrete and give impressions of competence and exactitude. So while this is useful on the one hand, it can also give a spurious reality to things that did not, in fact, ever exist; as well as compounding pre-existing, though sometimes exaggerated, impressions of Nazi efficiency.

Superlatives are perhaps even more perplexing. There is something about them that excites; and there is no doubt that the National Socialist ambitions were frequently formulated through the thrill of superlatives.[43] Relating superlatives, or using comparatives – pointing out, for example, that had the German Stadium been built, even today it would be the biggest stadium in existence – conveys what has been called Nazi 'gigantomania'. But highlighting the enormity of the Nazi enterprise also risks ushering in admiration, a dilemma of which guides are well aware, and that they carefully try to negotiate, as we see in Chapter 7. Here is something that they say to illustrate the perverse priorities and chilling ambition of 'gigantomania': the dimensions of the German stadium, they explain, were so vast that those seated at the rear would have had difficulty seeing the events. Moreover, the dimensions would have contravened Olympic regulations. When this was pointed out to Hitler, he merely replied that this would not matter for in future Olympic games would be held in Germany.

Doing with buildings

Even if the architectural ideas employed by the National Socialists were not always well thought through or coherent, and even though there were sometimes conflicts of opinion or aspects of the actual construction processes that meant that the buildings did not come out quite as intended, Nazi building design nevertheless employed a wide range of ideas about how to do things with architecture.

Size was one of the material relativities which was much deployed at the Rally Grounds site. Large size relative to the human body was understood to impress and give the individual a sense of awe. As Speer explained, what was involved here was a 'violation of human scale'.[44] Such a violation played into a calculated Nazi ideology of dwarfing the individual, and subsuming individual identity to the collective project. This ideology was explicitly stated in one of the slogans of the rallies: '*Du bist nichts,*

dein Volk is alles', 'You are nothing, your people is all'; and was part of the Nazi
'*Volksgemeinschaftsprinzip*' – the principle of 'national community' in which 'the
people' were a united mass (exclusive of outsiders).[45] The appearance of size was
also exaggerated by the use of repeating lines, as, for example, in the rows of closely
set pillars of the Zeppelin Building, which create a visual illusion of even greater
extent.[46]

The massive dimensions of the marching grounds also allowed for a mass –
though rigidly ordered – grouping of bodies, which was likewise intended to
have emotional effects on both participants and viewers. As well as incorporating
the individual body into the collective, this 'body work' was meant to generate
emotions of *Begeisterung* and *Faszination* – a heady mix of enthusiasm, awe,
fascination and excitement. These responses were understood to be spontaneous
and non-cognitive. Nevertheless, although affect drummed up at the rallies is
sometimes described as a kind of 'mass hysteria', it was also carefully controlled
and channelled.[47] This was achieved by extremely strict choreography, movements
of participants being minutely controlled, supported by the hard lines and strong
axiality of the architectural space in which they took place.[48] The rigidity and
orderliness of the architectural lines of the main spaces and buildings at the Rally
Grounds, and of the movements that the masses were to make within them, were
intended to help effect obedience and conformity. Moreover, as Bernd Ogan has
put it, the buildings' 'oppressive solidity and coating of monumentality were to
make the observer experience his compulsory situation as naturally-given and
unchangeable'.[49] Party hierarchy was physically set out on the tribunes, on which
party officials were ranked, above the flat mass of the crowd. And at the centre of the
Zeppelin Building, elevated above the crowd and pre-eminent among the officials,
was the pulpit-like so-called Führer podium from which Hitler made his speeches
to the masses below. The separation off of Hitler, as in his elevated position on the
Führer-podium was expressive of the '*Führerprinzip*' in which all state power was
invested in the leader whom the Volk was to follow in blind trust.[50]

The selection of materials too was shaped both by ideas about their connotations
and what were regarded as inherent properties. Granite was chosen for the Congress
Hall partly because of its hardness and durability.[51] The white limestone cladding of
buildings such as the Zeppelin building was selected to provide a striking and even
dazzling stage for the display of Nazi officials and the numerous banners – with
the Nazi red, black and white insignia – with which these were bedecked during
rallies. This choice of colours – made personally by Hitler – was itself an example of
the calculated 'impact on the eye' that he wanted to achieve.[52] In another Hertzian
material prompt, the colours are those which Berlin and Kay identify as 'basic'
and that Victor Turner sees as having the capacity to generate 'heightened bodily
experiences … informed with a power in excess of that normally possessed by the
individual' on account of their being 'the three colors representing products of the
human body whose emission, spilling, or production is associated with a heightening
of emotion'.[53]

Another aspect of buildings so valued by Hitler was their relative material durability
– that they were capable of lasting beyond even several generations of human

lifetimes and, thus, as he put it, being able to 'speak as eternal witnesses'.[54] They would, he hoped, leave a lasting legacy via a physical presence, which would remain in the landscape, capable of 'speaking to' future generations.[55] This idea of buildings as capable of speaking across time is also articulated in Albert Speer's famous and controversial 'Theory of Ruin Value'.[56] As he describes it in his recollections and in a book about architecture published in 1978, he was inspired by the fact that buildings from classical antiquity had retained a capacity to impress and generate feelings of awe over the centuries even as they fell to ruin. His 'Ruin Theory' thus aimed to take into account the ways in which buildings would decay, and to set out principles that would ensure that even as they did so they would remain capable of acting as what he called 'bridges of tradition'.[57] That is, that they would retain sufficient of their shape and qualities to remain able to 'speak'. If so, this sets up problems for the future in that it suggests that the buildings might continue to speak in ways originally intended. Whether such a theory was actually put into practice in the construction of Nazi buildings is, however, questionable. Certainly, those at the Rally Grounds, while outwardly impressive, have stone façades covering cheaper material, such as brick, and so have already decayed less attractively than have classical buildings. Nevertheless, as we will see in Chapter 4 in particular, Speer's claims themselves contribute to a fear about a possible continuing agency of the buildings and to the negotiation of this difficult heritage later.

Historical and religious referencing

In addition to these uses of materials, another aspect of National Socialist architectural calculation was historical and religious referencing. The Zeppelin Building, for example, was modelled on the west front of the Pergamon Altar, the structure previously topping the acropolis of Pergamos, celebrating the defeat of the Galatians in Greek mythology, and of which there is a large model in Berlin's Pergamon Museum.[58] The speaker's podium at the centre was consciously modelled as a pulpit to further enhance the image of the speaker – most often Hitler – as a religious leader (an analogy that was made at the time).[59] The quasi-religious effect was further stimulated by the use of light, Speer's 'Lichtdom' – a 'cathedral of light' – created by projecting numerous search-lights into the night sky.[60]

The Congress Hall too had classical antecedents, not only the Roman Colosseum, but also some Greek architectural features. As Paul Jaskot points out:

> this conflation allowed for the competing and often contradictory claims made about monumental architecture by National Socialist cultural administrators: Greek to emphasise the supposed racial connections between contemporary Germany and its Aryan ancestors, Roman to buttress the claims of Nazi Germany as a new and powerful empire. ... This architecture, like other monumental state and Party buildings, helped to support the emphasis on permanence which Hitler associated as early as the writing of *Mein Kampf* (1925) with both specific types of classical public architecture as well as the strength of any legitimate political regime.[61]

But it was not just the monumental, colossal architecture that was built to try to produce certain effects. In the cosy homey architecture of the Strength-through-Joy buildings, for example, the 'small farmer from the provinces' was supposed to feel at home, and safe in a warm, cosy (*gemütlich*) atmosphere. Giving Nuremberg's Old Town a more thoroughly medieval appearance was also linked to political ambitions – as evident in the decision to site the rallies in Nuremberg as discussed below. For the medieval streets of the Old Town – like the Rally Grounds – also acted as a backdrop for peopling by the masses during what have come to be called the Nuremberg rallies.

'Can't you feel their power?'

One day at the Rally Grounds I noticed two people with a video-camera, filming on the Zeppelin Building and approached them to ask whether I could interview them. They are English, a man in his late sixties and a woman, his daughter. When I explained that I was doing research about the place and was interested in knowing what they thought of it, the daughter laughed as she said her father would willingly talk to me for hours about it, and that it would be a great relief for her if somebody else would listen to him for a change. He proudly concurred that he was indeed the man to talk to for he had spent a lifetime researching 'the Third Reich and all that'. We talked for about an hour and a half, and again, more briefly, when our paths crossed later in the day.

It soon became evident that he – I will call him Mr Smith – was on a kind of pilgrimage. He had 'always wanted to come here' for he had read so much about it. He also collected Nazi memorabilia – he bet he had more than most museums in Germany. What Hitler was doing in Germany, he believed, had begun well and should be admired 'until it went wrong in 1936', but we should still remember the many excellent developments, including 'inventing motorways' and, 'with Albert Speer, building these amazing buildings'. 'They have such power', he said, 'you can really feel it'; then, to me, 'Can't you feel their power?' I think I smiled and wrinkled my nose. But he continued to press the question. 'Whatever you think about Hitler and everything that happened, you've got to admit that this place is pretty special. I can just see it all with the rallies, the crowds down there, the shouting. And Hitler just there, where I've just been standing … You've got to admit it, it's impressive. You can feel the power of the place, feel the power of the buildings. Can't you?'

I said that, yes, if I tried to imagine how the buildings were back then, and with rallies in place, then I could imagine how powerful it must have seemed to those there. But when I looked at them today, perhaps because I had spent so much time there and they had become so familiar, that wasn't really so. With all the weeds and broken bottles (evidence of both being around us), and with the side wings gone from the Zeppelin Building, they seemed more – I hesitated while trying to find an appropriate expression – 'pathetic really'. So, to me, I concluded, they didn't have the kind of power that he felt.

Mr Smith vehemently agreed that the removing of the side galleries was 'a crime' (though that had not been my interpretation). He also expressed annoyance at the sorry state of the building and said that it should be restored – 'back to its proper glory'. Then 'people will be really able to feel the power of it'. The words in stone would be able to speak properly, across time, not only to those like him – who could so readily picture the rallies and original buildings in their mind's eye – but also to those, like myself, lacking in sufficient imagination.

The encounter raised a question central to my research – that of how these buildings were understood and 'felt' today. It also made me aware, however, of a further dimension of my own willingness or otherwise to attribute agency to them. In short, there was no way that I wanted to stand on a Nazi staging ground and claim to be experiencing the power and spirit of the place alongside a Nazi pilgrim. At the same time, however, I did feel that the removal of the wings of the Zeppelin Building and its crumbling façade, together with days of seeing skateboarders and tennis players practising on it, made it seem much less impressive to me than it would have done otherwise. Pictures of it in 'its proper glory', bedecked with banners and crowned with a golden swastika in a laurel wreath, undoubtedly showed a more threatening – and powerful – edifice. Even when I first saw the building itself, however, I had difficulty reconciling its mutilated state with the images that I too had seen previously.

The party rallies

The rallies were 'mega-events', mass happenings in which thousands of participants acted in unison, and which formed a spectacle not only for those actually there but also, as noted above, at a distance.[62] From 1933 until 1938 they were held annually at the Rally Grounds site in Nuremberg, which was still in a state of construction. Over the period they increased in length from four days to eight as more events and lengthier spectacle were added to the programme of marches and demonstrations. Hundreds of thousands of people came to participate and spectate.[63]

Each of the rallies was given a name – Victory (1933), Unity and Strength (1934), Freedom (1935), Honour (1936), Work (1937) and Greater Germany (1938) – and to some extent the programme varied for each, though there were certain shared key events and a basic template. Each day of each rally was devoted to a key group. Thus, there would generally be days dedicated to displays centring upon the following: political leaders, the Reich labour service, the Hitler Youth, the SA (*Sturmabteilung*) and the Wehrmacht. All involved parades with large numbers of people standing and moving in orderly fashion or the shared enthusiasm of mass chants, in a physical, visual and aural manifestation of organised collectivity and unity of goal; and all included speeches by important party members, intoning the party and nationalistic messages, and helping to whip up fervour for the National Socialist project. There were too, displays of dances and gymnastics, also emphasising coordinated action as well as, variously, the beauty of German womanhood or German tradition; and there were performances not just of amassed human strength but of military hardware, showcasing the national war capability.

The rallies were thoroughly ritualised events. They were spatially and temporally marked as special – as sacred rather than profane. The very fact that such enormous effort and expense could be spent on a site that would be dedicated for this purpose and used for only one week per year was itself a symbolic statement of the ritual significance with which it was being imbued and of the might of a regime that could afford such effort in honour only of itself. The elaborate opening ceremonies indicated the beginning of a 'suspension of mundane time'[64] – a period of heightened experience and meaningfulness. Durkheim's idea of ritual as a means of constituting a social group and allowing it to experience itself collectively – and imbuing this with emotion and 'effervescence' to make the experience all the more effective – seems to capture well at least part of what was involved in the party rallies.[65] The repetition of action in unison, the rhythm of collective chants and dances, the dramatic use of lighting and fire, are all features often found in rituals, helping us to recognise them as such, and constituting part of what we might call the apparatus of affect.

While Durkheim understands ritual as confirming an already existing social order – that is, as mirroring the status quo – other theorists have pointed to the way in which rituals may be part of a motor of change, ushering in a new social order or, in some cases, allowing for different possibilities to be negotiated through ritual action.[66] The rallies were played out as rituals of an existing social order but they were also part of the means for mobilising support for the national socialist programme and thus bringing about their desired new social order. By dramatically playing out the appearance of mass support and total faith in the Führer, the Nazis were able to help make these become still more real and thus to further their wider objectives. As Don Handelman observes, the Nazi Party rallies were thoroughly 'declarative', with no hint of the interrogativeness of some rituals:[67] they were shot through with unambiguous statements and transparent symbolism. They were also characterised by what Handelman refers to as 'over-signification' – the 'very visibility of symbols throughout' and their 'plenitude ... exactness, replication, and uniformity in detail'.[68] The organisation of the rallies was marked by an obsessive attention to detail, with, for example, marchers being told the distance to the inch that they must keep between one other and the exact positioning of each of their fingers.[69] The design of the site itself was likewise part of the detailed means for structuring action; the granite blocks on the Great Road, for example, were precisely cut so that each would be of the right length for two 'Prussian strides'. This fastidious attention speaks of a will to control that was based not only in presenting an existing order (as Handelman seems to suggest) but helping to bring one into being.

The effectiveness of rituals and symbols also lies in their capacity to evoke other, existing symbols. Indeed, Connerton is critical of the idea that we necessarily need to know the intent of those who created a ritual (or, equally, a building) for this relies on an expectation that everything must be formulated in words and relegates the bodily or symbolic to a mere 'translation' of this, and fails to recognise the bodily – or the formal and performative – features of rituals in themselves.[70] The Nuremberg rallies employed numerous formal references to other rituals and symbols and established new ones in the process. The 'blood flag' ritual mentioned above, for example, draws on notions of baptism (each area flag being 'anointed' by contact with the blood flag) and martyrdom (in the symbolism of a military funeral), turning the original failed putsch into a

> sacred event, and one that points forward to another sacred event, that of … the seizure of power … Between the two events a mythic concordance is established … It was a rite fixed and performed. Its story was not told unequivocally in the past tense but in the tense of a mythical present.[71]

Rituals draw on ideas of the past to give legitimacy and rooted meaning to the present and simultaneously give events from the past a continuing relevance. They also turn what might otherwise be mundane or banal into something elevated. The 1923 putsch, which might equally have been seen as a failure, is transformed in the commemorative ceremonies into mythical prelude. More generally, the use of religiously-inspired symbolism in the rallies serves to present National Socialism not as just another political position or movement but as a creed, something to be related to not through debate and rational reasoning but through faith and emotional devotion; and Hitler was transformed from an ordinary political leader into a semi-deified figure, as when made to appear surrounded by an aureola of light.[72]

Accounts by those who participated in the rallies (as, for example, shown in the site's Documentation Centre today) give evidence of having been emotionally affected by the experience, some talking of *Begeisterung* (or its recensions). Generally translated as 'enthusiasm', the term *Begeisterung* shares more closely the original meaning of 'enthusiasm', namely, to be possessed by a god or spirit, than the more usual use of the English term today. 'I was enthused, completely enthused' doesn't quite grasp the sense of being overwhelmed inherent in the German term, which might here be better rendered as 'enthralled' or 'enchanted'. If you are *begeistert*, you are possessed and can, perhaps, hardly help yourself. While this cannot, of course, excuse participation in the Nazi project, it does express the emotional power of the rallies and their significance to the National Socialist movement. As we shall see in later chapters, one task for attempts to represent the rallies and Rally grounds in exhibitions since has been how to explain that *Begeisterung* and convey a sense of its power without recreating the experience itself.

Visual representations and reports of the rallies were, of course, carefully edited to convey a sense of enthralled unity. Marches that lasted several hours or speeches that consisted of reading out seventeen typed pages could be boring;[73] and not everybody who participated was necessarily *begeistert*, even if, as a woman I met on a tour of the Grounds described to me, they had to stand in the streets with their flag and look as though they were enjoying doing so. To try to explain popular support for National Socialism solely in terms of *Begeisterung* or *Faszination*, and its production through the choreography of mass events and image-management, would ignore

46

other, variable, aspects of both the agency and compulsion of the so-called '*Mitläufer*' ('fellow travellers'). Economic calculations, anti-Semitism and other forms of racism, brutalities, politicking and dissent were all thoroughly involved too. Nevertheless, propaganda was still crucial and the party rallies and Rally Grounds were a central part of the apparatus of affect through which Nazi terror was produced.

Siting the rallies

The Nazi Party rallies are still to the forefront of images of Nuremberg held by many foreigners in particular, as surveys such as that given to me by Michael Weber confirmed. Like him, and as we will see in later chapters, many city officials and inhabitants see this as in some ways unfair on Nuremberg, not only in that it ignores other aspects of the city's history and qualities but also because many in Nuremberg regard the fact that Nuremberg became the official City of the Reich Party Rallies (*Stadt der Reichsparteitage*) as largely outside the city's control. Not only does this understanding conceptualise 'the city' just in terms of some of its inhabitants, conveniently ignoring others as somehow not of the city, it also depicts the city 'as victim'.[74] Historian Neil Gregor shows this at work in recent years in Nuremberg as well as in the 1950s, as do later chapters in this book.[75] The question of why Nuremberg became the site of the rallies is, therefore, important, for the city has long resented having been singled out as a Nazi city and this has shaped the response to publicly representing that past.

Indeed, it is almost a mantra among many of those in Nuremberg that Nuremberg was not a particularly Nazi city, and to this end voting figures showing that the NSDAP did not have particularly high support there are generally quoted (see Chapter 5). As many of my Nuremberg interviewees, both lay-people and city officials, were keen to inform me, the city was known as 'red Nuremberg' and had solid social democratic credentials before the war, which postwar it has largely maintained – having had an SPD mayor for the whole of the postwar period with the exception of 1996–2002 when the CSU held office. As a publication about the Rally Grounds produced by the organisation that also organises walking tours explains:

> When the National Socialists considered Nuremberg for the role of 'City of the Reich Party Rallies' this was not based in a right-wing political tradition in the city; to a much greater extent, Nuremberg, as Bavaria's largest industrial and worker city, was a social-democratic-liberal stronghold, which also had wider regional significance due to a strong worker movement.[76]

Tour guides typically ask the groups that they are taking around the site why they think that Nuremberg was chosen as the city of the rallies and as part of the discussion that follows they emphasise the fact that Nuremberg was not especially 'brown' (see also Chapter 7). The message is that what happened in Nuremberg could have happened anywhere else.

The message is no doubt important in order to counter possible complacency among visitors ready to think that such pro-Nazi propaganda and enthusiasm could only issue from a strongly pro-Nazi place. Social historian Hermann Glaser, who as the city's SPD culture minister from 1964 to 1999 played a key role in initiatives to publicly display and debate the Nazi past, told me that it was also important for the self-identity of Nurembergers postwar to feel that Nuremberg – branded by the Nazis and the allies as especially Nazi – was 'a city like any other' (as I discuss further in the next chapter).[77] That Nuremberg has a long history of being politically 'red', and that this distinguishes it from its neighbours, especially Munich (which so often acts as the oppositional 'other' in Nuremberg self-definition), has also been useful to the Social Democrats in maintaining their political dominance over the years; and it is primarily, though certainly not exclusively, from their ranks that those involved in the public representation of the Nazi past have tended to come.

Nevertheless, as Neil Gregor has shown, the notion that Nuremberg was somehow unfairly 'picked on' by the National Socialists has the effect of directing attention away from local politics and it implies 'Nurembergers' were a homogeneous group, victim to Nazi policies. Those seen as responsible are 'others', either generalised 'Nazis' or particular Nazi individuals – most notably the city's notorious *Gauleiter* (the head of a Nazi administrative district), Julius Streicher, who published the virulently anti-Semitic newspaper, *Der Stürmer*. While there was some active opposition to the Nazi regime in Nuremberg as elsewhere, there was considerably more support for the National Socialists, endemic in many sectors of the city.[78] Moreover, the surrounding areas of Franken had been 'strongholds of anti-Semitism in Germany since the beginning of the twentieth century' and Nuremberg was the centre of anti-Semitic nationalist political movements.[79] Even in 1925, the Jewish community of Nuremberg made a complaint to the Bavarian minister-president, saying that 'today in Germany there is no other city in which political incitement and poisoning have reached such a level as in Nuremberg',[80] Nuremberg being at that time one of the few Bavarian cities that permitted National Socialist gatherings, which were banned in cities including Munich and Bamberg.[81] By 1927, when the Nazis held their first rally in Nuremberg, the city was home to one of the best-organised and most committed groups of Nazi supporters in Germany, including supporters among the police.[82]

Rather than having the title of City of the Reich party rallies thrust upon it, the evidence is that those in the city council at the time (1933) were keen to receive this 'honour' and the economic benefits that doing so was believed – also among Nuremberg businesses – would flow from it.[83] Decisions such as this were not simply made by Nazi high command and automatically put into effect, nor were they necessarily even pushed through by Nazi members – including the mayor – of the city council. Rather, they typically required at least the complicity of other council members, some of whom, for example, were non-party functionaries who had been in post during the previous regime too, such as the city's garden director, who might object on all kinds of practical or economic grounds. In the case of the Rally Grounds, the council – presumably especially swayed by the garden director – initially objected to the plan to cut down trees as part of the building programme. The decision was, however, overturned when Hitler said that he might give the honour of hosting the rallies to another city. While this shows the power that he was able to exert, it also shows that it was often more complicated than outright enforcement. Throughout the making of the Rally Grounds, as described well by Doosry and Jaskot, there were often fraught negotiations between different interest groups, such as architectural firms, the city council, and the National Socialist leadership.[84]

There were also certain practical features of Nuremberg that made it a good candidate to become City of the Party Rallies, as is often pointed out on guided tours for example. Positioned fairly centrally within Germany, it had good railway connections, an abundance of accommodation as it was already a tourist resort, and a large space which could be made available for construction. In addition to these practicalities, however, and surely doing more than just over-determining them, were Nuremberg's historical credentials.

Heritage attraction Nuremberg

Part way along the Great Road on the Rally Grounds, tour guides usually stop and suggest that visitors look north, back towards the city. Although now obscured by trees, the view leads directly to the Kaiserburg, Nuremberg's medieval – though since expanded and reconstructed – castle. The Kaiserburg is one of Nuremberg's most historically important and visually well-known sights, its outline forming the city's logo as well as being used on all kinds of local products, such as many brands of the famous *Lebkuchen*. The Nazis too used depictions of the Kaiserburg in their visual materials, such as posters for the rallies. They also, it is usually believed, designed the Great Road to point directly towards the Kaiserburg.[85]

That the Kaiserburg had been significant during a substantial period of the Holy Roman Empire (911–1806) was extremely attractive to the Nazi construction of the idea of their political regime constituting a Third (German) Reich. In their historical scheme, the Holy Roman Empire constituted the First (German) Reich (*das Erste (Deutsche) Reich*) and the German unity established by Bismarck in 1871 (and usually seen as lasting until 1918) the Second. The ambitions of their so-called Third Reich were cast in part as a recovery of the geographical extent of the First Reich. Incorporating the areas of present-day countries of Germany, Austria, Switzerland, the Czech Republic, Belgium, Luxembourg, Liechtenstein and the Netherlands, as well as parts of Poland, France and Italy, the Holy Roman Empire had no single capital city. Instead, monarchs roved from place to place, with various cities acting as *Reichsstädte* – imperial cities. Nuremberg was one of these and in this capacity held the *Reichstage* – the Imperial Diets – at least eleven times.[86] Its castle, the Kaiserburg, begun in its present form in the eleventh century, was visited by such important Kaisers as Frederick Barbarossa and Karl V. As Anne Kosfeld notes, Nuremberg was already drawing upon this history and presenting itself as 'holy capital of the Reich' well before the Nazis adopted this idea to their own ends.[87]

Holding the *Reichsparteitage* of the Third Reich in Nuremberg, although these were very different kinds of events from the *Reichstage* of the Holy Roman Empire, produced a fictive historical continuity, making the Nazis appear to be heirs to a long tradition that had only been unfortunately interrupted in the nineteenth century. But this was only one, albeit especially important, aspect of Nuremberg history that led to Hitler describing the city as 'the epitome of unequivocal Germanness'.[88] That

Nuremberg had been home to Germany's celebrated Renaissance painter, Albrecht Dürer, appealed to Hitler, a keen painter himself. So too did the fact that it was the setting for the opera *The Mastersingers of Nuremberg* (*Die Meistersinger von Nürnberg*) by his favoured composer, Richard Wagner.[89] The opera is set in the sixteenth century, when Nuremberg was still an imperial city and its renaissance culture was also flourishing. From 1933, the opera was performed in Nuremberg during every party rally.

City streets

Many of the streets around the area that was to become the Rally Grounds site were, in 1906, named after characters and places in the famous Nibelungen myth that had also been the subject of Wagner's famous opera cycle, *Der Ring des Nibelungen*. For example, Wodanstraße, over which Tram 9 trundles en route to Luitpoldhain is named after the God of War, as is nicely observed by Nuremberg poet Fitzgerald Kusz in his shortdialect poem, *bewältigung*.[90]

Bewältigung	overcoming
di wodanschdraß führd	wodan street leads
zum platz der opfer	to victims of
des faschismus	fascism square

'Restoring' the city to how it might have appeared at this time, or even as depicted on stage in Wagner's opera, shaped the heritage makeover of Nuremberg, various buildings in the old-town being given 'medieval' façades that they never previously possessed (as described above).[91] This provided an ideal First Reich backdrop for those parts of the Nuremberg rallies that took place in the streets of Nuremberg's Old Town. Hitler's procession could thus bear the imprint – an 'eye impact' – of imperial processions of earlier times.

War and after

A rally was planned for 1939 – to begin on September 2nd. Ironically, it was to have been called the Rally of Peace. But with the escalation of military aggression and with war imminent, it was cancelled. On September 1st, Germany invaded Poland. On September 3rd, Britain and France declared war. War efforts meant that construction at the Rally Grounds site was massively scaled down and by March 1940 was almost completely halted.[92] Nevertheless, planning and procuring the massive quantities of stone required for what was classified as a *Dringlichkeitsstufe 1* – top priority – project continued through to 1942, with a peak number (10,613) of workers being employed on quarrying in 1941; and prisoners of war were being brought to the Rally Grounds site as late as 1943 to work on the buildings.[93] For these, but also for other war prisoners, the barracks at the south of the site that had been erected for rally participants, were turned into a prisoner of war camp – 'Stammlager (Stalag) XIII D' – containing up to 30,000 prisoners at any time.[94] (Those numbers again.)

As the site of a large number of factories producing armaments and other hardware vital to the war effort, and as a main station on the west–east and north–south rail axes, Nuremberg was a prime military target and was subject to numerous bombing raids, the first main allied attack being in August 1942. Overall, there were over 40 major allied bombing raids on Nuremberg and from the summer of 1944, and as Schramm writes, hardly a day or night went by without the air-raid alarms sounding.[95] By the time of the last air attack on 11th April 1945 more than 6,000 people had died as a direct result of allied bombing.[96] On 2nd January 1945, in what has come to be called Nuremberg's night of horror (*Erschreckensnacht*), the Old Town was severely hit and turned into a blaze that could not be extinguished for several days.[97]

American troops entered Nuremberg on 16th April 1945 and fighting in what is sometimes called the battle of Nuremberg lasted until the 20th, Hitler's 56th birthday. A relatively small part of the battle took place in the Nazi Party Rally Grounds, mainly in the northern areas near to the SS barracks and in the Luitpold arena.[98] But for the most part the Rally Grounds were the site of little actual military activity. It was, however, bombed, though by no means to the same extent as many other parts of the city. As Schramm points out, it was hardly surprising that the allies did not 'waste' many bombs on this now disused propaganda site given the considerable number of factories building munitions which were located elsewhere.[99] Nevertheless, it was hit repeatedly. The Strength-through-Joy village was totally destroyed, as was the Luitpold hall. The stage of honour on the Luitpold arena was seriously damaged. The SS barracks suffered moderate bomb damage, as did some of the façades on the Zeppelin Building, and the Congress Hall, where scaffolding was destroyed and the façade burnt over a length of 150 metres.[100] Some more minor buildings and foundations were also destroyed or damaged; and others, such as the Mars Field were hit but not badly damaged; and the whole area was left littered with unexploded shells.[101] Overall, however, most of the main buildings and grounds were left relatively intact.

* * * * *

While much of Nuremberg was reduced to rubble, then, the Nazi Party Rally Grounds remained. What was left after the war was a large area of completed and semi-completed monumental buildings and marching grounds. Also left were images of the Rally Grounds thronging with enthralled participants – images that, as Tim Benton observes, convey 'powerfully the causes, effects and qualities of National Socialist hysteria'.[102] More mobile and more easily produced and reproduced than the buildings themselves, film footage and photographs were key technologies allowing the stones to speak out beyond the site itself. These, as well as the monumental architecture that remains, continue to inflect upon the ways in which the former city of the Nazi Party rallies is encountered. How this has been negotiated since – with words, silences, architectural interventions, pictures and physical movements – is the focus of the chapters that follow.

3

DEMOLITION, CLEANSING
AND MOVING ON

One approach to difficult heritage is to obliterate it – to remove it from view. Another, related, is to 'mutilate' or 'deface' it – a procedure that might make its origins unclear and that is often perceived as removing its power or ability to 'give testimony'. The Turkish demolition of Armenian churches and monasteries in Turkey, Ceauşescu's razing of 'ethnic' architecture in Romania, and the Chinese destruction of Buddhist monasteries in Tibet are just some twentieth-century examples of such demolition and mutilation as part of wider 'ethnic cleansing'. Nazi destruction of synagogues was one aspect of the elimination of Jewish presence in Germany – even while, at the same time, those in Prague were to be kept as part of a Museum of an Extinct Race.[1] Demolishing buildings or certain architectural features may also be implicated in demoting or forgetting particular political regimes and social orders. In postwar Germany, for example, the East German dictatorship cleared some buildings deemed 'bourgeois', such as Berlin's Schloss on Alexanderplatz. More recently, the current dismantling of the Palast der Republik – the building 'for the people' with which the GDR government replaced the Schloss – might in turn be seen as an attempt to excise a particularly visible and central reminder of Germany's socialist history.[2]

One way of at least partially avoiding having to continually negotiate the difficult heritage of Nazism, then, is to remove physical reminders of its presence. There are numerous examples of such removal, some of which involve the complete razing of Nazi buildings. In the immediate postwar years this was usually only of buildings that had sustained significant bomb damage. In Munich, for example, two Temples of Honour (*Ehrentempel*), built to commemorate the Nazis who died in the Beer Hall Putsch, were blasted away in 1947 and the Wittelsbacher Palais – that had been used by the Gestapo for internment and torture – was demolished by 1950.[3] In Berlin, buildings such as the Reich Chancellery and the former Gestapo headquarters were demolished in the late 1940s and early 1950s.[4] More often, however, especially 'lesser', Nazi buildings have remained in place, though stripped of their Nazi insignia of swastikas and eagles. Such buildings are often unmarked in cityscapes. In Weimar, for example, even today the massive Gauforum – a complex of Nazi buildings and vast marching square near the centre of the town – is simply listed as 'Weimar Platz' on most maps and has no signs on it to inform about its history (see Chapter 4). In Munich, buildings such as the House of German Justice and the Luftwaffe headquarters were not just maintained but were substantially rebuilt.[5] In Berlin, the

Olympia Stadium was stripped of its obvious Nazi insignia and has continued in use. It was even the venue for a spectacular light show – that reminded some critics of that used previously by Albert Speer at the stadium – during the 2006 Football World Cup finals.

In Nuremberg, until the 1990s most maps and guides produced for tourists either focused on the Old Town, conveniently leaving the former Nazi Party Rally Grounds just outside their frame; or else they indicated the camping site and stadium that are based there without naming the Rally Grounds.[6] Even in the late 1980s there were complaints about a lack of signs in the city about how to get to the Rally Grounds, with comments in the visitor books such as 'One can't simply deny the existence of twelve years of German history'.[7] Through this lack of locators, the Nazi buildings in the city were kept out of the gaze of all but the most dedicated tourists.

Hidden heritage

At a conference I fall into conversation with a delegate from Austria who, when I tell her about my research, recounts having attempted to visit the Rally Grounds with a group of friends in the late 1970s. They had asked at their hotel for directions, she relates. The woman at the desk initially told them that everything had been destroyed during the war and that there was nothing left to see. When they said that they were informed otherwise, she became defensive and challenged them about why they should want to go there. There were many other, much more attractive, places to visit in Nuremberg, she told them. They remained insistent. Finally, she gave them rough instructions but these were so poor that it took them a long time to get there, finally they managed it – though 'so late that we had hardly any time to look round'. How extraordinary, she said, that it was seen as so unsuitable to visit even then.

Although unmentioned on maps and guides, however, most of the Nazi buildings at the Rally Grounds were not demolished. When I have given seminars about this topic, audiences have often expressed surprise that they weren't completely razed after the war. Why leave such obvious relics of Nazi power in place, especially given their obvious attraction as a place of pilgrimage for neo-Nazis? Surely it would be easier to have removed this massive architectural stigma from the city's face and memory? Knowledge and memory are not, of course, necessarily anchored in physical presence; and physical absence does not inevitably equate with forgetting. All the same, continued material presence – especially of large structures like buildings – can make forgetting more difficult, and can become the focus for later commemoration or reflection.

In this chapter, I address the question of why the buildings were not completely destroyed and also look at some of the suggestions that they should have been, in whole or part. I also consider some of the partial demolitions of the site that have taken place and I examine a number of other examples in which the lack of mention of the site's history has later come to be seen as a surprising and even extraordinary silence, and perhaps as evidence of 'repression' of a troubling memory. In doing so, I seek to highlight as far as is possible how these matters were understood at the time, and also to explain the political structures through which negotiations about the site took place in the postwar years. The examples included here range from the immediate postwar period – when the predominant approach was one of removing swastikas – through to the early 1970s, when the site was listed under heritage protection legislation and a period of more extensive demolition was largely, though not entirely, brought to an end. By looking at these examples, my aim is to show some of the various possible impetuses to demolishing, mutilating or apparently ignoring difficult heritage.

Removing swastikas and denazification

Immediately after Nuremberg was taken by the allies, the Nazi Party Rally Grounds were occupied by the US forces. One of their first acts was to remove swastikas. On the 24th April 1945, following a military parade on the Zeppelin Field, and the awarding of medals for bravery to US soldiers on the Führer podium, the large central swastika in its oak leaf crown on the Zeppelin Building was draped in the Stars and Stripes before being detonated.[8] Press reporters from around the world recorded the event. Other swastikas were dismantled with less ceremony and drama, some of them being taken by US soldiers as souvenirs.[9]

One of my interviewees recalled having seen as a child what he supposed was a melted-down swastika shortly after the war. He described it as a large, twisted lump. In his choice of words and the tone in which he described this Nazi relic, it was as though he was describing what the regime really had been: an ugly mass dressed up as golden and ornate. The symbolic stripping of the regime of its façade reduced it to what it really was. This idea was clearly part of the allied 'undressing' of the Rally Grounds and other Nazi buildings. Swastikas came to be seen not just as a key representation of the regime but also as possessing agency, or what Paul Virilio has called an 'arresting power', a capacity to create a kind of 'paralysis of the spectator's gaze'.[10] The swastika was both feared for what it represented, and for its dangerous capacity, like Hitler's supposed hypnotic powers, to entrance. The removal of swastikas was thus an obliteration of a significant item in the Nazi apparatus of affect as well as of the pre-eminent symbol of Nazism.

Visions of endings

The ending of terrible regimes is often captured in visual images that become iconic of ending and new beginning. Photographer Robert Capa's image of a US soldier standing triumphantly in front of an enormous swastika (on the Zeppelin Building) is one such compelling, and widely-known, image of the end of World War II. The image teases with its intact swastika and soldier who could initially be mistaken as giving a Hitler salute. But his grin, and the title 'Victorious Yank', tell us otherwise. The image looks spontaneous and radiates an energy as such. But perhaps it was carefully staged.

Photographers and magazine editors know how a striking image can seem to sum up a moment and how it can lodge in memory. Creating and circulating such images is part of the stock-in-trade. Recall that of the statue of Saddam Hussein being toppled in 2003 – an image that perfectly depicted regime end, as well as US triumphalism. Later it was denounced as highly stage-managed, not only in the careful preparations at the time but also in the closely cropped frame that suggested more Iraqis hitting the statue with their shoes than were in fact there.[11]

The Nazi buildings and marching grounds themselves, however, were mainly left intact in the first postwar decade. An exception was the removal of the stands and stage in the Luitpold arena and the grassing over of its marching ground in the early 1950s. This followed a request in 1949 by a local residents' association for the area to be returned to its prewar state.[12] A main reason for the more common absence of such suggestions or discussions was no doubt simply that there was plenty else to be done

Figure 3.1 *Triumph.* Photograph by Robert Capa, shown on cover of *Life* magazine, 14 May 1945 (see: www.skylighters.org/photos/robertcapa.html)

in terms of rebuilding lives, dealing with those arrested and trying to establish new political and social structures. However, it also seems that for some, including the Americans, it was not deemed necessary. Denuded of their swastikas and flags, and occupied now by confident US soldiers, the buildings seem to have been regarded as effectively neutered by the euphoric victors, and, as such, they even acted as captured trophies, symbolising the defeat of National Socialism. Tourism to the site, which the Nazis had promoted, was continued by US soldiers who came to take snaps of these relics of fascist dictatorship. As Susan Sontag observes, cameras can act as 'predatory weapons', part of a means of 'capturing' and 'taming' that which they 'shoot'.[13] The great propaganda site of the National Socialists was – without its previous decorations and occupants – now 'captured' and seen as unable to work its 'magic'.

The removal of swastikas has parallels with the broader processes known as 'denazification' (*Entnazifizierung*) that were also underway at the time. The Nuremberg trials – the first such international trials and based on the model of a military tribunal – were set up in order to try those accused of Nazi war crimes.[14] Although there were good practical reasons for holding the trials in Nuremberg, in particular the large courtroom with adjoining prison cells, the fact that it was seen by the allies as the capital of the Nazi Party was also significant. Performed for a general public, the trials were simultaneously a ritual and drama of cleansing.[15] In this sense, they acted, as did the blasting off of swastikas, as a form of ritual purification, serving not simply to remove apparent defilement but also to mark the end of one period and the beginning of another.[16] Choosing what was seen as the centre of Nazi-dom for such symbolic performance made sense. Just as the historical resonances of Nuremberg had made it an apt choice of site for the Party rallies, the Nazi historical legacy made it an especially important site to ritually purge.

To say that the trials had a ritual function is not to say that they were mere ritual, though, as Kettenacker notes, they were surely seen as such by some, even at the time.[17] Nevertheless, questions can be, and have been, asked about how far the trials and other forms of denazification really did rid postwar society of Nazi tendencies. To what extent was this really the new beginning – the *Stunde Null* or 'zero hour' – that became an important part of publicly performed historical consciousness? On the one hand, insofar as the Nazi Party had been dissolved, its principal leaders killed or removed from power, the Wehrmacht disbanded, new forms of government established, and cities left in rubble, the old regime had clearly come to an end. On the other, it has been argued by many scholars that denazification remained superficial and did not properly ramify through German society.[18] The Nuremberg trials focused on those in positions of power, and thus limited blame, avoiding the idea that the whole German people was collectively guilty for the crimes committed in their name. This included a tendency that grew stronger in later years to engage in what Reichel calls the 'demonisation of Hitler' – the focusing of blame on the Führer, the leader.[19] While every member of the German population had to give answers to 131 questions about their roles and activities during the war (in the infamous *Fragebogen* – the questionnaire), and while these were considered by German denazification committees, this led to relatively few convictions.[20] There was widespread resentment and criticism of the denazification processes, which made attempts to carry it out effectively increasingly difficult; and this was compounded in the Western zones by attempts to bring the process to a close by the end of the 1940s.[21] Far from being only about purging, denazification procedures were simultaneously processes of rehabilitation. By going through what was, after the initial months, hardly a rigorous process and being cleared, individuals were able to claim that they had been tried and found innocent. Denazification thus allowed them to take up jobs and hold office once again. Perhaps even more consequentially, as Lutz Niethammer argues, it allowed people to avoid critically examining their own complicity or actions.[22]

Blasting swastikas off buildings was analogous to – and part of the same historical consciousness or approach to the past as – official denazification procedures in that it acted as a powerful social ritual to publicly mark the end of the Nazi regime and to make Nazi discourse and symbolism taboo. Showing the swastika in public places was prohibited, and anybody in positions of power expressing sympathy for Nazism, or using its discourse, risked being drummed out of office. But while rituals undoubtedly help to perform – in the sense of 'make happen' – that which they articulate, Marxist theorists in particular have pointed to the ways in which they may provide an appearance that mystifies what is really happening.[23] Just as denazification procedures allowed real soul-searching to be avoided, so too, at the level of material culture, did removing swastikas. The buildings themselves – undoubtedly stripped of some of their allure – could, and did, remain standing, at least for the time being.

Postwar political organisation and negotiation

In 1948 the allies officially returned to the city the land – including buildings such as the Congress Hall and Zeppelin Building – that had been taken by Nazis for building the Rally Grounds, although they continued to control the use of some buildings and areas. As elsewhere in the Western zones, there was a move by the allies soon after the war to try to establish local and regional governments, including rebuilding a civil service. In doing so, they had to seek out people for office whose track record did not implicate them too heavily in the previous regime but who would, nevertheless, be competent. This was not an easy task. In Nuremberg, the first acting mayor (*kommisarischer Bürgermeister*) had been a member of the NSDAP, though he only held office for a few months before being replaced by a member of the SPD; and then, after democratic elections were established at the end of 1945, an SPD 'full mayor' (*Oberbürgermeister*) took up office, and the SPD maintained the mayor's post and a majority on the city council until elections in 1996. Others who had been part of the Nazi local government became fully part of postwar governance for much longer, though only in non-elected posts. Most notably for the story that follows, Heinz Schmeissner (1905–97), who was Nuremberg's Buildings Minister (*Baureferent*) from 1949 until he retired in 1970, had been a member of the NSDAP and had worked in the buildings ministry in Nuremberg during the war, having been director of the main buildings office (*Hochbauamt*) from 1940. He was convicted by the military government in 1945 on a relatively minor charge and later pardoned, and shortly afterwards was voted by the city council to take up post with particular responsibility for reconstruction.[24]

The political structure that emerged postwar, then, was one of local (including city) and regional governance by Germans, the higher levels of which, especially the state Minister-Presidents, were appointed directly by the allies and accountable to the Office of Military Government of the United States (OMGUS). While the latter undoubtedly kept a close eye on many of the more important activities, they left the dealing with most day-to-day affairs in the hands of the local administrations.[25] There were, however, negotiations and even conflicts between OMGUS and the city council. The Rally Grounds were a significant site of such negotiation. In 1946, for example, the city council asked to be able to use the former SS barracks, with its opulent offices, as its own base – in other words, as the *Rathaus*, the town hall. Such a request might seem curious from a 'new regime' council. But it reflected the dearth of suitable office space and the culture of relentless pragmatism that characterised the period. The US rejected the request on the grounds that it was itself using the building complex and wanted to continue to do so.

Other parts of the grounds being used by the US military included the Zeppelin Field, which was used for military exercises and sport; and the Great Road, which from 1951 was used as a runway. Of most concern to the city council, however, was the municipal stadium, which had been Nuremberg's main stadium prior to having been taken over by the Nazis and without which the city lacked a significant amenity. The struggles over the use of buildings led to a conference on the matter in 1953, during which city officials maintained that the city was being dealt an unjustified double blow, having first lost their stadium to the Nazis and then to the allies.[26] Despite the conference, however, the disagreements were not fully resolved. The stadium was not vacated by the military until 1961; and the SS-barracks – which remained a contested site – was only fully vacated and handed over to the city in 1992. In other cases, however, such as the Zeppelin area, joint usage was successfully achieved. As well as being used by the military, from 1947 it was used for annual motor racing, tens of thousands of spectators occupying the Zeppelin Building and surrounding seating to watch the show.[27]

US military parades

During the period of US occupation, the American military not only used the Grounds for training purposes and for practical matters such as holding prisoners and housing displaced persons and refugees, they also used them for their own military rituals. Generally two parades per year would be held by the US military, with, from 1948 onwards, at least one of these being held at least partly in the former Nazi Party Rally Grounds, most usually on the Zeppelin Field. Thus in 1948 an Armistice Day parade was held there. The local newspaper, the *Nürnberger Nachrichten*, which had been established with a postwar US-approved anti-fascist editorship,[28] seemed to signal a coded note of disapproval of the US use of flamboyant military parades in its brief and cool report and observation that 'only a few Germans came to enjoy the spectacle'.[29] That the parades were intended as much to be observed by the German public as they were a ritual for the military itself was still clearer in 'American Army Day' which also came to be held annually. This typically included parades of infantry,

Figure 3.2   US military parade, 'Day of US Airpower', 1952

tank and airforce units through the town, sometimes on routes hardly different from those that Hitler had taken during the Reich Party rallies, and an array of military displays on the Zeppelin Field – something which also had taken place under the Nazis. Of the 1949 parade, the *Nürnberger Nachrichten* reports that the number of German viewers was greater than before, though does not estimate a number.[30]

To carry out displays of military might, and to seek to impress the public, on just the site on which the National Socialists had done the same thing earlier, might seem in poor taste or even a failure to learn from history. However, as with US soldiers giving a Hitler salute on the Führer podium, it was part of a desecration typical of war triumphalism. Moreover, the US parades were part of their own military tradition, and they were not expanded into the extravaganzas that the Nazis had staged. Nevertheless, if the Germans are accused of using the site unreflectively postwar, and if this is seen as a symptom of a broader failure to properly acknowledge their difficult heritage, we must surely conclude that the Germans were not alone in this: the occupying forces were doing likewise in some respects at least.[31] The Rally Grounds were being approached by both within cultural frameworks that made the uses to which they were put appear appropriate and reasonable. The effect of those frameworks, however, was to set up blind-spots, in which participants did not see what their own preoccupations excluded, and also did not see how their actions might appear to others.

On pragmatism

The fact that the buildings could be put to use – by both the US military and the city council – was no doubt especially important in a city in which so many buildings had been destroyed or seriously damaged. Nevertheless, the emphasis on usability and the pragmatic, reiterated time after time by the city council and also in later accounts of what was done (or not), is itself cultural.[32] In another 'culture' a different course of action might seem obvious or the pragmatic thing to do. In postwar Germany, emphasising practicalities and economics was not just taken for granted, it also had moral connotations and implications for the fate of the physical heritage.

Until the 1970s – and continuing as a major approach since – the predominant language in which negotiations about the Rally Grounds was conducted was that of practicalities and costs. At the end of the 1950s, for example, there were debates in the city council about whether or not to spend money on repairing parts of the Congress Hall that were used for storage. The local newspaper invited suggestions from the public about what to with the *Erbstück* – 'heritage piece'. But despite the fact that the newspaper tendentiously described the building in this way, the printed selection from the flood of suggestions received shows none mentioning the past of the building at all, with the exception of one who cautioned that there should be no attempt to build the roof that had originally been intended for the building, for to do so would be to 'posthumously endorse a mania'.[33] Others made practical suggestions, such as that the building should be given a nylon roof, and all supported the idea that money should be spent on repairs if this could increase council revenue.

Likewise, debates during these years recorded in council minutes about the fate of the Congress Hall and other former Nazi buildings were overwhelmingly concerned with how much this or that course of action would cost; and virtually never considered the symbolic meanings of different courses of action. There were, however, some exceptions. In 1958, for example, in making a case for the Congress Hall becoming a football stadium and multipurpose event venue, Building Minister Schmeissner (who, as noted above, had also been buildings minister during the Nazi period), supplemented an argument about making use of the 'astronomical sums' already spent creating the building with a (specious) claim that it need not be seen as 'exclusively the spiritual product of the twelve brown years' because the plans to make some sort of exhibition building had been begun in 1929.[34] If the building remained undeveloped, he argued, it would retain its Nazi identity as 'the Congress Hall' in public memory – despite attempts by the council to refer to it as the 'Exhibition Building' (*Ausstellungsrundbau*); whereas, if it was altered, then it would take on a new identity as 'the Arena'.[35] The emphasis on forging a new identity did not only come from those who had been part of the previous regime, however: it is also evident in the German Architects Association recommendation in 1963, discussed below, to raze the Congress Hall from the landscape.

In making their economic cost–benefit calculations the SPD-majority council not only included projected future sums and amounts that could be raised as rent income (running to some tens of thousands of deutschmarks (DM)) but also, as in Schmeissner's argument, they often invoked the amounts that had already been spent – 'invested' – in the site. Exactly how much money the Nazis had expended on the Rally Grounds was difficult to calculate, though it was undoubtedly enormous. There had, of course, also been the immense human cost, though perhaps because this, unlike the financial expenditure, was not perceived as being 'of the city', perhaps because it was not easily calculable or perhaps because it was morally difficult to contemplate, it was not mentioned.[36] But by casting the financial expenditure as 'investment' – 'diese riesige Investierungen', 'these gigantic investments' as the buildings department expressed it in a 1955 document about what to with the Congress Hall [37] – the council undoubtedly strengthened its arguments for making use of the buildings rather than destroying them. 'Investment' is expenditure from which gains are only expected in the future: it is expenditure made for this purpose. Describing the money spent on the Rally Grounds as 'investment', and as 'Nuremberg's money', council members of all the main political parties turned the possibility of not using the buildings into the equivalent of throwing away the city's resources. As a newspaper report about the debates about removing the Luitpold arena put it, 'Amortisation' – gaining repayment on investment – 'is the keyword'.[38]

The council did not necessarily need to look at things in this way but by doing so, especially in a period in which so much else had been lost, it constructed what appeared to be a strong moral argument against unnecessary waste. If the Third Reich had squandered vast sums at this site, so the reasoning went, the least the city could try to do was to recuperate some of this and to turn it to the advantage of the city that had been so badly treated by the Nazis. In this way, the arguments of the council contributed to a growing tendency to locally understand Nuremberg as having been swindled by the Nazis and as now having to struggle to make good – a struggle in which the occupying allied forces were also sometimes seen as adversaries.

Celebrating construction: the German Building Exhibition

One example of making the most of the Nazi building investment was the use of the site, especially the Congress Hall, for holding the German Building Exhibition in 1949. In several books published in the 1990s and since, as part of a new wave of looking at Nuremberg's past, this is highlighted as a conspicuous example of the city's postwar failure to acknowledge the city's history, or even to 'repress' it.[39] While there does seem to have been a good deal of reticence about the identity of the exhibition's location, looking further at some of the documentation highlights the cultural frameworks within which such a 'silence' occurred as well as suggesting that the lack of explicit reference was evident to at least some participants, as was the all-too-recent history of the site.[40]

The 1949 German Building Exhibition was the first such exhibition held postwar and Nuremberg's council was undoubtedly delighted to have worn the contract, especially over their rivals, Munich.[41] The decision to hold the exhibition at the former Nazi Party Rally Grounds was made primarily – as part of the pervasive culture of pragmatism – on the basis of the fact that the Congress Hall made an ideal exhibition space. On maps produced for the exhibition, the Congress Hall is indicated simply as 'Exhibition building'. A massive event, the Building Exhibition attracted hundreds of exhibitors from all over Germany and some from overseas. These were categorised according to a taxonomy of trauma, in which countries were divided into two groups: one of countries that had suffered destruction – Austria, England, France, Holland and Italy; and one of those that had not – Sweden, Switzerland and the US.

German cities were further categorised to serve as examples of, variously, complete reconstruction, structural attempts to divide the city into living and business areas, and heritage protection. Nuremberg was included in the latter.

The exhibition attracted numerous visitors, many more than had been anticipated, from throughout Germany, including the eastern zone. On the middle Sunday of the exhibition 70,000 attended, even though a message was put out on the radio requesting the Nuremberg population not to come due to overcrowding. The event was a cause for celebration and the festival newspaper argued that this was the first time since 1938 that the town was bedecked in flags – 'in full festival decoration' ('*in vollem Festschmuck*').[42] As it further commented, however, this was 'not the sign of a shrieking "movement" (*Bewegung*) for power and mastery over the people' but 'the new sign of a reestablished German state brightly expressing its wish to be part of the so important rebuilding of Europe'. The admittedly rather indirect reference to the National Socialists through the term 'movement' is evident too in other references and allusions in articles produced about the festival. While somewhat coy, they are nevertheless there, and usually used, as with this example, in order to mark the present as different from the past.

Nowhere in the exhibition catalogue or guide, however, is any indication given as to who constructed the Congress Hall and surrounding buildings or the purposes for which they were used and intended. That there was some awareness of the evasion involved, however, is evident in a joke included in one of the exhibition magazines:

> Last Sunday an exhibition visitor asked one of the Exhibition organisers: 'How long have you needed to build this splendid area?' The man from the [exhibition organisation] replied, 'We began with the technical preparations in May'. The other: 'And in such a short time this giant building was completed?'[43]

Perhaps one of the most striking examples of silence over the Nazi site is in a part of the exhibition on the subject of granite, held near to the exhibition entrance, in the granite-covered cloistered walkway of the Congress Hall. Organised by the *Deutsches Granitverband* (German Granite Association), this exhibit spells out the advantages of granite as a building material, above all its durability. Mounted on the granite blocks of the congress hall, each one of which would have cost lives of concentration camp workers, was a motto that could equally well have been engraved by Speer on the building itself: '*Granit. Der Stein für die Ewigkeit*', 'Granite: The Stone of Eternity'.[44]

The principal theme and rationale of the exhibition was the destruction of German cities. This was part of a wider, understandable, concern with the devastation that cities such as Nuremberg had suffered; and with the task of building that was the exhibition's focus. The opening speech by Nuremberg's mayor, Otto Ziebill, reproduced as the first article in the exhibition newspaper, began: 'Nuremberg, once called the imperial treasure chest, is one of the most severely destroyed cities in Germany'.[45] Practical suggestions for new housing models or what to do with war rubble all reminded of 'this terrible chaos', as the 'teaching show' exhibit puts it.[46] And a trip to a café set up on the terrace at the top of the Congress Hall was recommended

Figure 3.3   Great German Building Exhibition: Nuremberg's Night of Horror

in order to take a look 'at the so badly destroyed, but still beautiful, Nuremberg' (as well as to 'get a good impression of this extraordinary gigantic building', namely the Congress Hall itself, though the building's own history is again not mentioned).[47] The most visually striking and direct of the references to destruction in the exhibition was a panorama model of Nuremberg's *Altstadt* after the night of the 2nd of January 1945 on which it was severely bombed (the *Schreckensnacht*). The article describing this in the exhibition newspaper is one of the only references to the background to the destruction and even here it is far from direct. It calls the exhibit a 'menacing reminder for all not only of rubble, the depressing sight of which is all too familiar in daily life and whose impression can hardly be taken away from us in the future, but also of the mindless destruction of the culture of our forefathers by small characters acting big [*von kleinen Gerngroßen*]'.[48]

Arguably, the cryptic form of reference here could be to the allies rather than the Nazis. The ambiguity is, perhaps, significant. Whichever, the construction here is of the present population as a victim (see previous chapter) – of the Nazis and of allied bombs. In such a construction, images of the city destroyed come to visually represent that victim status and trauma, and they can also act as a visual shorthand for the Nazi legacy. In this context, reconstruction takes on even more importance. It is not simply about providing places to live and work, vital though these are, but becomes a spiritual and moral task, a means of overcoming the mindless destruction that has been wrought upon the innocent city and its inhabitants. The exhibition catalogue describes the activity of building as 'the biggest, most important and most beautiful task that it is necessary to undertake for our people'; and intones the imperative '*Wir müßen bauen!*', 'We must build!'.[49] Medical metaphors are also employed to the same end, the exhibition catalogue describing an 'unbounded housing misery that is spread through the community like a terrible illness in the organism'.[50] The official motto of the exhibition is 'Healthy towns and houses offer the best guarantee for peace and well-being', and the task of the exhibition itself is to make sure that visitors understand this message.[51] Building is described as 'a good omen for the future of the German people',[52] and as an act 'for freedom' being undertaken for the 'reconstruction of destroyed Europe'.[53] Encoded here too is the idea that looking to the future, and leaving the past behind, is the healthiest response to the devastation suffered.

All of these heady claims were aimed not only at the visiting German public but also at international visitors and exhibitors. The speeches, exhibition newspapers and catalogue are generally careful to refer to the rebuilding of *Europe* rather than Germany specifically, and they cast rebuilding as necessary for peace rather than as part of regaining German strength. The Building Exhibition provided a significant opportunity to present the world with a different Nuremberg from that so recently established in international memory as the place of the trials of Nazi war criminals, as well as the only slightly more temporally distant role as city of the Nuremberg laws and rallies. As Nuremberg's mayor concludes in the exhibition guide:

> I express the hope and expectation that the 1949 German Building Exhibition in Nuremberg will contribute to our city regaining the old good name that it possessed for centuries, and that it will make us new friends at home and abroad.[54]

Cleansing, reconstruction and return

Mayor Ziebill may have really believed that holding events such as the Building Exhibition would be enough for Nuremberg to 'regain its good name'. The idea that he expresses, that it will be possible to return to the pre-Nazi status, is one that is also articulated by others, both verbally and through action. President Theodor Heuss, visiting Nuremberg in 1952 for the celebrations to mark 100 years of the Germanic National Museum, announced that Nuremberg's name had been sullied by history (*von der Geschichte verschmiert*) and that the task ahead was to make it clean again (*den Begriff Nuremberg wieder zu reinigen*), as though the Nazi years were a superficial smear that could be rinsed away to reveal the clean history lying beneath.[55] It was analogous to blasting off swastikas and filling in the denazification *Fragebogen*.

Much of the physical reconstruction was also concerned with trying to return to a pre-Nazi state, so forging continuities with the earlier past. In this way the Nazi period could be contained, turned into a blip within a longer, more meaningful history. As elsewhere in Germany, many of Nuremberg's older buildings were painstakingly reconstructed.[56] The Altstadt was rebuilt stone by stone, restoring buildings such as the Kaiserburg, the Frauentor, the Frauen and Sebaldus churches and the Dürer House to as close as possible to their prewar state. In some cases, such as the Heilig-

Geist-Spital, this meant restoring them to the enhanced medieval appearance given them by the Nazis, though as the aim seemed to be to restore as much as was old-looking as possible this was not raised as a matter of concern. What was at issue was restoring another, longer history. In this way, the city addressed what the guidelines of a 1947 competition for plans to rebuild the Altstadt referred to as '*die Verantwortung gegenüber der Vergangenheit*'[57] – the responsibility or accountability for the past. It was as though the past was being rescued through the city's heritage.

An exhibition held in the Congress Hall to mark Nuremberg's 900th birthday in 1950 provides another instance of this 'historical skipping' and restitution through heritage reconstruction. Part of the exhibition included an overview of Nuremberg's history with the following subheadings: 'Pre- and early-history'; 'The Blossoming of Nuremberg' (mid-fifteenth century); 'The later imperial city era'; 'The Bavarian period'; and 'Nuremberg from tomorrow'. There is no mention anywhere in this of the Third Reich, though the 'The Bavarian period' ends with a depiction of the Altstadt 'before the destruction of 1945', and the final section is a call for reconstruction together with models of how this could be achieved.[58]

Part of what was at work here was turning Nuremberg into a museum of its former self. This was explicit too in the founding of the Altstadt Museum in the reconstructed Fembo House in 1953. As a guide produced by the city's Transport Association – the branch of city government responsible for tourism – explained:

> The purpose of this unique museum is to keep alive the memory of Nuremberg's great past – especially after the severe damage which the Old Town suffered during World War II – and to give visitors an idea of the culture and the splendid architecture of the former imperial city of Nuremberg.[59]

But as was evident in the coupling of Nuremberg's admirable history with what the Nine-hundredth Anniversary Exhibition referred to as 'Nuremberg from Tomorrow', this was not simply about remaining in the past but providing a different – more comfortable and longstanding – historical trajectory for 'moving forward'.

The idea of 'moving on' was still more evident in an alternative approach which took the idea of a 'zero hour' – a new beginning – seriously.[60] This was *Aufbau* – the construction of functional modern buildings. While practices of rebuilding – *Wiederaufbau* – entailed a 'reprojective' returning to a less problematic history as a base for development, *Aufbau* was explicitly framed as leaving the past behind. In many parts of postwar Germany there was a 'bitter power struggle between the advocates of reconstruction (*Wiederaufbau*) and of new construction (*Aufbau*)'.[61] In Nuremberg's Altstadt, the symbolic heart of the city, the former held sway; but in the outskirts there were new constructions, though their design was typically plain rather than innovative, and due to the dire need for housing, municipal and industrial buildings, they were often built in haste.[62] Nevertheless, their rather austerely modern style, as devoid of *volkisch* references as possible, was conceptualised as a break from the immediate as well as more distant past. Paradoxically, however, the 'pared-down functionalist style' adopted was scarcely distinguishable from the kinds of buildings that the National Socialists had constructed for 'low-ranking party, military and public' purposes.[63] This meant that such buildings constructed by the Nazis, such as Nuremberg's main post-office, could – once stripped of their obvious Nazi insignia – blend into the postwar cityscape. Extraordinary though it might now seem, there may even have been, as Iain Boyd Whyte claims, the hope that the buildings of the Party Rally Grounds – such as the Congress Hall – could also be reappropriated and blended into the landscape in this way.[64]

Commemoration

That buildings could be blended into new landscapes was evident in the way that the *Ehrenhalle* war memorial that pre-dated the building of the Rally Grounds had so readily done so. Postwar the memorial was again used for commemorative services – a 'return' that might surely seem especially problematic, though which again seems to have raised little comment at the time (and see following chapter).

This first remembrance service after the Second World War took place on *Volkstrauertag* – Remembrance Day, or literally, 'people's sorrow day' – in 1952. This was part of events held throughout the Western zones that had only been permitted by the allies after considerable debate, and in recognition of a need for some kind of ritual to commemorate the dead of both world wars. By changing the date of the earlier *Volkstrauertag* – which had also been celebrated as *Heldengedenktag* (Heroes Commemoration Day) under the Nazis – and by insisting that memorials also included mention of the Nazi victims, there was some attempt by the allies to counter the 'hero-ising' dimensions of such events.[65] On the rear wall of the *Ehrenhalle*, then, the names of Nuremberg soldiers, regiments and places of death in World War II were added to those from the First World War, and a new inscription was engraved on its front central wall. This followed a formula approved by the allies and used throughout Germany, and runs as follows:

Den Opfern der Kriege	To the victims/sacrificed of the wars
1914 bis 1918 † 1939 bis 1945	1914 to 1918 † 1939 to 1945
und der Gewaltherrschaft	and of the tyranny
1933 bis 1945	1933 to 1945
Die Stadt Nürnberg	The city of Nuremberg

Bringing together those who had died in war and those who had been victims, in whatever way, of the National Socialists glosses over differences between victims and perpetrators in what Peter Reichel has called a 'generalising victim formula' (*generalisierende Opferformel*) and Harald Marcuse nicely dubs 'victim soup'.[66] The blending involved was enabled by the fact that the German term '*Opfer*' covers connotations of both 'victim' and 'sacrifice', that is, as fully passive and having a purposeless death or as dying for a higher end.[67] Prior to 1945 the active sense, 'sacrifice', was more common, especially in war memorials, whereas post-1945 'victim' has become predominant, thus removing culpable agency from all of those who died, though at the same time preserving the ambiguity and thus allowing different groups to interpret it in line with their own understandings.[68]

Despite the changes to the inscription, which were also echoed in the language used in the mayor's speeches, the ritual itself was almost identical to its post-WWI form. Wreaths were laid, braziers lit, and large numbers of veterans, widows and other relatives of dead soldiers attended. As these had also been employed by the Nazis at this site, the ceremony bore some resemblance to the Nazi rituals that had taken place there. But this was legitimated locally by a strong sense that earlier precedent should prevail. That victims of the Nazi regime could find themselves standing alongside those who had been fully part of it, was also blended over by the construction of Germans, or more specifically Nurembergers, as all victims of a terrible time from which they were still suffering. So even though war commemoration was a moment in civic life that entailed an explicit looking back to the war and its consequences, it too was contained within a predominant historical consciousness that did not cast the use of a space or ritual forms appropriated by the Nazis – nor of the lumping together with those who might be classified as 'perpetrators' – as in any way improper for commemorating Nazi victims. Later, however, as we see in the following chapter, it was to become so.

Leisure, pleasure and events

A return to the pre-Nazi era was also evident in the uses to which the area was put by the public. Even though the military was occupying part of grounds, other areas were used by the local population again for the leisure purposes for which it had been used prior to having been taken over by the Nazis. The remaining green and wooded areas were used for walking and picnics, and the lakes for bathing and boating – as they had been before the war. Return – going back to the 'innocent' time prior to Nazi power – was one of the most compelling ways of negotiating difficult heritage, and rather than being at odds with the notion of a forward-moving temporality, it was understood as being part of it. Moreover, using the site for leisure was not necessarily about forgetting the immediate use of the area, but was rather a reclaiming by the local populace.

In this spirit, new and reconfigured leisure uses of the site also emerged. For example, the great fire braziers from the ends of the Zeppelin Building filled with water and were used by children as paddling pools. While it would be fatuous to think of this as a form of resistance, nor should it necessarily be seen as any kind of repression of historical awareness. There were also new activities: one of my interviewees told me that she remembered barbecuing (referred to as 'grillen' in German), still very popular today, being introduced by 'the Amis'. She also recalled being given sweets by American soldiers and her own attempts to say 'Thank you very much'. The site thus also became one of the meeting grounds – formal and informal – between the local German population and the US authorities.

In 1953 the Volksfest was moved to the site, to an area right next to the Congress Hall – an area in which it is still held biannually. There seems to have been no sense of a possible contradiction of locating this place of pleasure on a Nazi marching ground: the fact that in the 1920s the Volksfest had taken place at a location nearby, and the wider Dutzendteich area had been used for other festive events, gave a historical legitimation to its being held here.[69] That children should come to take a ride on a merry-go-round, or adults to drink a mug of beer, in the shadow of an enormous fascist building which had been built only a decade before was presumably not seen as untoward by either the council who authorised the location or the crowds of Nurembergers who attended. More important to the council was trying to find a site on which a festival could be held that wouldn't look as though Nuremberg was just 'baking small bread rolls' in comparison with Munich's Oktoberfest.[70]

Invisibility

'The picture is well known: on the left the half-circle of the Congress Hall, to the right the whole circle of the ferris wheel and in front bright and intriguing beer tents and stalls selling sausages, raffle tickets and sweets, and dozens of rides. Twice a year – in this almost cosy proximity – the Volksfest takes place. What is reckoned to be the gloomiest building in the city becomes a symbol of its gaiety. That isn't meant to sound cynical. But it is disquieting that nobody is disturbed by this bizarre mixture, that nobody's jolly mood is upset. The secret is: the Congress Hall can only be seen by foreigners. To Nurembergers it is invisible. It stands in a blind spot. Nobody will deny that it exists. But nobody can really perceive it. This is because from early childhood they have been trained, by visiting the Volksfest twice a year, to develop a blind spot. For decades this has functioned so perfectly that all NS-buildings have existed completely outside the awareness of Nurembergers'. Gerhard Liedtke.[71]

As well as the Volksfest, the Nazi Party Rally Grounds were also used for other leisure events, such as motor racing. This drew vast crowds and was coordinated by Motor Sport Club Nürnberg – an independent organisation of enthusiasts that continues today as an active lobby group for its sport. There were also other plans over the years to increase the sporting offer at the site. Some of these, such as the idea to build a football stadium in the Congress Hall, never happened; the latter after years of debate and a final decision from the council that it would be a 'senseless shredding of money'.[72] Other ideas, such as turning the Congress Hall into a cinema, or, later – discussed in the next chapter – a leisure and shopping centre, were also shelved, usually on the same grounds. Nevertheless, the number of sporting events and parts of the grounds allocated to sport has increased: to include, in recent years, a new ice stadium and the building of more football fields and the holding of matches as part of the World Cup in 2006.

So too have musical events been held. The Meistersinghalle – a purpose-built modern concert venue – was constructed in the 1960s at the northern end of the site, in a location that had previously been part of the Luitpold marching field. In 1986 a wing of the Congress Hall was developed as a 'Seranadenhof' – an open-air romantic concert venue – in which concerts, especially from the Nuremberg Symphony Orchestra (which also has practice rooms nearby), are regularly held in

Figure 3.4   Volksfest and the invisible Congress Hall, 2007

Figure 3.5   Motor-cycle racing *c.*1949

Figure 3.6   Motor racing – Norisring, 2006

the Summer months. And in 1978 the first Rock Concert was held on the Zeppelin Field, featuring Bob Dylan – a sign to many, as local poet Fitzgerald Kusz observed, that 'the times they are a-changin''.[73] Since then many others such as the Rolling Stones have also played there; and one of Germany's largest rock festivals – Rock im Park – has been running since 1997, bringing numerous well-known bands from around the world.

The area also came to be used for mass gatherings by groups which had in some sense been persecuted by the Nazis or had suffered in consequence of war. For example, on 1st May 1947, Labour Day speeches and events were held on the Zeppelin Building and Field; and in 1955 half a million people came to participate in Sudetendeutsche Day – an event to commemorate the expulsion of Sudeten Germans from Czechoslovakia at the end of World War II – and which has been held annually since.[74] In 1969 Jehovah's Witnesses – a group persecuted by the Nazis – held an international congress of over 100,000 participants there. This was not the only mass religious event held at the site. In 1963, American Evangelist Billy Graham preached to a crowd of thousands; and in 1988 a massive religious festival called 'Christival' also took place on the Zeppelin Field.[75] While on the one hand the use of the site for mass religious events might seem to continue the religious staging employed by the Nazis, a widespread perception of religion – especially Christianity – as a form of cleansing and overcoming turned these events into a symbolic triumph of good over evil. This was not the first or last instance of trying to harness the perceived redemptive powers of Christianity as we will see below. It can also be seen elsewhere in postwar Germany, as, for example, in Christianised imagery of the Käthe Kollwitz sculpture added to the Neue Wache in Berlin in 1990 as a memorial to victims of the Nazi regime or the erection of chapels at former concentration camps, including Dachau and Flossenbürg, as well as in locations outside Germany, such as the building of a Carmelite

Figure 3.7   Bob Dylan concert on the Zeppelin Field, 1978

Convent at Auschwitz; or in the Christianised imagery of some 'national' postwar commemoration in Germany.[76]

Until the late 1980s, the holding of events on the Zeppelin Field – the most used site – had to be agreed with the US army. Their main concern seems to have been health and safety. In the early 1980s, for example they decided no longer to allow rock concerts due to the litter and damage caused to what they saw as their training field.[77] Once the US had left the area, decision-making was devolved into different

Mass events

In 1969, when the Jehovah's Witnesses held their world congress at the former Nazi Party Rally Grounds they believed that the world was soon to end – in 1975. My friend, the anthropologist Regina Römhild, recalls having been taken there as a child by her mother. 'Everything there seemed enormous – like a gigantic football field, visually strongly divided into large blocks with rows of seating, each marked with letters or numbers'. She has distinct memories of such details as the dreadful dark red hat that she had to wear, the people from different countries speaking different languages, a disturbing play about the imminent Armageddon, and having forgotten the number of her seating area and being temporarily lost. Nobody told her, she thinks, what the place was; and this is something that she came to reconstruct for herself later. But she thinks that the location – as part of the machinery of oppressing the Jehovah's Witnesses in the Third Reich – was surely significant, and alluded to in the disturbing play. For her personally, however, there were other parallels to be made between systems which used speeches, graphic representations and collective participation to put individuals under pressure to conform.

Figure 3.8   World Congress of Jehovah's Witnesses, at Zeppelin Building, 1969

council departments, especially the *Ordnungsamt* (town clerk's office), responsible for health and safety, and the *Liegenschaftsamt* (property office), responsible for matters such as liaising with local populations over noise levels and so forth. Other departments, such as the *Sportsamt* might also be involved, depending on the type of event. Overall, as was explained to me by officials today, 'It is fundamentally the case that the type of event is more decisive for how it is dealt with than the place in which it takes place'.[78] The allocation of bureaucratic responsibility had the consequence that practical matters were given precedence over symbolic ones. While this could, of course, be something of a front for justifying decisions made on symbolic grounds – as was surely partly the case in preventing neo-Nazi events on grounds of public disturbance – it certainly seems from the records available that it also allowed such questions to fall off the agenda.

Demolition

While the former Nazi Party Rally Grounds were never fully razed but were for the most part just denuded of their swastikas and used in multiple ways, there was nevertheless some selective demolition from the late 1950s, through the 1960s and even into later decades. For the most part, this destruction wasn't invested with the same high levels of symbolic significance as the removal of swastikas, though nor was a symbolic dimension lost on participants. Physically more difficult than the removal of swastikas – requiring more dynamite and producing large amounts of rubble – the destruction sometimes highlights what might be called the 'material agency' of the buildings but shows that while this could prove suggestive to interpretation it had no direct correlation with the attribution of agency by participants.

Below, I look at two cases of physical destruction of buildings and chart some of the players, negotiations and attributions of agency and symbolic meaning involved. The first example is of the total but relatively uncontroversial removal of the massive towers of the former Mars Field at the south end of the site in 1966 and 1967. The second, discussed in the following section, is the 'amputation' of the Zeppelin Building which mainly took place in 1967, though with some further – and especially controversial – destruction of parts of the building in 1976. These are not the only examples of such physical changes to the site. In particular, as noted above, the damaged stage of the Luitpold arena was removed in the 1950s, and then in the early 1960s its remaining stands were disassembled as part of the building of a new concert hall, the *Meistersingerhalle*. In 1963 the Association of German Architects proposed that both the Congress Hall and the Great Road should be demolished. The terms in which they couched their arguments are interesting – as well as rather melodramatic. These structures, they maintained, could not be 'overcome' (*bewältigt*) by just planting greenery around them. The Congress Hall's

> macabre monumentality contradicts every contemporary building conception. The whole area suffers from this representation of a crazed dictatorship. It can and should not be the responsibility of democratic institutions, which should not have to spend a single Deutschmark on its continued existence. It remains a contravention of the spirit of the new city to have to even contemplate a use for it. We have the responsibility to erase this sign and to sacrifice it ... and so to set a symbol and give evidence of the will of this generation to engage in this humble form of *Wiedergutmachung*.[79]

The Architects Association partly makes its argument in financial terms – suggesting a monetary 'sacrifice' now as a form of 'investment' (by saving money) for the future. But in employing the topical and emotive vocabulary of sacrifice (*Opfer*, which, as we have noted can also mean victims) and *Wiedergutmachung* – literally 'making good again' (but entering public discourse increasingly as restitution, including financial restitution) – it infuses this with moral considerations. Destroying the Congress Hall, the Association tries to argue, would not only prevent further, morally challenged, expenditure on a Nazi relic, it would also be a kind of moral restitution – though the problematic consideration of to whom is not addressed. The innovative architects' argument did not, however, gather the public support for which they called – despite their provocation that 'Whoever doesn't take part [in making decisions about the development of the City] is not a quiet citizen but a bad one!'[80] – and it was never acted upon. Both the Congress Hall and the Great Road remained intact. The Mars Field towers and the Zeppelin Building, however, did not.

Overcoming a towering presence

The Mars Field towers were located at the south end of the former Rally Grounds site. Here, in areas that had previously included the various rally accommodation areas as well as the Mars Field, housing developments had begun postwar with financial assistance from the US under the Marshall Plan. In 1954 there was a competition to develop the whole area in order to create a new suburb or 'new town' (*Trabantenstadt*) called Langwasser.[81] The winning design integrated the eleven towers, mainly as air-raid shelters. However, years of negotiation followed between the US military, which used the towers for storage, the city council and the Wohnungsbaugesellschaft der Stadt Nürnberg. The latter was an organisation that had originally been set up after World War I by the city council on the model of English Development Corporations – the first time such a model had been used in Germany.[82] A non-profit-making organisation, formally and financially independent, it had the remit to provide affordable social housing in the city (its costs being recouped later through rents). From 1957 it was formally charged by the council with the Langwasser project. As part of its task, it also gathered up views about planning projects; and these provide a glimpse into some of the ways in which the material heritage of Nazism was being approached.

One controversial suggestion, proposed by the Catholic Church, was to build a church tower around one of the towers, something which, it was suggested, would not only be symbolically redolent – a sign of 'the triumph of the cross over the swastika' (a phrase that works better in German, with the 'Kreuz' being victorious over the 'Hakenkreuz') – but would also 'present an interesting architectural challenge'.[83] As has been pointed out, however, the Church had not offered any significant resistance to the Nazis,[84] and so the symbolic suggestion was disingenuous, as perhaps the Church well knew in its giving a second reason too. Nevertheless, the proposal was part of a persistent trend in the history of the site to try to 'convert' it through the transformative capacities of Christianity. Such conversion offered another route to starting again and moving on.

The original plan to integrate the towers was also dispensed with, partly due to objections gathered by the Development Corporation that these would not be an attractive sight for those living in the new accommodation, and partly because it was argued – again – that maintaining the towers would be expensive.[85] Initially, it was hoped to dismantle the towers but that too was dismissed as too expensive, compared with blowing them up.[86] A plan to use the material for building 700 flats was shelved when the stone resisted, proving too hard to be used in this way. The vast amount of rubble was instead used to build a wall to protect part of the suburb from traffic noise.

The blowing up of the towers attracted media interest from across Germany, the idea that this was a significant removal of a difficult heritage being evident to commentators When some of the towers failed to fall at the first attempt, the director of the Development Corporation remarked: 'It is not so easy to overcome the past'.[87] Nevertheless, the towers were removed – and with no other opposition than that they put up themselves. 'In 54 minutes the spectre was gone' was one newspaper headline.[88] But the idea that the spectral past could – or should – be eliminated so easily was not one that later many commentators would hold. When in the 1990s parts of the Mars Field foundations were uncovered during building work, the city's building department decided to leave these visible and – as in other parts of the former Rally Grounds – to erect an information board explaining the history of these traces.

Amputating the Zeppelin Building

Of all of the buildings at the former Nazi Party Rally Grounds, the Zeppelin Building is most iconic of Nazism. Widely familiar from images of the rallies, its massive length and distinctive design make it for many visitors the most imposing of the site's buildings. During the 1960s and 1970s, however, the side-galleries and end towers of the building were demolished, leading, as Tim Benton has written, to an appearance of the building being 'amputated' and thus 'disarmed'.[89] Not totally obliterated in this case, then, the building's potential 'eye impact' was nevertheless substantially altered. Denuded of its side galleries, it was visually fore-shortened, making it appear stunted. This impression does not only rely on a contrast with its earlier state, but also on a bodily parallel that draws on a common way of apprehending buildings.[90] The story of this amputation – as far as it can be unravelled – shows an interesting mix of players and attributions of agency.

Despite the grand claims by the National Socialists that they were building for a thousand year reign, and despite Speer's ruin theory claims, the Zeppelin Building was showing signs of wear and tear within thirty years of having been completed. This has been attributed to minor bomb damage and the fact that it was built hastily

Figure 3.9   Amputating the Zeppelin Building, 1967

and is mainly a limestone façade on an underlying brick construction.[91] How to deal with this came to a head in the 1960s.

It did so after a visiting student from Israel claimed in 1965 that Nuremberg still had swastikas open to public view.[92] These alleged swastikas were on the ceilings of the side-galleries of the Zeppelin Building – part of a design that is also on the ceiling inside the building, in the so-called Golden Hall (though this was not open to the public at the time; see Figure 2.3). In response to the claims, the Mayor of Nuremberg's personal minister declared that 'nowhere on the former Zeppelin Field did there still exist swastikas in the form used by the National Socialists. All such emblems had been removed immediately after the end of the war'.[93] The ceiling design was, the minister emphasised, a classical meander motif that had been seen as nothing more than a pattern from classical antiquity by numerous visitors, including 'Americans of Jewish background'. The Director of the city's art collections, Dr Wilhelm Schwemmer, was also called upon to show images of ancient vases with the same design, in an attempt to show that the pattern on the Zeppelin Building could not be interpreted as having a Nazi meaning. (The fact that the swastika itself had an older history and could have been made subject to the same arguments was never noted.)[94]

Swastika stories

It is a hot day in August 2003 and a middle-aged man sits, bare-chested, reading a newspaper on the steps of the Zeppelin Building. I have seen him there on other days. I approach him to ask whether I can ask him some questions. He tells me that he lives nearby and comes here often when the weather is good to relax and 'recover from stress'. My question about what he knows about the history of this place provokes not only the usual accounts about its use in the Nazi era but also some of his own memories of coming here as a child and wondering what the massive braziers could have been for. He also tells me, rather conspiratorially, about the 'real reason' why the side-galleries of the building on which we were sitting had been blasted away. It was because they had a swastika design, he explains, and visitors to Nuremberg noticed this and accused the council of being Nazis. And so – he winks and gestures towards the empty space where the galleries would have been – now we have to sit here on this hot day without any shade.

The council's hyper-defensiveness was a function of a postwar determination to be seen as having effectively 'denazified'. Despite the arguments that were made at the time, however, two years later the council resolved to dynamite away the Zeppelin Building's side-galleries – those containing the swastika design. In taking this action, the council emphasised that their decision was a purely material one: the galleries had become structurally unstable – cracks had appeared in the ceiling after frost and, therefore, there was a risk that they might fall and cause injury.[95] Certainly, in all of the recorded minutes from the meetings of the council, only material problems with the side-galleries were reported, and the ceiling design was never mentioned. Some consideration was given to the possibility of repairing the building and turning it into a monument (*Denkmal*) – and detailed calculations produced – but this was dismissed as being too costly. Furthermore, Schmeissner – who was still in office until he retired in 1970 – explained, there were more worthy calls upon the limited funds available for heritage protection and there was no way that this building could be 'kept from being eaten up by the tooth of time'.[96] The agency for the destruction of the galleries was, thus, located in the building itself: it had brought about its own demise by becoming unsafe. This could also be inferred to be ultimately the fault of the Nazi builders and architects, for the poor workmanship involved in the building's construction. Whichever, though, the originating agency of the council was deleted: they were merely carrying out the inevitable.

The council was clearly aware that political motives might be attributed, however. In announcing the decision, Buildings Minister Schmeissner stated that it 'had nothing to do with getting rid of a Zeitgeist'.[97] Some letters to the newspaper, however, deemed otherwise, writers commenting variously that it was right that Nazi buildings should be removed as the Nazis had got rid of buildings such as the synagogue, or that the council were acting as 'Jewish knaves' (*Judenknechte*) by destroying an architectural heritage which was compared to that of Ancient Greece.[98] Surprisingly, however, none of the reports or letters made the link with the student's claims, though later, getting rid of the embarrassing swastikas that the student had pointed out, widely came to be seen as one of the motives for removing the galleries.[99] At the time, however, the protests against the demolition of the galleries were not voiced in terms of compelling the city to remember and address its past, but came instead from Nazi sympathisers – among whom there were signs of new, albeit minority, activity in Nuremberg at the time – and from the Motor Sport Club which was concerned that motor racing would be disrupted by the demolition work.[100]

Even after the building was 'disarmed' in this way, negotiations continued about its safety and future. Despite Schmeissner's refusal to recognise the building as 'heritage' – 'it only possesses worth as a curiosity'[101] – in 1974 it was listed as such under new heritage legislation emanating from Munich. As I discuss in the following chapter, the city went ahead with further amputation of the building – blasting off the towers at each end – even after the listing; though never the complete demolition of the building that some council members had called for.

* * * * *

In this chapter, I have looked at examples ranging from the demolition of difficult heritage, through its semi-destruction, to cases of apparent looking away or ignoring historical significance. In doing so, I have sought to highlight ways in which these matters were negotiated at the time. The location of agency in swastikas or in the failings of buildings, the format of financial calculations, the self-perception of acting pragmatically, and certain understandings of temporality, were all, variously, mobilised in the negotiations and actions taken. It was such understandings and frameworks, manifest and produced by historically and socially located actors, rather than more generalised and dehistoricised psychological mechanisms of repression or notions of haunting, which provided the impetus for action.

What is also evident here is that while the Nazi past was recognised as a problematic legacy immediately after the war, the idea that Nazi buildings were a heritage that might be preserved as a means of documenting that history or educating about it was scarcely voiced in Nuremberg before the 1970s. Such suggestions as there were in the 1960s that the buildings be considered as a heritage to be preserved tended to come from those with Nazi sympathies and were usually robustly rejected by those in charge of the site's management. That some of those making such robust rejection, most notably the city's building minister, also had personal grounds not to want to be reminded about the Nazi past was surely significant to the response. But it was not the only reason.

These observations have relevance for debates about German memory cultures in the postwar years. What is clearly being shown by collective scholarship of the period is that there was not a single, unified approach to remembering and forgetting, but that this was fragmented and located variously in specific social practices or areas of public culture. So, on the one hand, the Nuremberg trials and the flood of images of atrocities from concentration camps which were reproduced in newspapers in the early postwar years ensured that the National Socialist legacy was kept in public view. So too, in other ways, did living with the devastation of bombed cities, public and private encounters with returning prisoners of war, and mourning ceremonies for those killed in war or still missing.[102] Moreover, by the 1960s there was evidence of more willingness of parts of the German media, institutions and public to reflect upon Nazi crimes and signs of the beginning of the 'working through' of the past that Theodor Adorno called for in a celebrated 1959 lecture.[103] In Nuremberg this was especially manifest in the establishment in 1965 of an annual event, the Nuremberg Forum (*Nürnberge Gespräche*), specifically dedicated to discussing such questions. The first, for example, was entitled 'Perceptions and Misperceptions in Germany' and brought eminent speakers – including Jewish scholars such as Adorno's former colleague Max Horkheimer – to Nuremberg from Jerusalem, London, New York and Paris as well as from various parts of Germany.[104] Founded by Culture Minister Hermann Glaser – who has been a motive force in many of the city's other progressive educational programmes related to the Nazi legacy – the Nuremberg Forum was part of a much wider, and more longstanding, current of attempting to 'work through' the Nazi past in Nuremberg by some members of its population, as Glaser argued in an interview with me. As he also acknowledged, while the Forum was intended to keep questions about the past in public consciousness, there was also a strong postwar emphasis on seeing Nuremberg as 'a city like any other' – something that he and others acknowledged as important both for reasons of historical accuracy (i.e. recognising that Nazi crimes were not especially confined to Nuremberg) and for its citizens' own self-awareness in the postwar years.[105]

On the other hand, there were also areas of public culture – and no doubt also private life – in which the emphasis was elsewhere, which were not imbued with memory, and in relation to which the predominant discourses were those of moving on, rebuilding lives and being essentially no different from other Germans. The account here of the negotiations over this one particular part of the National Socialist legacy highlights aspects of the historical consciousness that shaped what were later seen as conspicuous lacunae in public memory.

My argument is not, however, that what is described here is a past historical consciousness that no longer has currency. While, as we see in the next chapter, demolition of the buildings at the Nazi Party Rally Grounds became more difficult in the 1970s, after they were listed under monument protection legislation, many of the same ways of thinking about them, and about the relationship between past, present and future, continued afterwards, alongside and sometimes interwoven with, new approaches. And as we see in later chapters, many of these continue into the present – and can often be found elsewhere too.

4

PRESERVATION, PROFANATION AND IMAGE-MANAGEMENT

In the previous chapter, we saw how a site of difficult heritage could be left largely intact not on account of any idea that it should be preserved for posterity but for a range of other reasons, including, in the Nuremberg case, the location of its 'power' in a surface symbol, the swastika; and the idea that the financial 'investment' in its physical fabric should be put to practical use. Increasingly, however, sites of difficult history, like many other kinds of places that are perceived to be carriers of history, are being actively preserved through legislation and conservationist practices. That is, they are being turned into 'official' heritage – a status that has implications for how they can be treated and also for their reception. This can set up particular problems for difficult heritage, which may deal with a past that many might prefer to forget or dissociate from ongoing self-identity. It also risks giving a special allure – a 'heritage effect' – to such spaces and histories.

The Nazi Party Rally Grounds were listed under heritage protection legislation in the 1970s. This considerably constrained the opportunities open to the city to somehow 'cleanse' its image by 'wiping away' the memory of the past, whether by removing the buildings or just ignoring them. Not only did blasting away Nazi structures become more difficult – though not altogether impossible – the city was also compelled to spend money on halting their decay. What also began to change during the 1960s – though it did not really become widespread in approaches to the city's Nazi architecture until the 1980s and even more so during the 1990s – was that the idea of 'moving on' and trying to leave the difficult past behind, or skipping this past in a return to a longer history, came to lose its status as an obviously 'healthy' response to traumatic events. The city's image could no longer be managed by trying to keep Nazi remains out of the frame, as with the tourist maps mentioned in the previous chapter. Instead, alongside, though never fully supplanting notions of 'moving on' and 'containing', emerged an idea that the difficult past should be addressed and, as Adorno had put it, 'worked through' for the psychological and moral health of the body politic. This had implications for negotiating judgments of what were appropriate or inappropriate ways of dealing with the physical remains of the past – which came increasingly to be seen as not just the remnants of previous 'investment' or as dirt or detritus in the cityscape but as 'witnesses' or 'documents' of the past, and even of what might remain imminent in the present.

In later chapters I look at some of the more specifically educational attempts to negotiate the former Nazi Party Rally Grounds into being as material documentation and historical witness. In this chapter, however, I look first at the contested matter of the official turning of the Rally Grounds into 'heritage'; and then at a range of other attempts to 'counter' – or, in the language that the Tourism Minister had introduced me to, to 'profane' – what was increasingly cast as the symbolic power of the buildings, and that was partly a consequence of their new heritage status.

Preserving difficult heritage

The idea that sites of difficult heritage – especially sites of atrocity, trauma or perpetration – should be preserved and treated as 'heritage' has been controversial in many parts of the world. In Rwanda, for example, Susan E. Cook writes that 'tensions will always exist between those advocating remembering the genocide and those who advocate forgetting it'.[1] Moreover, she points out, even among those who call for some kind of preservation there can be tensions between documentation and memorialising, which can produce very different forms of site, with differing emotional resonance.[2] Arguments about the form and nature of the site of the twin towers in New York – a site of trauma – have likewise highlighted complex questions about the 'appropriate' way to preserve cultural memory at such a site.[3] While there are long and various traditions for commemorating atrocities – including through monuments and war memorials – the preservation of sites where atrocities occurred has by and large been more recent, and has certainly become considerably more prevalent.[4] Paul Williams even speaks of 'the global rush to commemorate atrocities'.[5]

In Germany, many former concentration camps have become sites of commemoration and education, though they were not generally preserved intact from immediately after the war.[6] Many buildings were destroyed, often due to concerns about disease or simply because there was no thought that these were sites that should be conserved. Nevertheless, some were used by the allies immediately to act as evidence of the atrocity that had taken place. German citizens were taken into sites such as Buchenwald and Dachau as part of forcing them to witness the atrocity committed.[7] In some cases, as at Dachau, educational exhibitions were mounted in the months straight after the war, though these were later removed and other, sometimes more extensive, though often 'cleaner' and less graphic, exhibitions came to replace them. In many cases, exhibitions and educational programmes began much – even decades – later. For example, the Gestapo 'educational work camp' near Kassel was only begun to be turned into a memorial museum in 1982; and concentration camps at Moringen, Drütte and Neckaretz, near Heilbronn, in 1993, 1994 and 1998 respectively. Many, especially in the allied zones, were also memorialised through art works or the addition (or sometimes adaptation of existing) religious spaces, such as chapels. Dachau, for example, now has on site or nearby, a Catholic chapel (dedicated in 1960) and Carmelite convent (1964), a Protestant church (1967), a Jewish memorial building (1967) and a Russian Orthodox chapel (1994), as well as several striking art works.[8] All of these developments altered the original sites; and in some cases they went alongside more extensive revision – and sometimes demolition of parts of the site (as at Dachau where barracks were pulled down in the 1950s and also 1990s). There have also, however, been examples of reconstruction. To take the case of Dachau again, barracks buildings and watchtowers were reconstructed in the late 1950s and 1960s, as were parts of a ditch around the site in the 1980s.

Many other kinds of sites connected with Nazi terror have only more recently come to be actively preserved and exhibited. So, for instance, the Wannsee Villa opened as a museum in 1992 (having been used by the military, and later as a school in the meantime), as did a Gestapo headquarters in Dortmund. The remains of the former Gestapo, SS and Reich Security Service headquarters in Berlin, uncovered in the late 1970s were provisionally exhibited as the Topography of Terror in 1987, after considerable debate. Another a decade of argument followed before the decision was made to create a more permanent exhibition.[9] Another decade later it is still not complete.[10] Sites connected with Nazism but which were even less directly connected with victimhood have also, usually even more recently, come to be displayed to the public. A documentation centre at the vast Strength-through-Joy holiday camp complex of buildings at Prora opened in 2000; and in the same year the first tours of the courtroom in which the Nuremberg trails were held, though only at weekends owing to the fact that the room is still in use.[11]

Exhibiting does not, however, necessarily go hand-in-hand with official preservation. Many sites have been exhibited and even preserved without such legislation. And on the other hand, there are buildings connected with the Nazi regime – such as the monumental Gauforum in Weimar, mentioned in the previous chapter and also below – that are listed under heritage protection legislation without being displayed to the public. This is the case too with many less substantial buildings.

Between its listing in the early 1970s and the opening of the first exhibition at the site a decade later, this was so for the former Nazi Party Rally Grounds in Nuremberg too – though with the difference from some of the other examples in that much of the overall site (if not most of the individual buildings) was open to the public. It was not, however, actively presented to the public – this was a development that came later (Chapter 5). And although many people came to the site, most did not do so to visit Nazi heritage. In the remainder of this chapter I look at the background to the site's listing and some of the struggles with, and sometimes against, this new status. This shows well some of ideas implicated in, and consequences of, becoming official 'heritage', as well as, in this case, awkward negotiations and struggles with which it became entangled.

Making a monument: heritage legislation

The legislation under which the former Nazi Party Rally Grounds were listed as worthy of protection as heritage was the Bavarian State Historic Preservation Law of 1973. Although there was already considerable preservationist activity – not least that bound up with post-bombing restoration and reconstruction – this was the first time that at state level there had been detailed legislation for identifying heritage and regulating its protection.[12] Indeed, it set a model for other West German states; and although altered in part it has remained the basis for heritage protection up to the present.

In 1974, the Bavarian Conservation Department, based in Munich, drew up lists of buildings and other monuments throughout Bavaria that it recommended should fall under the new heritage protection legislation (*Denkmalschutzgesetze*). It was a vast list, with 100,000 'monuments' listed in Bavaria as a whole. Part of the reason that it was so vast was that its remit was considerably broader than 'high culture', allowing buildings of 'an already completed era of architectural history that no longer exists in the present' to be considered, including those erected as recently as 1945.[13] As Gavriel Rosenfeld observes in his account of Munich's postwar dealing with Nazi architecture, rules which had not specifically been designed to include Nazi architecture thus 'automatically' included them.[14] However, as he also notes, this did not lead to any consternation in the Conservation Department for the officials viewed the buildings from what he calls a 'normalised perspective', that is, as just another kind of historic edifice.[15] In Nuremberg, by contrast, the listing did cause consternation. This was partly due to the inclusion of Nazi buildings, as I discuss below, though this did not arise immediately. The initial and primary concern was what the city council saw as the excessive number of buildings and 'ensembles' (groups of buildings) – 2,700 – listed (though Munich had 8,000) and the fact that the Old Town was listed as a single 'ensemble', thus restricting any new developments or change in the whole area.[16]

While the listing imposed considerable limits on alterations and new construction, and it obliged the city to undertake conservation and restoration, it also offered the opportunity to apply for financial assistance to help do so, the Bavarian Conservation Department having a substantial sum (over 40 million DM per year) at its disposal for helping with such work. A good deal of negotiation followed the initial listing and resulted in a much smaller agreed final list of 1,023 'objects' (either buildings or ensembles) in September 1976. But although the former Nazi Party Rally Grounds were identified by the Council's Building Committee as requiring more debate, this seemed to be passed over in the face of other concerns and they were duly listed. They were so as a single 'ensemble' on the grounds of the historical significance of their fascist *Kolossal* style of architecture, and significance as 'witness of the past' (*Zeuge der Vergangenheit*). Like the other buildings listed, the Nazi Party Rally Grounds would, henceforth, officially be a *Denkmal* – heritage.

Under the new legislation, making alterations to listed buildings or sites was to be avoided as far as possible and would require permission from the Bavarian Conservation Department to be carried out. However, partly because it was new but also because the implementation of heritage legislation is a negotiated rather than mechanical practice,[17] various changes were still carried out, and not always with the approval of the Conservation Department. In particular, nipping in just before the listing was finally settled, in June 1976 the end towers of the Zeppelin Building were removed. As before, the official reasons were structural instability and the consequent danger to the public. The decision to take this action had initially been made in 1973, before the listing of the building though it was already known that it was likely to be included. At that time it had been concluded by the city council's Building Committee that this was a much more economical measure than would be 'a securing of the building along heritage preservation principles [which] would cost millions' and even compared with the complete demolition of the building that one SPD councillor called for.[18] Members of Nuremberg's Building Committee were nevertheless described as 'gnashing their teeth' about the fact that they were going to have to spend more money on the Zeppelin Building, and that having invested in trying to shore up the foundations with concrete was just going to have the consequence that 'this building from a despicable time would be cemented into the catalogue of all those buildings that according to the new Bavarian heritage protection legislation are deemed worthy of preservation'.[19] The consequence of not having demolished it previously, in other words, was that, especially once defined as heritage, it was going to continue to act as a drain on the public purse, and even to do so to a greater extent.

While this demolition of part of the Zeppelin Building was the last major example of dynamiting away bits of the former Rally Grounds, other changes have also been undertaken since. In the 1990s, after US personnel vacated the former SS-barracks, there was considerable debate about what should be done with the building, the city council initially proposing to tear it down in order to develop a business park.[20] There was some confusion over whether it was already protected as part of the Nazi Party Rally Grounds ensemble or not but nevertheless the Bavarian Conservation Department objected to the plans and maintained it should be treated as heritage. In the end, a degree of compromise was reached, with the building itself retained but part of the surrounding land being given over to a business area. The development of the building for use as an office for the processing of foreigners' claims for asylum and refugee status entailed some alterations, such as replacing some ceilings with reinforced versions capable of bearing greater weights, that were judged by the conservation officers to constitute a 'partial destruction'; though they won some concessions, such as retaining the original windows. More recently, parts of the land at the south end of the site have also seen new developments, especially the extension of the trade fair land and, in 2001, the construction of an ice stadium. As these did not involve direct change to buildings the heritage protectors were unable to intervene.

But there has not only been nibbling away at the edges of the protected area over time. There have also been examples of restoration as well as educational projects to provide information about the history of the site. Below I consider some of the examples of, and negotiations involved in, restoration; but first turn to a process that I call 'oscillation' in cultural politics.

Oscillation

Reading through sixty years of documentation about the former Nazi Party Rally Grounds, I was struck by the fact that alongside changes in ways of dealing with the site, there was also considerable evidence of a tacking back and forth – or oscillation – between different approaches. So, for example, partial demolition or new construction on part of the site might be followed, not necessarily immediately, by some restoration work or perhaps an educational project – and vice versa. Political oscillation is familiar in systems in which there is a constant swing between different political parties being in power, each seeking to revoke or redress the policies put into place by the others. In the Nuremberg case, however, the oscillation does not usually map onto shifts in power-holding. Throughout most of the period the SPD held the Council and, while there were some party political differences over how the Rally Grounds should be dealt with in relation to some specific events, which I will discuss further below, most of the decisions taken could not be located along party lines in this way, and the oscillation was not an outcome of differently achieved compromises. Some of the differences can, however, be referenced to different parts of city policy and government. Thus the educational projects, which became especially significant from the 1980s on, emanated mainly from the Pedagogical Institute – a semi-independent branch of city government (see next chapter). And building projects – including restoration and demolition – were generally proposed by the Building Committee.

Rather than being straightforwardly the product of different social or organisational positions, however, the alternative tacks taken in political oscillation were as much a realisation of a more endemic ambivalence over how to deal with the difficult past, and with struggles over perceptions of its agency. Whether the right or appropriate thing to do was to preserve the buildings or to leave them 'to the tooth of time' – as Buildings Minister Walter Anderle explained to me in 2000 – was not a settled matter; and only rarely coalesced into clear socially positioned approaches. Instead, as Daniel Boyer has argued in relation to what he calls a dialectic between 'spirit' and 'system' – which he traces through a long tradition of German thought as well as in contemporary journalists' everyday concerns and talk – central tensions pervade the ways of knowing involved.[21] In his account, journalists from the West and East tend to position themselves, and position each other, differently within the dialectic in ways that are not fixed but rather, in the terms that I use here, negotiated. Likewise, the oscillation between preserving or neglecting the Nazi heritage – as between attending to that past or ignoring it, or between remembering and forgetting – could take place within individuals as well as between them. At the same time, some individuals could be relatively constantly positioned much more towards one end of the spectrum than another. Neo-Nazis, for example would always argue for the buildings' preservation – this being one reason for the ambivalence that many others felt about maintaining the site.

The oscillation was not, however, only a function of the ambivalence over remembering and forgetting. As I discuss in the following section, it was also part of a tacking forth between preserving or restoring the Nazi legacy and finding means of countering or reflecting upon it. This in turn could be part of a struggle to deal with the perceived Nazi agency that might be retained or even unleashed by preservation and restoration. Moreover, oscillation could also be part of an exculpatory cycle in which – as some accused locally (as we will see below) – acts of reflection could seem to act as 'alibis' to allow wider neglect, destruction or even questionable restoration.

Restoration

In the run up to the fiftieth anniversary of the Nazi seizure of power, the city council approved a recommendation from the Building Committee to apply to the Bavarian Conservation Department for funding to help with the restoration of the Golden Hall inside the Zeppelin Building so that the room could be used for exhibitions and events, especially those reflecting back on 1933.[22] This was clearly a rather different tack from that of blasting away parts of the structure and could be seen as making some amends for the earlier destruction. Moreover, the restoration would involve repairing a ceiling that was very similar to that in the side-galleries that had been demolished – including a design that could be regarded as containing swastikas.

Although the restoration was surely questionable in the same terms as had been raised by the Israeli student over a decade earlier, it was largely supported by Nuremberg's history workers. Hermann Glaser told me that while he was aware at the time that restoring the building, especially its swastika ceiling, could be seen as restoring some of the Nazi aura, he had been in favour of doing so partly because this would also provide a space in which the history of the Rally Grounds could be addressed.[23] Moreover, while there was a small circle of people who would be attracted to the Nazi architecture because it was Nazi, the majority, he said, were simply interested to know how it looked – something that couldn't easily be gained from the outside of the building given its poor condition, or from its other pokey, gloomy rooms. Conveying the allure – the fascination (*Faszination*) – of Nazism, he added, was also an important aspect of information about it; and without the swastikas this building was not readily distinguished from the mainstream of European gigantic buildings of the time. So, in what looked like an exculpatory oscillation, an exhibition – entitled 'Fascination and Terror' (*Faszination und Gewalt*) – was opened in the 'fascinating' Golden Hall with its restored swastikas (Figure 2.3).

That there was a danger that restoring buildings might be seen as Nazi homage was evident in a report in the *Sunday Times* in 1983 in which, according to the local Nuremberg press, it was maintained that the city wanted to restore the buildings on the Zeppelin and Mars Fields back to their former glory as a way of establishing Nuremberg's reputation as the 'cradle of National Socialism'.[24] Not surprisingly, Nuremberg's authorities were furious about the claim.

The restoration of the Golden Hall was not the only restoration of parts of the former Rally Grounds over the years; though it was unusual in its restoration of swastikas and in that it opened up a Nazi space to the public that would not have been visible otherwise. Other examples of restoration were repairs to the roof of the Congress Hall, as mentioned before, more of which were also needed subsequently. Rather than being entangled in heritage discourse, however, these were all negotiated through cost analyses of repair in relation to the income that could be gained by continuing to be able to use the rooms for storage. Another case of restoration that led to more complex negotiation, however, was the repair of the Great Road – the granite-paved road running south from the Congress Hall – in the early 1990s.[25]

Initially the city planned to repair the road by replacing many of the original paving stones. Even that was going to cost 270,000 DM; but despite misgivings over the sum involved the Council concluded that it was worth doing primarily because of the importance of the road for car-parking, especially during the Christmas markets. The Bavarian Conservation Department intervened, however, and refused to allow repairs of this sort to go ahead. Instead, they demanded restoration of the road; and they criticised the council for showing 'no sense of responsibility in dealing with the legacy of NS-architecture' [26] – a criticism that must have rankled in the city given that a persistent theme in Nuremberg's self-identity is that it has been left with a Nazi stigma while Munich has managed to get away without doing so. The costs for a fully 'responsible' dealing with the heritage, however, were projected as in the tooth-gnashing millions. In the end a compromise was reached – even this costing 14 million DM, of which the Conservation Department paid almost half. In a scaling of authenticity, a stretch of 200 metres of the road, at the north end, would be retained as far as possible in its current state – as a 'museum piece', 'documenting the transience and decay of the "Thousand Year Reich" ';[27] though further decay was to be prevented as far as possible by barring it to traffic. The next 650 metres would be laid with original undamaged stones – so illustrating the road as it would have been originally. The remaining 650 metres – which were most important for traffic, especially to the trade fair site (the *Messe* – built in the former tent accommodation part of the Rally Grounds in 1971) and that were also used by local people to repair their cars and for holding barbecues – would be replaced with a new concrete structure. In this way, a range of approaches to difficult heritage were covered, from one end of the street to the other – though 80-year-old Nuremberger Robert Müller, member of a group of those who had been persecuted as Social Democrats by the Nazi's, denounced it as 'rehabilitating a Nazi monument'.[28]

Profanation

Heritage protection turned the Nazi Rally Grounds into heritage. That is, it identified them as historically significant, as special, as worthy of preservation and attention. In doing so, it gave the site symbolic value and seemed to demand particular ways of treating and viewing it. Not all in Nuremberg were happy with this heritage effect, however, and some feared that it might play into the hands of neo-Nazis. When in 2000 I asked Michael Weber, Director of Tourism, about the fact that so few of the maps produced by the Tourism Department over the years had included reference to the Rally Grounds, he immediately responded that they had not wanted to make it easy for neo-Nazis to find or to 'give it recognition' (*Anerkennung geben*) – a phrase which in German as in English also carries a connotation of according worth. While the idea that neo-Nazis would not have been able to find the site without publications produced by the Tourism Department might seem unlikely (though it certainly stopped others getting there and perhaps neo-Nazis were no better informed), his comments convey the concern of tourism authorities to avoid looking as though they were pandering to Nazi pilgrims. The dilemma faced here by those responsible for city tourism should not be underestimated. On the one hand, if they did not include the site in brochures, maps or tourist itineraries they looked as though they were trying to hide or ignore the Nazi past. On the other, if they included it, they risked looking as though they were regarding it as just another heritage attraction – part of the 'local colour' available for tourist consumption. This could be accused of 'normalisation'. Faced with such a dilemma, it is perhaps not surprising that 'profanation' should have seemed like an attractive strategy.

The banality of evil

Hermann Glaser explains that his ideas about the significance of the banal or trivial use of the Rally Grounds was based in his academic engagement with the history of National Socialism and German cultural history – on which he had already published several books by the time that he became Nuremberg's culture minister (SPD) in 1964. In particular, it was shaped by Hannah Arendt's notion of the 'banality of evil' (*Banalität des Bösens*). The Nazi regime was characterised in general by an aestheticisation of barbarity; and that led also to the aestheticisation at the Rally Grounds, with the films of Riefenstahl and so forth. But this aestheticisation of barbarity was always bound together with the banality of evil. In other words, he continued, what was involved was not so much a demonic leading of a people but also what he had described in one of his books as a '*Spiesserideologie*' – a petit-bourgeois mentality. A gigantic building like the Congress Hall was demonic, and that was why he was attracted to the idea of using it for trivial purposes – to find a way that, just in a glance, the banality of evil would also be conveyed. Also important, because from around 1900 ruins have been regarded as fascinating, was to avoid the aura of the ruin.

The notion of 'profanation' – *Profanierung* – is widely credited in Nuremberg to Glaser, though he tended to prefer the term *Banalisierung* (and also sometimes used *Trivialisierung*). Creating an exhibition could be seen as one way of 'working through the past' and trying to counter the potential 'enchanting' or 'fascinating' effects of the heritage site. (*Übertrumpfen, widersprechen* and *bewältigen* are some of the words that have been used to express this idea.)[29] Profanation, however, was seen as a means of countering it through more 'trivial' or 'banal' means, as its local synonyms made clear. Rooted in philosophical arguments about the nature of National Socialism (briefly indicated in the intervention above), profanation basically entailed doing ordinary things that did not 'give recognition' to there being anything special about the site. As such, it became capable of incorporating most of what was already going on – including much that might otherwise have looked like neglect or failure to address the past. So the ordinary uses of the buildings for storage – of school furniture, impounded cars, traffic signs, the boat club's canoes, and so forth – or for activities such rehearsals by the Nuremberg orchestra or fire-fighting practice by the Association for the Prevention of Accidents, or even for events such as motor racing or rock concerts, all became instances of profanation. As Glaser put it of rock concerts, whose impressive light effects might have been seen as recalling Speer's aesthetic staging, 'The synthesisers and flood-lights of rock bands trump the fascist monumental aesthetic à la Riefenstahl'.[30] Local people's daily dog-walking, or their perfecting of their tennis strokes against the Zeppelin Building were, likewise, transformed into acts of profaning the Nazi legacy.

Figure 4.1 Profanation? Banal uses of the Rally Grounds site. Rear of Zeppelin Building, 1984 and 2006

In articulating the concept, however, Glaser was also addressing a more specific problem – that of restoration versus ruin. Restoring the buildings was a problematic strategy because it potentially returned at least some of their original power to attract. Letting them fall into ruin, however, was equally hazardous, for to do so would fulfil Hitler's and Speer's hope of a future of the buildings as ruins. Moreover, the 'aura of the ruin', which as he pointed out was rooted in nineteenth-century romanticism, seemed to hold a dangerous allure for the German psyche. Glaser was not the only one to suggest this – these were arguments that had wider currency in Nuremberg in the 1980s, as well as more widely. For example, in a city council discussion (of the shopping centre proposal discussed below) in 1987 a CSU representative also argued that there was a danger that if the buildings were neglected they would become 'mythologised as ruins' – and he called for 'demythification' (*Entmythologisierung*) to help address this danger.[31] 'Profanation' – which entailed leaving the buildings in a state of unsightly semi-disrepair – was one such form of 'demythification'.

While the concept of profanation was eagerly taken up by the tourist authorities and continues to circulate today, as we have seen, it was also subject to criticism. In the council debate just mentioned, for example, Green councillor Sophie Rieger argued that the notion of 'demythification' was misconceived because there 'was no myth, no saga, just bitter reality'.[32] In other words, the very notion of profanation defined the site as in some sense 'sacred'; if it was not sacred, it could not be profaned. Arguably, this missed the point that, whether or not individuals 'gave recognition' to the site, heritage legislation had already in effect defined the site as not ordinary or profane, which – as in anthropologist Mary Douglas' terms – meant that it was effectively 'sacred'.[33] But even for some of those who did not object to the idea on

Rock concerts – counter-events?

In Sung Hyung Cho's subtle and insightful documentary film, *Full Metal Village* (2006), about the arrival of a heavy metal festival in the small village of Wacken, north Germany, one of the teenage girls talks about her grandparents' experience of Nazi times, participating in rallies. She wishes, she says, that she could have the chance to go back to those times, just for a day, to see what it was like. Later in the film we see her at one of the festival concerts as a Black Metal band screams about death and destruction and the crowd chants and punches the air in unison.

I think about a tour guide holding up a picture of a Nuremberg rally and contrasting it with one of a Bob Dylan concert (Chapter 7 and contrast Figures 2.1 and 3.7). He points out the different body postures as participants as the latter sprawl across the grass. Yet, the body postures at rock concerts are not always quite so different, as *Full Metal Village* shows. Walking around the Rally Grounds site while a large rock festival – Rock im Park – is on, and feeling the presence of so many other people, gives me the closest experience in all of my own visits of what it might have been like to be at a Nuremberg rally.

Figure 4.2   Rock concert participants at Nuremberg Rally Grounds, 2007

these grounds, profanation could easily just seem like an excuse for doing nothing and continuing with business as usual.

Nevertheless, the idea that there could, and should, be steps taken to somehow 'challenge' the symbolism and potential agency of the site was one that grew in the 1980s – and that was expressed in a greater range of negotiating tactics. Some of these had precedents. Thus attempting to 'redeem' the site through Christianity, as we saw in the previous chapter, was also evident in some new proposals, as we will see below. Trying to counter Nazi evil through nature had been in evidence from immediately after the war, with the emphasis on returning some parts of the site to public park land and to plans to cultivate the areas along the sides of the Great Road. While the Association of German Architects' bold plans of 1963 had argued that just planting some greenery around the existing Nazi buildings would not be sufficient to 'overcome' (*bewältigen*) them, their proposal nevertheless saw the use of nature as a particularly appropriate way to deal with the razed site. Should any remaining bits of the demolished building stick out among the plants as ruins, however, the architects suggested that this would be a poetic reminder to citizens of their own success in having 'triumphed over [*überwunden*] a time that deserved to be forgotten'.[34]

A proposal in 1988 from a working group of the city council to hold a Federal Garden Show in Nuremberg also saw a plant-centred use as especially appropriate for the Nazi site. They planned to turn the Congress Hall into a gigantic greenhouse, known as Plantopolis or Ökopolis; and the Zeppelin Building into a 'flower arena'. The plans were rejected, however, primarily on grounds of cost, though a couple of council members suggested it to be an 'inappropriate' way of dealing with the Nazi buildings.[35] While there were differences of view, this attention to, and negotiation of, what was and what was not 'appropriate' for what were increasingly explicitly referred to as 'NS-buildings' (*NS-Bauten*), was being invoked to a new extent in city council debates by the late 1980s.[36]

Below, I look at a controversy that took place shortly before the suggestion to turn the Congress Hall into a greenhouse – and in which questions of appropriate use of Nazi heritage came to the fore. This was a proposal in 1987 to transform it into a shopping and leisure centre. In a sense, this was a continuation of the leisure uses that had been underway since the war, and that had gained a new status as profanation, but it took it to new levels, and also coupled it with a more blatantly commercial dimension. The controversy shows the first major public questioning of the seemliness of a proposed use of a Rally Grounds building. First, however, I want to turn briefly to some examples of protests at the Rally Grounds that also took place in the early 1980s. These show the Rally Grounds becoming entangled in a more radical politics of questioning existing relationships to the Nazi past – though they also show that, unlike in the shopping centre controversy that follows, the provenance of buildings was not yet a central issue.

Protest

As part of a more active peace movement growing in Germany during the 1970s, questions had been raised increasingly frequently about the military ritual of Remembrance Day ceremonies. In the early 1980s this resulted in disruption of the services at the war memorial on the Nazi Party Rally Grounds. Protesters interrupted the speeches, unfurled banners and gave out leaflets, before being arrested.[37] In 1985 the Greens organised a second Remembrance Day service at the Southern Cemetery, which sought to avoid any elements of 'hero-isation'.[38] Despite this reflexive criticism, however, the fact that the war memorial was located on the former Nazi Party Rally Grounds – and at a memorial that had been a centrepiece of Nazi military ritual – was scarcely mentioned. So, for example, in an interview in 1985 with Erika Sanden, a representative of the VVN (an anti-fascist organisation *Vereinigung der Verfolgten des Naziregimes*, Organisation of Victims of Nazi Persecution), about the alternative ceremony, she explained the decision almost entirely in terms of the troubling military form of the ritual. Even in response to a leading question by interviewer Rolf Wolf – 'The Luitpold field is marked as a part of the Nazi-era Reich Rally Grounds. Why [will the alternative ceremony be held at] the Southern Cemetery?' – she replied only that the Southern Cemetery contains graves representing a broader victim group: Russian prisoners of war, Nuremberg citizens killed in the bombing of the city and young people who Hitler enlisted towards the end of the war.[39]

In subsequent years, the SPD city council toned down the military character of the ceremony at the war memorial. No longer were there uniformed and armed soldiers standing to attention on the memorial's stage, no more burning flames in the crucibles and no singing of 'Good Comrades'. In response, some CSU representatives stayed away and held an alternative commemoration at the memorial to pilots at the back of the war memorial.[40] There was, however, no suggestion of an alternative location and Remembrance Day continues to be commemorated at the memorial on the former Nazi Party Rally Grounds today.[41]

Another peace protest took place at the former SS-Barracks in Nuremberg in 1983. In this case, the provenance of the building was noted as a secondary factor, the continued presence of the US military being the primary one. The event was attended by Petra Kelly, a founder of the Green Party, who gave a speech; and participants stood in a circle holding hands, and decorated a tank with knitting wool and a banner reading 'Bread and Roses for the World'.[42]

Nazi Heritage as 'shopping paradise'

In March 1987, after over a year of consultation and preparation, a private Nuremberg company – Congress & Partner – put a detailed proposal to the council to convert the Congress Hall into a shopping and leisure centre.[43] In the oscillations that I have argued have been typical of the negotiations of the site over the years, this was hot on the heels of the opening of an exhibition about the site's history in the Zeppelin Building (see next chapter); and at a time when there was greater engagement with Nazi history in Germany more widely. In Nuremberg it was at the beginning of a new wave of reflective activities, discussed in the following chapter. Also, however, it followed yet more reports about the necessity to spend money to maintain the crumbling buildings, which seemed to be raising increasing frustration with the heritage protection laws. In a council meeting in July 1986, for example, the city's treasurer, Dr Hans Georg Schmitz (SPD) maintained that the decisions of the Bavarian Conservation Department should not all be taken as 'expressions of the highest wisdom' and rhetorically asked 'who is going to protect us from heritage protection?'.[44] Particularly galling to him was the fact that more was being done to

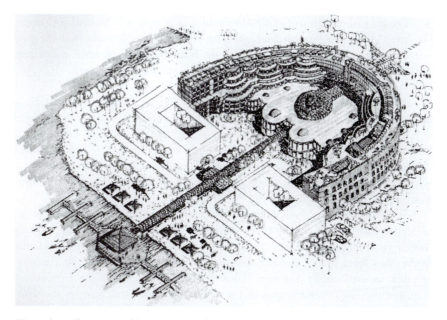

Figure 4.3   Shopping and leisure centre plans, 1987

protect Nazi buildings than some other, earlier, heritage. While the Greens on the council disagreed with his sentiments, he expressed a widely shared frustration that forms part of the backdrop to the receptiveness to the proposal from Congress & Partner the following year.

Under the proposals the main shell of the Congress Hall was to be retained but substantially developed in order to contain 'elegant' and 'exclusive' shops, restaurants, luxury flats, cinemas, discos, sports facilities including swimming pools, tennis courts, squash courts, gyms and golf-driving ranges, and an older people's home. The mottoes of the project were 'Property with personality' and 'The world's money to Nuremberg'.[45] It was projected to cost 500 million DM. When the plans were put to the city council they were initially broadly welcomed. That Nuremberg lacked such a facility, that it could help build up commerce, especially in the south of the city, and that it would finally create a use for the building that would generate enough income to cover any future repairs, were all identified as attractive points in the plans' favour. Treasurer Schmitz also commented that he felt it appropriate 'in the spirit of demythification [to] bring life into the building'.[46] The only reservations expressed initially were over precisely how it would be financed and possible problems with traffic and for existing retailers in the area. Even Nuremberg's Monument Protection officials were in agreement with the proposals as long as the outer form of the building was not altered.[47]

Members of Nuremberg's public, however, were not so convinced. Letters were sent to the local newspaper opposing the plan, and not just for the practical reasons raised by some on the council.[48] Many of these were dripping with sarcasm. One, for example, wrote:

> Congratulations on this extraordinary idea. Not only will Nuremberg's inner-city ... become a treasure chest again, no, even as unlovable a relic from the great days of the Nazi Rallies will become the finest shopping paradise in Franken. There's no better way, 42 years later, to repress misery and atrocity.

Observing that 'a monument (*Mahnmal*) to national socialist megalomania is to be turned into a monument to commercial megalomania', one writer predicted that if the trend continued 'the prison cells in the city hall would be turned into a cellar disco'. Another argued that as consumerism could help people to forget about the poverty and hunger of the Third World that was caused for our wealth, there was no better place to build a 'shopping paradise' in Nuremberg. One writer simply wondered whether the proposal might be a carnival or April Fool spoof.

Several writers also talked about the past having been 'repressed' (*verdrängt*) or 'alienated' (*verfremdet*), and of the importance of these buildings for an ongoing 'working through' of Nazi history. Such ways of talking were relatively new in relation to the Nazi Party Rally Grounds, though they had become increasingly common in other areas of public discourse about the Nazi past.[49] While the terminology employed was not necessarily part of a psychoanalytic discourse, many of the terms had become popularised after the publication of a book entitled *The Inability to Mourn* published in 1967 by Margarete and Alexander Mitscherlich. Selling in the hundreds of thousands, the local newspaper could simply say 'Mitscherlich' as a shorthand for their ideas without any further explanation.[50] Even over thirty years later this was the book most often pointed out to me during my fieldwork as significant for understanding German approaches to the Nazi past. It was not so much the Mitscherlichs' specific Freudian arguments about Germans having been unable to mourn the father figure of Hitler that became part of public discourse, however, as a more general perception that German society was suffering from all kinds of psychic ills because of having repressed and denied the past. Such a perspective inflected upon ways of evaluating approaches to Nazi 'heritage'. What might previously have simply been seen as pragmatism, moving on or even profanation was now cast as a symptom of a failure to face up to the past, and even of a wider moral failure to acknowledge the consequences of present-day actions.

The strand of public opposition evident in the letters solidified further into an official challenge – a 'citizens' initiative' (*Bürgerinitiativ*). According to the five citizens who mounted the initiative, the plans 'hushed up, repressed and concealed' the city's past.[51] For forty years, the citizens charged, the city had shown no understanding of the significance of these buildings for remembrance. That the buildings should somehow act as such was a point that had also been made by Professor Michael Petzet, chief conservator of the Bavarian Conservation Department, who had contacted the city council to express his reservations to the shopping centre proposals. The Congress Hall was, he argued, 'one of the most important witnesses (*Zeugnisse*) of the gigantomania of National Socialism'.[52] Rather than using the building for the commercial purposes proposed, he argued that it should be left unused to act instead as a *Mahnmal*. The term 'Mahnmal' – which had also been used in some of the newspaper letters – is difficult to translate into English and is part of German's twentieth-century extensive and differentiated memory vocabulary. Klaus Neumann explains it as follows:

> The term *Mahnmal* is a composite of the verb *mahnen*, 'to admonish', 'to warn', or 'to remind', and the noun *Mal*, 'sign' or 'mark'. In contrast to a *Denkmal*, which is to function merely as a reminder of a past, or an *Ehrenmal*, which honours somebody or something from the past, a *Mahnmal* is a critical statement about the past. It is to serve as an admonition – lest the past recur in the future. The term *Mahnmal* is a product of the twentieth century and has been used most often to designate memorials that are ostensibly warning present and future generations not to allow the horrors of the Nazi years to repeat themselves.[53]

Referring to the buildings of the Nazi Party Rally Grounds – places not of victims and suffering but a stage for Nazi propaganda – as a *Mahnmal* and as a 'witness' was also relatively novel in the site's history. It was, as Neumann's explanation indicates, a significant distinction from the buildings just being *Denkmäler* – heritage as a 'reminder of the past'. Now it was also to be a warning for the present and future.

The citizens' initiative likewise called for the Congress Hall to be left largely unused – in what they called 'planned demise' (*geplanter Verfall*) – in order to function as a *Mahnmal*. This was not, however, simply envisaged as neglecting the building, as had happened in the past. Instead, they proposed erecting a barbed wire fence across its inner courtyard in order to symbolise the idea of 'barring National Socialism from our lives'.[54] Moreover, they also proposed that exhibitions should be mounted in part of the building – a negotiating tactic of 'making explicit' (see next chapter).

On 15th July there was a heated debate in the city council about the proposals.[55] Introducing the debate, Treasurer Schmitz made clear his support for the shopping centre proposals. While this support was mainly on grounds of relieving the city from its ongoing financial burden – and even promised increased income – he reiterated that he was also in favour of the 'demythification' of a Nazi building that he saw the plans as offering. Moreover, he argued, Nazi Gauleiter Julius Streicher's former headquarters – the so-called 'Brown House' – was being used by the *Nürnberger Nachrichten* without this being seen as problematic. The CSU also argued in favour of such 'demythification'. This was eloquently criticised by Green councillor Sophie Rieger, as noted above, who also reported that the Greens had letters expressing strong opposition to the plans from former Jewish citizens of the city. Some SPD councillors also spoke against the plans. These included Arno Hamburger, the head of Nuremberg's Jewish community, who criticised the argument that the shopping centre could be compared to the use of a former Nazi building by a left-leaning newspaper. They also included Peter Schönlein, candidate for the position of mayor, who declared himself unconvinced by the business side of the plans and concerned that the council risked making a 'historical mistake' given the importance of the Congress Hall as 'an expression of the megalomania of the Nazi time'. The council vote was close – 39:31 against the proposal.

The shopping centre case has been seen in Nuremberg as a turning point in the city's dealing with the Nazi Party Rally Grounds.[56] Although not totally absent previously, the controversy brought to the fore the ideas that the buildings could act as 'witnesses' and as '*Mahnmäle*'; and it heightened the stakes in the debate about 'appropriate' usages by casting some as 'repression' or even a conspiratorial 'hushing up'. Concerns over 'city image' – so central in earlier years too – resonate through these debates but they also take a different turn. As Rieger made clear in her arguments, and as one of those involved in the citizens' initiative, Eckart Dietzfelbinger, had pointed out on the basis of his experience of giving guided tours to visitors from overseas, Nuremberg would be judged by the outside world in terms of how it treated this past. Hushing it up or turning it into a shopping paradise would reflect badly on the city. New approaches were needed.

Another shopping paradise in Nazi heritage

On a rainy day in early 2007 I visit Weimar. On my 'to see' list is the former Gauforum, the monumental headquarters of the Nazi administrative district – a vast square of offices and marching grounds close to the centre of this town, so famous for its Goethe heritage and as capital of the former Weimar republic. Somewhere near to where I think the Gauforum should be I stop at a tourist information office, which is on the top floor of a smart little shopping centre, amidst some kitschy Italianate reconstructions. When I ask the woman at the tourist office for directions, she smiles and tells me that I have found it. The shopping centre, opened in late 2005 is in part of the Gauforum. This was allowed, she explains, because the original external structure of the building has been kept under its cover of advertisements. Outside, it is possible to peep between buildings and see the grassed-over marching square and its surrounding buildings. But I can find no signs indicating the presence or history of the building.

Klaus Neumann has written insightfully about Weimar's dealing with its past, especially its attempts to disassociate itself from Buchenwald, the concentration camp on its doorstep. While for many years city authorities largely managed to make this disassociation, he writes in a book published in 2000, 'in the 1990s [they] were unable to quarantine Weimar from the name "Gauforum" ... In fact, they were to explain it to the many international visitors expected in Weimar in 1999' when Weimar became a European City of Culture.[57]

What had happened in the intervening years to put it under wraps again – this time literally? Why had it become possible to turn it into a shopping centre and what negotiations had taken place? Looking into the latter, I discovered that there had been a series of seminars organised during the discussion phase to which expert speakers from elsewhere were invited.[58] One of these was Eckart Dietzfelbinger, one of those who had mounted the original citizens' initiative against the shopping centre proposals in Nuremberg and who now worked at the Documentation Centre in the Congress Hall. One thing that the Weimar Gauforum case so clearly showed was that the idea of a straightforward move over time to being more explicit, to flagging up the Nazi past, was certainly not unequivocally underway. I found myself wondering too, had Nuremberg turned the Congress Hall into a shopping centre in the 1980s would it now be relatively forgotten and simply used? Or was that site, and that vaster and more distinctive building, somehow different?

The burden of history and image-management

The shopping centre controversy led to a realisation that there needed to be public debate about the future of Nuremberg's Nazi heritage. The council decided to hold a symposium on the subject the following year; and all of the political parties then issued reports on what they thought should be done. Officially unrelated to the controversy, the Tourism Department also decided to commission a report on the city's image and how this could be managed.

The symposium, entitled 'The heritage – dealing with Nazi Architecture' ('*Das Erbe – Vom Umgang mit NS-Architektur*') – was held at the Germanic National Museum in July 1988. Organised on behalf of the council by a group of

Figure 4.4 Shopping Centre 'Atrium' in Weimar Gauforum, 2007

organisations, including the Pedagogical Institute (which was itself campaigning hard for more support for an expanded exhibition at the site, see next chapter), it included talks by many renowned historians, architects and artists, who provided comparative examples as well as ideas.[59] The tone was set in the opening talk by Ralph Giordano (b. 1923), who had recently published a book entitled *Die zweite Schuld oder von der Last ein Deutscher zu sein – The Second Guilt or the Burden of being a German*, which had been widely discussed in Germany and reported on at length in the local newspaper. The idea that being German was a 'burden' was not unusual in public discourse and was usually deployed, as in Nuremberg earlier, as part of a complaint about having to still bear the stigma of history. Giordano, however, used the term differently to argue that Germans had tended to deny all guilt, and to not face up to their historical duty. This failure to atone for the past constituted 'second guilt'. In other words, the burden of being German was one that had to be openly accepted rather than resented or ignored, otherwise the guilt was compounded. This had clear implications for the way in which Nuremberg should approach its Nazi 'heritage-burden' (*Erblast*).

The local newspaper summarised the outcome of the symposium:

> None of the symposium participants called for the demolition [of the buildings], because all were unanimous that they must be retained for future generations as a reminder (*Mahnung*) and definitely should not be allowed to fall into a state of romantic ruin, in which even now a seductive magic lurks (*verführerischer Zauber*). And there was also general consensus that a commercial use, like that under discussion last year, should not be considered under any circumstance, for to use this building [the Congress Hall] just like any other would be to play

down (*verharmlosen*) the National Socialism for whose deadly megalomania it was erected.[60]

Not only did conference participants agree that the buildings should be treated as *Mahnmäle*, however, they also argued that if Nuremberg did so it would be dealing with its Nazi heritage better than other cities. Contributors pointed out the failings in Berlin and Munich, where Nazi buildings were simply put into new usage, and said that what Nuremberg faced was not so much a burden as a *chance* to do things better.[61]

When the SPD and CSU subsequently published papers about their recommendations for the future of the Rally Grounds, they broadly agreed with the consensus at the symposium and made many of the same points. Even the CSU was clear that, as the document's author Hans K. Frieser put it, 'a flight from the responsibility for the past is no longer tenable … just to leave the buildings as a diologue with our past is insufficient' – to which a newspaper editorial archly remarked 'you don't get such a clear word from the ranks of the Christian Socialists every day'.[62] What the CSU proposed for the site was to extend the existing exhibition in the Zeppelin Building and make it available all year round, and also to offer more tours. At the same time, however, Frieser also argued for recognising another 'historical phase' of the site, its pre-Nazi state – 'in the era of the liberal mayor Hermann Luppe', as he diplomatically pointed out – as a public park. This should be realised in a 'leisure belt' stretching from the north to the south of the area.

The SPD document, published early the following year, went further in its call for a documentation of the past.[63] Instead of extending the current exhibition, the SPD wanted to establish a foundation charged with producing a documentation centre and a museum for contemporary history. This foundation, they recommended, should be answerable not only to the city but also to Bavaria and West Germany, and even to the EU and UNESCO. Clear in the symposium and the documents was that it was broadly accepted that Nuremberg's 'image' would be judged by how it reflected upon – and was seen to reflect upon – its Nazi heritage. Ignoring it, or dealing with it inadequately, was now recognised to be what Schönlein called 'a historical mistake' (above).

While the symposium and the documents were directly concerned with the Nazi heritage, however, this still remained marginal in other approaches to the city's image. A report produced for the Tourism Department just a few months after the symposium – *Reflections on Nuremberg's Image: The Case for a Unified Image-management* – shows a highly professionalised approach to 'image-management', with the employment of concepts such as '*Wir-Gefühl*' ('belonging' or literally 'we-feeling') and '*Enttäuschungseffekt*' ('disappointment effect').[64] It begins: 'Image-management is one of the most important tasks of every business enterprise. But for a city like Nuremberg a comprehensive positive image is downright essential'.[65] The problem is not only that 'foreigners still often associate the name Nuremberg with the Nazi period', but that Nuremberg fails to project itself as a lively, modern, creative city in which businesses will want to invest.[66] For the most part the report concentrates on how to address the latter, with little attention to the Nazi history.

So while on the one hand, in the symposium, the city of Nuremberg was being personified as a moral witness with a responsibility to address its history, on the other, in the professionalised concerns with image-management, it was being defined as a business whose most important task was creating a positive impression. These were not necessarily wholly contradictory, for, as the symposium suggested, being seen to deal with the history adequately might enhance the city's image. Nevertheless, the latter was not yet a perspective that many were ready to adopt, and so these tended to feel like uncomfortable alternatives. Only later would addressing Nazi history come more widely to be accepted as a *part* of the image-management that the Tourism Department called for.

* * * * *

There can be many different impetuses to the preservation of the material remains of the past – not all of which, as evident in the previous chapter, are part of an intentional or moralised saving for posterity. This chapter, by contrast, has looked at the initiation of active attempts to preserve, and at what was, in effect, the transformation of inherited stuff into a heritage deemed worthy of conservation for the future. This status as heritage also contributed to heritage effect dilemmas: once defined as significant in this way, might this prompt positive evaluation of a reprehensible regime?

Alongside attempts to counter this – and other developments for which this was sometimes used as an excuse – were also other shifts in the way that material culture was being understood. Increasingly, the moral compass of the buildings was not only considered in terms of the Nazi period itself but also in terms of how they had been treated since. They became evidence not only of the Nazi period but also of post-Nazi identity, of how those 'coming after' related to this past. This understanding, or way of reading material culture, was also entangled with the popular spread of a psychoanalytically influenced idea that not 'facing up to' the past, not addressing it openly, was a 'second guilt' (in Giordano's terms); and that it was a form of 'repression' that could lead to other symptoms in the body politic, such as the inability to recognise moral failing. While the call for a 'working through of the past' was not new – Adorno had called for it in 1959 as we have already noted – this became increasingly psychologised during the 1960s and increasingly widely popularised thereafter.

Bringing buildings within this orbit was not, however, immediate – at least in Nuremberg. The basis for doing so was nevertheless laid already. Not least, the work of postwar rebuilding, of recovering from destruction, made the treatment of buildings into a sign, to be interpreted; that is, it made buildings into a metaphor of postwar identity. This was developed still further in the new field of image-management, in which city identity was to be projected in part through the urban surface. But if all of these contributed to an idea that the state of city buildings could be read as a sign of identity and health, they also opened the way for interpreting other buildings – including Nazi buildings – through the same lens. And this was often uncomfortable and problematic in ways that we have seen – and will see again.

Legislation was a powerful, but not uncontested of fully determining, element of the turning of the site into heritage. There were struggles against both the practical and symbolic implications of the new heritage status. But the heritage designation was only a part of turning the site into full-blown heritage. Other heritage paraphernalia are also a typical part of the heritage assembly – guidebooks, information boards, tours, exhibitions and so forth. Their production was called for, and put into effect, by various history workers in the city. And it was also prompted by consumers – that is, the increasing numbers of visitors to Nuremberg who were seeking out the site, as part of a growing form of cultural tourism dedicated to witnessing such history, and seeking out 'difficult heritage' and especially sites connected with the Holocaust. The following chapters turn to these developments.

5

ACCOMPANIED WITNESSING

Education, art and alibis

By the end of the 1980s there was agreement in Nuremberg across the main political parties that the city needed to expand its educational provision about the Nazi past in general and about the Nazi Party Rally Grounds in particular. As one of the authors of an SPD paper about the future of the site explained in an interview: 'We do not want to leave people alone with their emotions and impressions of this monument (*Denkmal*), but want, rather, to explain it there and then'.[1] This felt need to 'accompany' visitors as they encountered the site was an effect of seeing it as having a power to 'fascinate' or 'enthral'. Such a way of seeing had been increasingly articulated in the years following its designation as heritage; no longer was this perception restricted to swastikas. In the 1980s, material qualities such as the size of the buildings, their distinctive architecture and even their signs of decay were accorded significance and potential agency; and, as we saw in the previous chapter, attention was increasingly paid to trying to tackle this agency. Two further important negotiating tactics employed were education and art.

Barbara Kirshenblatt-Gimblett notes that 'Walter Benjamin spoke of "the appreciation of heritage" as a "catastrophe"'.[2] Whether of not we agree that the appreciation of heritage in general is a catastrophe, the appreciation of 'difficult heritage' is clearly potentially especially so. As we saw in Chapter 2, Hitler hoped that Nazi architecture would have an 'eye impact' that would somehow speak directly to the emotions. Leaving people to view the heritage alone might, thus, potentially allow such an affective process to continue to work. As the Chairman of the government's culture working group recognised when he visited Nuremberg in 1989, the difficulty that the city faced in presenting this heritage was doing so in a way that 'awakened neither nostalgia nor obsession'.[3] He, along with others, called for more on-site education.

This call for education about the site on site was also motivated by the fact that in many areas of Germany there were moves to provide and extend education about the Nazi past. This was prompted in part by a psychologisation of the relationship between present, past and future, and of a growing social and popular history movement that took the Nazi past as its focus.[4] Both of these cast such education as a healthy 'openness' and honesty: a making explicit that was also a performance of not being in denial. Implicated here too was the idea – which spread during the 1980s – that 'authentic' sites were especially important for revealing the significant 'traces'

(*Spuren*) of the past and for their pedagogical potential.[5] All over the country local groups were established to look at the past in their area. In Nuremberg, this included an organisation called *Geschichte für Alle* (History for All), established by university history students in the mid-1980s, which became an important force investigating the history of the Rally Grounds and creating educational resources about it, including publications and guided tours (discussed further in Chapter 7).

These developments also came together with an understanding by some in authority that the city's international image might be better served by addressing its Nazi past than by appearing to be 'hushing it up', as the citizens' initiative had accused. Not speaking of the past could be justified less and less by the claim of simply having better things to do – such as building the future. Moreover, the fact that people were now growing up who had no direct memory of the Nazi period, and that Nuremberg was receiving increasing numbers of international visitors, also made providing information about the Nazi heritage seem more vital than ever. A local newspaper report in 1981, for example, noted the increasing number of German and foreign television and film companies wanting to use the site for documentaries in advance of the fiftieth anniversary of the 1933 Nazi seizure of power; and they quoted young visitors as worrying evidence of dwindling historical knowledge: ' "It must have been like a pop festival here" and "It was good that something like this was built, because of unemployment" '.[6] And another report in 1983, in a glossy local magazine, *Nürnberg Heute*, noted how after one television programme about Nuremberg in the series *Europe under the Swastika*, the television company and Nuremberg's mayor received numerous letters. While many of these complained about the oversimplified presentation of the past and the programme's insinuations of continuities with the present, viewers called for *more* information and coverage rather than for abandoning the topic. One respondent was quoted as typical:

> I believe that the worst kind of dealing with the past (*Vergangenheitsbewältigung*) is to repress (*verdrängen*) and keep silent about this appalling part of German history, as has mostly been the case up until now.[7]

The article also quotes some French visitors:

> We wanted to come and look at the Rally Grounds and its buildings. But it was not easy to find our way here because there was no indication anywhere. It surprised us that there was no plaque here, no name or anything like that. Also, no stand or wall of photographs where one can find out about things from those days … Perhaps the people here are ashamed, or they do not want to know about it any more. But to provide no information is dangerous, because then it can happen again.[8]

That such views were feeding back into the local context, and increasingly finding fertile ground, all helped to prompt and legitimate an expansion of informational provision.

As we will see below, by the late 1980s there had already been some significant on-site educational projects, as well as increasing numbers of artistic installations, intended to intervene in people's emotions and impressions as they gazed upon Nazi heritage. Before the unexpected breaching of the wall dividing Berlin in November 1989, and unification the following year, there was already agreement that the existing educational provision was inadequate. Unification, however, made the need for improvement even more pressing. The politics of public memory became even more intensively negotiated as the different ways in which West and East Germany had represented the past – especially their last shared history, the Nazi period – were compared. Westerners were particularly critical of the German Democratic Republic's ideological use of historical sites, especially concentration camps, to sustain an image of the East as the bastion of political resistance to Nazism.[9] One of the accusations from the East was that the West had never properly denazified and had tried to bury and ignore the Nazi past and its possible continuing presence. A neglected site such as the Nuremberg Party Rally Grounds looked like good evidence for such a criticism.

In this chapter, I look at some of the educational and artistic projects and plans at the Rally Grounds both before and after unification. In doing so, I want again to probe some of the ideas and key strands of negotiations that were involved, as well as to outline some of the players. Although the reflective dimensions of education and art clearly add to the site – they provide more 'company' to think with – I continue in this chapter, as in previous ones, to pay attention too to some of what is not addressed in such approaches. In particular, I look at some of the tensions between various kinds of 'local', 'national' and beyond national (e.g. European) which are mobilised and side-lined in the projects discussed.

Telling history

In 1977, the city council, under the direction of its Culture Minister, Glaser, published a short leaflet called *Nürnberg 1933–45*, with which, according to at least one retrospective on Nuremberg's historical activities, 'an historically aware dealing with the former Nazi Party Rally Grounds began'.[10] The leaflet was made available at locations such as the public library; though originally it was not available on the open shelves of tourist offices, allegedly in case this made visitors think that Nuremberg was advertising its Fascist past.[11] A sixth edition of 1990 (which had a print-run of 20,000) was still available in 2000 at an exhibition in the Zeppelin Building. It consisted of a two-page preface by Glaser, followed by a two-page text about the city 'under the National Socialists' and twelve pages of images and text about the main buildings (excluding the SS-Barracks) of the Nazi Party Rally Grounds. As implied by the fact that it was produced in English as well as German, the leaflet was intended for tourists as well as local people. Its introductory and background text strongly emphasise the 'red Nuremberg' narrative (Chapter 1), and the local version of the 'victimisation myth' that Harold Marcuse argues was one of West Germany's 'founding myths'.[12] Nuremberg's local variant – of the city as not especially Nazi – was argued by Glaser to be important for postwar identity in Nuremberg (as explained in Chapter 2). He contributes to such an account in the leaflet's preface:

Yet up to 1933 Nürnberg was one of the most fervently republican cities in the Weimar Republic and it cannot bear the blame for becoming the city of the NS rallies. But unlike Munich – the capital of the NS movement – or Berlin – the capital of the Thousand Year Reich – Nürnberg has remained the symbol of the history of National Socialism.[13]

This is tempered with a statement that 'it must be admitted that when the National Socialists seized power they found in Nürnberg as everywhere else a not inconsiderable response which was deeply-rooted in the feelings of the German people'. Nevertheless, the overwhelming impression conveyed is of Nuremberg having been unfairly picked on by the National Socialists, and having had to bear this stigma ever since. In a flatteringly misleading presentation of figures from the last election before the Nazi seizure of power, the leaflet states of Nuremberg: 'Even in the elections of March 1933 the NS only achieved 0.1 per cent'. In those elections – in which over 90 per cent of the Nuremberg population voted – the National Socialists achieved 41.7 per cent of the votes cast. I finally figured out, after much puzzling over this apparent error that had survived so many reprintings, that 0.1 per cent is the difference between the proportion of the vote received by the SPD and KPD (Communist party) put together and that of the NSDAP – though this is not explained, and is hardly such a categorical rejection of Nazism.

The fact that the booklet is primarily a description of the Rally Grounds buildings supports the victimisation narrative. The buildings can readily be seen as imposed onto the cityscape – as the work of 'external' and 'megalomanic' Nazis. Moreover, as part of the architecture of enchantment, this focus plays in well to an impression of 'the German people' being 'tricked' (as the leaflet puts it) by the National Socialists. What is ignored in such an account, as noted in Chapter 2, is the extent to which National Socialism was embedded into local life – how, for example, certain local entrepreneurs and firms embraced 'opportunities' offered by National Socialism such as the use of forced labour or the acquisition of 'bargain' formerly Jewish properties in order to enable them to gain a business advantage. So while the leaflet was indeed an important development, not least because it included the Nazi Party Rally Grounds on a potential tourism agenda, it simultaneously defined 'Nürnberg 1933–1945' as restricted to this site, and as outside the city itself. It was not the last educational negotiation of Nuremberg's Nazi past to do so.

The preface of the leaflet also looks forward to '[t]he creation by the Nürnberg city council of a multi-media show entitled "Fascination and Force" on the site of the rallies'. This was a 'sound and light' show, intended to be opened in 1983 to mark the fiftieth anniversary of the Nazi seizure of power, but eventually opening at the end of 1984.[14] It is worth looking briefly at this exhibition and criticisms of it, partly because its title – *Faszination und Gewalt*, translated as *Fascination and Terror* in later versions – and orienting idea has been retained by later exhibitions. It shows well some of the dilemmas involved, and matters that later exhibitors would also have to address.

Exhibiting fascination and terror

As with so many other developments, the financing of the project was problematic. Initially 727,000 DM were deemed necessary to cover also the further necessary renovations to the Zeppelin Building, including improving the toilet facilities. CSU council members argued that this was excessive; and not only suggested that there should be support from the state of Bavaria but also that the exhibition creators should demonstrate 'the courage to improvise'.[15] As the amounts necessary for repairing the building rose, it was clear just how much improvisation was going to be necessary to produce an exhibition on a shoe-string.[16] In the end, only 80,000 DM was available to the Pedagogical Institute, a semi-autonomous branch of city governance which was charged with the task under the direction of Glaser.[17] With these limited means they created an hour-long sound and light show that opened in late 1984. This projected photographs and clips of film onto the walls, and some specially built extra internal walls, of the Zeppelin Building; in sections entitled 'Weimar and the seizure of power', 'Consolidation and persecution', and 'Final victory and final solution'.[18] In the two weeks that it ran in 1984 it was seen by 8,000 visitors, and some were turned away as it was booked out.[19] While it was praised as a significant attempt to provide some kind of reflection on the site, it was also much criticised as difficult to understand. The local newspaper provided a thoughtful account pointing out that the long stretches of Leni Riefenstahl's *Triumph of the Will* could be misunderstood; and that the fact that the Rally Grounds buildings were never actually visible in the images shown made the connection difficult for the viewer. And perhaps of most concern, the equipment often broke down with the result that, for example, visitors' experience might end – as it did at the première – with the cancelling of the 'Rally of Freedom' in 1939 rather than the Final Solution.[20]

Visitors also voiced such criticisms in questionnaires filled in after the show and at an open discussion evening that Glaser held in early 1985 in preparation for revising the show for re-opening. The central problems articulated were that 'The show provided too little information, explanation and commentary; it didn't indicate reasons and political background … and the local and regional situation was absent'.[21] In response, Glaser emphasised that the aim of the show had not been to transmit information but to 'be a motivation for information'. Rather than being a 'teaching show about National Socialism', the aim had been to convey 'the danger that had grown from the exuberant emotion and symbolism of the rallies'. But, the critics argued, this was to put too much emphasis on *fascination* – which they said was 'almost glorified' in the show – and too little on *terror*. Some schoolteachers said that the show should only be seen by pupils in the upper stages of school and who had been thoroughly prepared in advance, because otherwise seeing all those crowds of people 'under a spell' and in 'ecstatic fascination' risked awakening a 'secret admiration' among young people;[22] and others argued that they shouldn't see it at all: 'They come back [after seeing the show] and are totally enthralled by the Nazi regime' claimed one.[23]

The criticism highlighted some of the dilemmas of presenting this kind of difficult heritage. How could the attraction of the rallies and participation in the

Nazi project be conveyed without seeming to 'glorify' them? And how, at a place in which terror was not for the most part experienced by participants, could links be made to the regime's violence? These are dilemmas that continue over the years; and similar problems are faced at other sites of difficult heritage. How, for example, in an idyllic holiday location like Hitler's Eagles Nest do you make links to Nazi atrocity? Or how at a site of atrocity do you – and should you – try to convey what took place? In relation to concentration camps, for example, there has been considerable debate over what should be depicted; and whether there should, say, be attempts to reconstruct aspects of the camps – such as crematoria – that had been destroyed.[24] Are the piles of shoes or suitcases that have become standard ways of signalling the mechanised extermination of so many people anywhere near adequate to the task or, is it so impossible that it is misguided to even attempt to do so? Versions of these questions have repeatedly been raised in relation to the representation of the Holocaust in various media, many of them beginning from Adorno's famous warning that writing poetry after Auschwitz had become untenable.[25] Is any kind of aesthetic representation of such an event legitimate? Is it inherently redemptory?

The representation of perpetration also raises further difficult questions, on which there has also been considerable debate. These include: to what extent should there be an attempt to understand perpetrators? Is to try to understand somehow to condone – or is such understanding vital in order to help prevent repetition in future?[26] There is also the question of affect, which is raised in different ways in relation to the direct representation of atrocity, and is more generally an area of considerable importance, and as yet insufficient understanding, for heritage presentation. How far is it legitimate to try to 'convey' a particular emotion in an exhibition? Is this to engage in emotional manipulation, a practice in which the National Socialists were themselves so expert? Some pedagogical approaches argue that effective education requires making an emotional engagement; and it is often maintained that a key reason for experiencing 'real sites' is that they are more likely to generate an emotional response. But others suggest that, especially in difficult cases like these, heritage presenters should try as hard as possible to avoid affect and to simply 'present facts'; or that too much emotion interferes with learning.[27] Clearly, these are awkward and contested matters, which have been the subject of extensive and often sophisticated discussion. Here, rather than look at them in the abstract, however, we can see how they might play out in practice. For representing these Nazi buildings for the public not only turned certain moral and epistemological positions into material form, it also made them available for negotiation by audiences.

Exhibiting emotion

After the 2001 Fascination and Terror exhibition has opened, I sit with Hans Christian Täubrich, its director, leafing through past versions of plans and talking about some of the various ideas that were originally planned but later rejected. 'One might have imagined', he tells me, thinking back to early days, that we would have confronted the visitor much more strongly with the question: 'how would I have behaved?' Or, where did this fascination come from? The current exhibition as it has been completed is much more factual … It might have looked completely different conceptually. But it was decided, with the scientific advisory committee, for the version that is there. There were difficult decisions to make about how to talk to a young audience, 70–80 years after the events, and which might need to be spoken to in very different ways.

Laying out the facts – the direction which was taken – was one way. But to try to bring the visitor into the experience more, other, more emotionally-directed exhibits were contemplated. As Täubrich explains:

It is very difficult and the devil also hides in the detail … There were suggestions for a media-installation in which a lone visitor goes into a room and sees a mass of people; and whatever they are all doing in unison, whether they are shouting 'Heil!' or are simply standing in awe, he gets caught up in it – 'Yes, I'll join in!' It's easy to see; it works like that. But this suggestion was never worked up in any detail because the comment [from the scientific advisory committee] was that such an emotional involvement of the visitors was a long way from the factual documentation. So sometime or other we cut it and said, 'First we'll do our homework'. But in an accompanying programme, in future, artists can tackle those other directions much more effectively with their own individual language.

In the wake of the sound and light show, the Pedagogical Institute argued strongly for the need for more funding to create a more 'comprehensive' exhibition. The city council agreed to provide a small amount more and in July 1986 another exhibition, also entitled *Fascination and Terror* but with the subtitle *Nuremberg and National Socialism*, opened in the Golden Hall. In contrast to the light show, the exhibition did not so much seek to convey particular impressions as to provide information. This it did primarily through panels of text and photographs; and there was also a room showing videos. As the panels had a background of wooden planks, looked rather hand-made, and were simply leant against the walls of the building, the aesthetic was stripped and unembellished, as though this was only the bare facts (see Figure 2.3). The same central motif – the link between fascination and terror – was, then, here presented rather differently from in the show; and, in particular, there was more attempt to highlight the terror side of the equation, for example by including images of victims. Nevertheless, there were criticisms of this exhibition too, not least from those working for the Pedagogical Institute which had produced it. Because of the lack of heating in the Zeppelin Building, the exhibition could only be open in the summer months. Moreover, although they managed to expand parts of the exhibition over the years – for example, in response to criticism that there was too little about the trials – they did so with shrinking means (their budget of 100,000 DM was cut in 1987 by 20,000 DM and in 1988 by a further 20,000 DM) and a minimal staff;[28] and the prospect of the permanent exhibition or museum that they continually argued for was repeatedly shelved. In frustration, members of the Pedagogical Institute themselves argued that this gave the impression that their work was just serving 'an alibi function' for the city.[29]

Despite its short opening season, the exhibition attracted increasing numbers of visitors. In 1989, for example, there were 35,000 visitors, more than twice the number of the previous year, and in 1990 there were 46,000.[30] This was partly accounted for by increasing numbers of school groups visiting; though staff speculated that a spate of neo-Nazi activity in Germany – some of which was also in evidence at the Rally Grounds – was also prompting many other citizens to engage in self-education about the Nazi past and perhaps even to visit such an exhibition as a sign of their own anti-Nazi commitment.[31] It was also part of a broader expansion of interest in this topic not only in Germany but also overseas, as indicated by visitor statistics.[32] These largely continued to increase during the life-time of the exhibition, which in the end remained open until 2001 when a new permanent exhibition (discussed below) was finally opened.

The changing climate is also indicated by the tourism authorities who in 1987 decided that this topic, which they now openly said they had so long regarded as 'taboo', was now over; and, partly in response to the evident interest in the subject shown by visitors to the Zeppelin Building exhibitions, created a cassette of information about some of the site's buildings that visitors could borrow to listen to on headsets.[33] In addition, both the Art Pedagogical Institute of the Germanic National Museum and the newly founded History for All began programmes of guided tours of the Rally Grounds; and by 1989 the first information boards at the site were erected. At last, commented the local newspaper, 'tourists would not have to be left alone with their impressions'.[34]

Figure 5.1   Information boards at Nazi Party Rally Grounds, 2003 (These information boards were replaced in 2006)

Art

In addition to this informative or documentary company, visitors could also increasingly encounter the site in the company of artistic reflections. Especially during the late 1980s and mid-1990s, and to a lesser extent since, avant-garde installation art works and plays have repeatedly been staged at the Rally Grounds. That many of these were touring productions is evidence too of the topic's currency elsewhere in Germany. In 1988, a bumper year due to a 'culture circus' in June, the following touring works were shown in the Golden Hall: a play by Peter Sichrovsky called *Born Guilty*, about interviews with the children of Nazi murderers; a performance about Adolf Eichmann, *I Have Followed*; a dance piece by Rosamund Gilmore about Hitler's invasion of Austria; and an installation artwork by Hans-Jürgen Breuste entitled *Litzmannstadt* (a reflection on the German-renamed Polish town that had been a massive ghetto).[35] A pair of Breuste's sculptures, made from spent munitions, entitled *Overkill I and II*, was also moved in this year from a school elsewhere in Nuremberg (where they had been since 1971, but were now deemed dangerous as children had taken to using them for gymnastics) to stand outside the entrance to the Zeppelin Building.[36] Others works were created specifically for the site. For example, in 1987 an installation called *Spaces for Perpetrators and Victims*, by Tobias Wartenberg, was staged alongside *Fascination and Terror* in the Golden Hall. This consisted, as a report described it, of

> a prayer stool in front of a flashing traffic light as an altar, a wash tub together with a bar of soap, brush and hand towel, in front of a plaster board with synthetic roses and a surrounding of plaster stones, wheelbarrow and national pennants.[37]

According to Eckart Dietzfelbinger, who had special responsibility among Pedagogical Institute staff for the exhibition at the time, this left almost all visitors baffled.[38]

The role of art at a site like this, as more generally in relation to difficult heritage of various kinds, is undoubtedly problematic. Perhaps, it might be argued, it doesn't matter whether visitors are puzzled, as long as they are made to think; or perhaps art works on a 'different level' anyhow and so visitors' feelings of incomprehension are irrelevant. The notion of 'eye impact' has currency beyond Hitler, being, for example, implicated in Glaser's ideas about 'profanation'. Some artists and theorists argued that, especially as the Nazis had employed aesthetic strategies, it was crucial to address these through aesthetic means, rather than relying on educational and informational approaches. This was well articulated, for example, by artist Gottfried Helnwein, who wanted to stage a spectacular one day 'action against the bad spirit (*Ungeist*)' at the Rally Grounds. As the local newspaper reported:

> He does not want to 'commemorate', neither to rationally explain. He wants to work with the medium of art … He is convinced that the aesthetics of Fascism can only be worked against through a different aesthetics. The irrationality of

Nazism, its sensory melodrama can only be overcome through other pictures and dramatic actions, not through rational analysis.[39]

In the end, this particular 'action' – which was projected to include provocative pictures and a 'Euthanasia Ballet' performed by children with Downs' syndrome – did not manage to raise the money necessary to take place.

Overkill

Children often clamber onto the plinths of *Overkill I* and *Overkill II* – sculptures by Hans-Jürgen Breuste – which seem to guard the massive doors of the Zeppelin Building. Made of munitions waste, they initially look like cannons or massive guns. One day I see two boys, one at each statue, play a game of blasting away some imagined enemy. As I hang around the Building to do interviews several visitors ask me what the Breuste objects are. When I say that they are sculptures, some ask whether they were made by the Nazis, or from munitions from Nazi times. I usually explain that the sculptures used to be somewhere else and that they were not made specifically for this location. (It is only later that I learn that they are created from US military waste from the Vietnam war.) For some visitors, this seems to add to their sense of puzzlement. 'I don't see why they put them here', a student tells me, 'to make this building look even worse?' 'Perhaps to remind us of war?' I venture. 'Yes, but we know about that. They just look like part of it, not like a critical reflection'. What would such a 'critical reflection' look like, I wonder later. For other visitors, the fact that the sculptures came from elsewhere seems a relief, as though they don't have to worry further about their connection to this place. One woman points to a graffiti-covered metal hulk further along the Zeppelin Building frontage: 'And that one?' That, I explain, is a skate-boarding ramp (see Figure 4.1). We laugh as she jokingly exclaims 'Modern art!' But all these visitors make me think about the relationship between art and location, as well as comprehensibility, and how much this might matter. Should art just unsettle or should it point in a particular direction?

Animate stones

Another, particularly contested, art work was that of Karl Prantl (b. 1934), exhibited in Nuremberg's art gallery in 1991. This raises a number of key questions about the role of art in relation to difficult heritage, as well as questions about materiality and meaning. The work consisted of granite paving stones mainly from the Great Road of the Rally Grounds, some of which had been engraved by Prantl. He had begun his work on the stones at the Rally Grounds in secret in the early 1970s and the two stones that he had initially worked on had remained in place until the late 1980s when they were removed as part of the preparation for the restoration of the Road.

Figure 5.2   Overkill I

Initially the monument inspectors are said to have assumed that the mysterious markings on the stones were some kind of special signals to the marching troops.[40] According to the gallery catalogue, however, the markings were ones that the stones themselves inspired Prantl to make. Rather than conceiving the role of a sculptor in terms of 'conquering dead material, bringing it to life and breathing a soul into it', Prantl was said by contrast to

> understand stone itself as an individual being with a soul, and his endeavour is to uncover that soul ... One of his most important concepts is 'reacting' (*Reagierens*). The artist reacts to the signals and demands of the stones.[41]

These were stones, the catalogue explained, on which

> the National Socialist military had marched and were supposed to be marched on for centuries longer. Brought together from many quarries in Europe, prepared by hand by forced labourers and prisoners in the concentration camps of Mauthausen and Flossenbürg, these stones lie today as a carelessly neglected treasure in Nuremberg's ground – a treasure in a double sense, witnesses of human work, human suffering and countless human fates, every stone a fingerprint of those who hewed it, and stones of great beauty and rarity, whose qualities have remained unnoticed heretofore.[42]

The 1991 exhibition not only included the stones that had originally prompted Prantl to his carvings but also others, removed from the Great Road, whose souls he was also permitted to reveal. Considerable debate about the merit of this work followed, especially in light of a suggestion that the art work might be bought for a collection elsewhere – galleries in Munich, Graz and Vienna having shown interest. The SPD proposed that they should remain in Nuremberg and should be used to 'open a discussion' by becoming part of a new 'Peace avenue' on the Rally Grounds.[43] Hermann Glaser, however, who had recently stepped down as Culture Minister, published a scathing critique of Prantl's work, suggesting that the 'conceptual discrimination' of those who were supporting it was 'suspended by their naivety'.[44] It was, he argued, a 'perversion of history' and 'moral indifference' to allow these supposedly 'naïve stones' to be shown in a 'historically naïve' way, as 'treasure' offered up for sensory appreciation. The museum director, Lucius Grisebach, hit back by saying that this was

> the well-worn argument of the blind intellectuals who only know how to deal with art if its message is presented in a literally illustrative and schoolmasterly manner ... They obviously have not managed to learn that form has its own language.[45]

It was also suggested that Glaser might be piqued due to criticism of his own suggestion the previous year that the buildings of the former Rally Grounds might be used to display Nazi art that was being returned to the city from the US.[46]

In the end, the city bought Prantl's art work for 374,000 DM (more than three times the annual budget of the Pedagogical Institute) and installed it not at the Rally Grounds as had originally been suggested but in the Altstadt next to the Lorenz (St Lawrence) Church[47] – where, from my own observations, it seems only rarely noticed by passers-by. A plaque to accompany the work reads:

> And stones also live. They are bones of the mother earth. Misuse of stones is like misuse of people. The fourteen flagstones come from the Great Road of the National Socialist Reich Party Rally Grounds. They were worked piece by piece by slave labourers and prisoners in concentration camps. Every stone is a fingerprint of a misused and maltreated person. (Karl Prantl 1991. *Nuremberg Crossroads (Kreuzweg)*)

This case highlights well some of the difficulties of using art – especially non-representational art – in relation to a theme such as National Socialism. According to Prantl and his supporters, he was working with the materiality of the stones and using a form that was not reducible to words. His sculpting – which removed the edges of the stone to make the inside visible – was giving recognition not just to the 'individual interior' of the stones but also the lives that had been imprinted into their surface. To dismiss Glaser's criticisms as incapable of understanding the non-verbal was, however, to forget that his own proposals about profanation or trivialisation had also employed such ideas. What he objected to in Prantl's work was that it did not

Figure 5.3   Kreuzweg

seek to unsettle, as did profanation, but instead 'smoothed over' history and made it 'harmonious'.[48]

According to James Young, in his analysis of post-Holocaust art, a key feature of successful and ethical pieces is that they avoid being 'redemptive in any fashion'.[49] Prantl's recuperation of the stones and presentation of them as 'treasure' could surely be seen as a form of redemption. It is also not clear that he meets another of Young's criteria for a successful and ethical post-Holocaust artwork, namely incorporating in the work 'the experience of the memory act itself'.[50] Prantl's portrayal of his role as an artist as one of 'reacting' to the agency of the stones in effect precludes any further analysis or reflection on his own acts of memory. As in so many apparently very different contexts in the history of the Rally Grounds, according agency to the materials themselves side-stepped other, possibly more uncomfortable, reflections. As Prantl emphasised, insofar as his work was about 'the preservation of memory', it was so 'without emotionalism, without accusation or allocation of guilt'.[51] Yet could or should emotion and accusation be evacuated from the memory of objects which had been part of the architecture of a Fascist regime? Some argued that Prantl's claim was in any case disingenuous, for he was surely capitalising – artistically and financially – on the emotional resonance of the concentration camp; and in any case, it was pointed out, his claim that the stones had been hewn by slave labourers was incorrect as they were produced before this policy had been instituted.[52]

Ambiguities of irony

Difficulties over the interpretation of art works came to a head again a few years later in relation to a work by local artist Michael Munding (b. 1959). This was funded under a Nuremberg art initiative called *One City for All* (*Eine Stadt für Alle*), which was intended to create works to be displayed in the city's underground railway stations that would act as signs against racism. Munding created gigantic postcards with contemporary scenic images of the Nazi Party Rally Grounds and the words 'Greetings from Nuremberg' (*Grüße aus Nürnberg*).[53] Nuremberg lawyer, Rainer Roth, wrote to the scheme organisers saying that these were 'Nazi propaganda' and should be removed. The organisers, however, stood by the artist's claim that the pieces were obviously ironic, and even commented that it was arrogance on the part of Roth to think that other people were so stupid that they would not grasp this. A quick questioning of underground passengers by a local newspaper showed, however, that not all viewers did 'get' the ironic stance. When asked to describe the Munding piece, for example, one observed 'landscapes with castles – typically German'.[54]

Examples of the use of irony elsewhere have shown that it can easily fail to be appreciated as such. The now classic case in the museum literature is that of the Royal Ontario Museum's *Into the Heart of Africa* exhibition about colonialism, in which ironic captions and comments were read literally by some visitors, contributing to widespread outcry about the exhibition's presumed racism.[55] Michael Munding himself was clearly aware of how his work might be seen: 'I reckoned on hysterical reactions', he commented, but 'Art can't just be unambiguous. Making people more tolerant – that's the job of educators, priests and mayors'.[56]

There were over the years a small number of art works that were more positively received. In the same year as Prantl's exhibition in the art gallery, for example, a video collage called *Pleasure to Kill* by Thomas Schadt (b. 1957) shown in the Zeppelin Building received good reviews in the local press.[57] Five monitors each played a different series of images: a 1930s film of people practising using gas masks; computer screens of hitting targets; film heroes such as John Wayne and Rambo committing murderous acts; scenes of sex and crime in music videos; and documentary horrors of war and death. While this was more representational than the work of Prantl, it was not directional or unambiguous. Lacking commentary, the continuously looping videos constantly threw up new combinations of images, simultaneously registering a common experience of mediated memory. This work seemed to succeed in unsettling the potential redemption offered by aestheticised images of glamorous violence, as well as by suggesting links between past and present, fiction and documentary, and pleasure and killing. In so doing, it also addressed the central theme of the exhibition of the Rally Grounds site itself – fascination and terror – but in a way that positioned these fully within viewers' own temporalities and experience.

On a solution and insolubility

By the late 1980s, as we have seen, there were many different approaches to the difficult heritage of Nazism in play on the Rally Grounds site. While many of these were conducted under various parts of city government, they were not for the most part coordinated with one another. So while the Zeppelin Building became the focus for informational and reflective artistic activity, most of the rest of the grounds lacked these except for the half-dozen scattered information panels. Instead, they were used for numerous other heterogeneous purposes, from commemoration to sport. In addition, new uses were introduced that hardly conformed to the idea of a new more reflective period. For example, as noted in the previous chapter, in 1988 a supposedly romantic concert hall was opened in a wing of the Congress Hall. The following year, its gloomy and forbidding storage rooms were used, to some citizens' dismay, for giving new East German citizens their 'greeting money' – hardly the best first impression to give of Nuremberg commented an editorial in the local newspaper.[58] To some, such as Hermann Glaser, the multiple and apparently contradictory uses of the site and the *Ratlosigkeit* – the state of being confused or at a loss as to what to do – were entirely appropriate. There should not, he argued, be any attempt to find a single 'solution' to the problem of presenting this difficult heritage.[59]

His successor to the post of Culture Minister, Karla Fohrbeck (b. 1942), of no political party, disagreed. In 1990 she presented what she described as a 'small bomb': detailed plans that she had drawn up for a *Gesamtkonzeption* – a whole or overall conception – or new representation of the former Nazi Party Rally Grounds.[60] Produced in the wake of German unification, she argued that the piecemeal approach of the previous years was no longer appropriate. Nuremberg would increasingly be confronted with problems of its image, she said, partly because of how people from the East would see it but also because the world would look to a place like Nuremberg as an indicator of whether there needed to be 'fear of a repetition'.[61] Especially in light of increasing neo-Nazi activity, 'with reports of over 10,000 right-wing radicals in the GDR', it was important that Nuremberg take a stand. It could do so, she proposed, by turning the former Nazi Party Rally Grounds into a 'central place of explanation, non-repression, consciousness, gratitude, love of humanity, many-sided understanding, tolerance, reconciliation and expressions of peace'. This, she argued, was not just a task for the city itself, but was also a means of expressing 'the truth-seeking spirit and thoroughly undeniable soul of Germany'. This was especially important in light of the fact that now Germany was 'whole' again, 'foreign countries' would be ready to point their finger and judge the country, perhaps as too narrowly 'materialist' or even as ready to rise up as a 'Master Race' again. Nuremberg should become, she stated, 'the "Heart of Europe"'.[62]

To this end she recommended not only an extension of the current exhibition but a major reworking of the whole site to turn it into a 'Place of Peace'. Drawing on ideas that she had gathered through speaking to artists and also from examples elsewhere – especially, she said, Israel's Holocaust Memorial, Yad Vashem – she proposed erecting pillars of reinforced glass around the grounds, especially along a 'Way to Peace'. These would be engraved with quotations from 'the three World Religions' – Christianity,

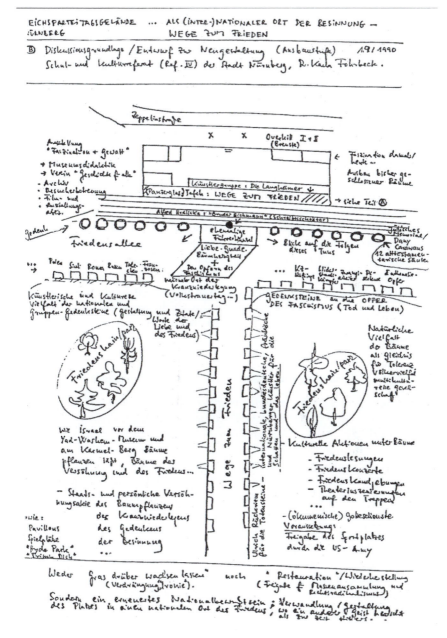

Figure 5.4   Fohrbeck 'whole concept' sketches, 1990

Judaism and Islam. If neo-Nazis desecrated the pillars, their graffiti could be left as an indication of growing right-wing radicalism, and 'relativised' rather than 'repressed'. (Her sketches of the pillars, with suggested quotations, even included projected Nazi graffiti.) In addition to the pillars there would be memorial stones (*Gedenksteine*) 'for all victims of Fascism – Poles, Russians, Czechs, Sinti and Roma, the French, Americans and many other nationalities, and also forced labourers, euthanasia victims, concentration-camp prisoners, deserters, resistance fighters and so forth'.[63] Jews, 'who had suffered a particular fate' under the Nazis, would have a special memorial; and there would also be a large memorial stone at the Führer podium of the Zeppelin Building. Alongside the memorialising, the plans also entailed planting trees and inviting artists to create art works at the site, so presenting: 'art and life against dictatorship and death, trees against stone, individuality and variety against uniformity and monotony'.[64]

These were thoughtful and ambitious plans that, for the first time, suggested a major revision of the whole site and a centring on commemoration. The idea articulated at the symposium the previous year (discussed in the previous chapter), namely that Nuremberg's heritage should not be seen as a burden but as an opportunity to play a significant role in a wider national and even international task, was thoroughly evident in Karla Fohrbeck's proposal. It was also widely seen as part of a purposeful break with what was referred to as 'the Glaser era' or 'Glaser's heritage' – something

Removing the stigma from Nuremberg's name

In an interview in 1995, Arno Hamburger, head of Nuremberg's small Jewish community since 1972, emphasised his constant attempts over the years to 'remove the stigma from Nuremberg's name'. This has included, for example, setting up friendship links with Israeli groups, who are invited to visit the city. Initially, his emphasis on giving a good image of the city puzzles me. Born in Nuremberg in 1923, Hamburger had to flee in 1939 because, as he put it, 'it was worse in Nuremberg than in any other city in the then German Reich'.[71] Remarkably, when he returned to Nuremberg in 1945 he found his parents had survived, though other relatives had not. Since then he has remained living in the city, first working as a translator during the Nuremberg trials, and in 1972 becoming an SPD councillor. Over the years he has initiated or been involved in some commemorative developments, such as the erection of a memorial on the site of Nuremberg's former synagogue in 1973. But for the most part he has striven to show another side of Nuremberg – as a 'democratic city', the kind of city that elects a Jewish councillor, as he puts it. By doing so, he explains, he sees himself 'as doing everything I could, to free Germany – where I had grown up – from the brown spectre'.[72] Moreover, he says, Nuremberg was not much different in many ways from other German cities and he does not want the image of the city to remain as shaped by Julius Streicher, the city's Nazi Gauleiter.[73]

compounded by the fact that Fohrbeck also controversially replaced some staff who had worked with her predecessor.[65]

There was a good deal of support for the plans, with, for example, a CSU councillor describing them as 'decidedly clever'.[66] However, reservations quickly emerged – many of which were familiar from the course of debates over previous proposals. One set of objections concerned current uses of the site, especially for motor racing, about which the initial Fohrbeck plans had remained silent.[67] A second set were concerned with Nuremberg's image. 'Why', asked an opinion piece in a local newspaper, 'wake the world from its sleep' and burden Nuremberg with the moral demand of being the country's 'watcher city', especially 'just when it seemed at last to be coming out of such a spotlight?' This wasn't an argument for suppressing the past, the author was quick to emphasise, but for allowing 'the quiet, unremarkable process ... of nature and time' to take place.[68] Local SPD head, Jürgen Fischer (b. 1937), argued that all German cities should be 'watcher cities', not just Nuremberg, and he made the usual comparison with Munich having managed to shrug off its heritage as city of the Nazi movement.[69] Even the head of Nuremberg's Jewish community, SPD councillor Arno Hamburger, expressed reservations that Fohrbeck's plan might make 'Nuremberg the scape-goat of the Third Reich'.[70]

A third set of criticisms addressed the more specific matter of the memorial forms proposed. Eckart Dietzfelbinger (b. 1953), of the Pedagogical Institute and former citizens' initiative, argued that it was inappropriate that a place of perpetration should become a national memorial site (*Gedenkstätte*).[74] Like a number of others, he was also critical of the lack of attention to political context in the proposals.[75] Hermann Glaser expressed concern that the plans would contribute to an *'Auratisierung'* – imbuing with 'aura' – of the place.[76] The overwhelmingly religious emphasis of the plans was also cause for disquiet, voiced among others by members of the Green party. Historian Günther Schödl dismissed the proposal's 'pseudoreligious emotionalism' and pointed out that Fohrbeck's understanding of the Holocaust as essentially a war over religious belief was misguided.[77] Moreover, as with the earlier proposal to build a church spire from one of the Mars towers, discussed earlier, some thought that to use religious imagery was unacceptable in a context in which the churches had not offered any significant resistance to Nazism, especially given that Christianity had a long history of anti-Semitism. By James Young's criteria, Fohrbeck's proposals can be seen to contain a strong element of redemption. This was evident in some of the quotations that she suggested for the pillars, such as, from the Lord's Prayer: 'forgive us our sins as we forgive sins committed against us'. Rather than the site remaining an 'open wound', as Glaser argued,[78] her stated aim in the plans was to contribute to a process of 'long healing' and a 'spiritual and psychological "making good"'.[79]

After much public discussion the small bomb largely fizzled out when it came up for discussion in a council meeting. A cheeky summary of the outcome in the local press put it this way:

> The politicians decided, as politicians always decide when they don't know what to do about a problem: to hold a conference, to set up a competition for the

development of the Rally Grounds, to collect ideas. In short: to delay deciding anything.[80]

Nevertheless, the Fohrbeck plan stands as a particularly intriguing counterfactual of a route that the city might have taken. It embodied key negotiations, some longstanding, and caught a wider interest and significant local support. The Berlin-based art magazine *PAN* commissioned a survey of the public in Nuremberg, according to which 47 per cent said they were in favour of the Fohrbeck proposal.[81] Not entirely compatibly, over 80 per cent also declared themselves to be both in favour of a competition for new ideas and of the view that existing uses of the site for motor racing and pop concerts should continue. This, perhaps, spoke more strongly for *Ratlosigkeit* and confusion than for any kind of whole concept or solution to the city's difficult heritage.

Remembering and deconstructing

In the early 1990s there was a flood of debate, symposia, publications, exhibitions and proposals about what to do with the former Nazi Party Rally Grounds. Two expensive and richly illustrated books about the site that were both published in 1992 are good indications not just of the new level of interest but also of the sophisticated nature of the debate and scholarship. *Kulissen der Gewalt. Das Reichsparteitagsgelände in Nürnberg* (*Staging Terror: The Nazi Party Rally Grounds in Nuremberg*) was produced by the Centrum Industriekultur Nürnberg, a recently opened museum of industrialisation that took a broad and often innovative approach to its subject.[82] The other book, *Faszination und Gewalt. Zur politischen Ästhetik des Nationalsozialismus* (*Fascination and Terror: On the political aesthetic of National Socialism*), acted as a catalogue for the *Fascination and Terror* exhibition and also contained essays based on those presented at the *Heritage* symposium of 1988 (discussed in the previous chapter) and at a series of talks entitled *Architecture and Barbarity* (1991).[83] Alongside pieces about the history of the site, both volumes contained reflection on how it had been treated postwar, how it might be treated in future and comparative examples.

Drawing on and contributing to some of the debate about aesthetics, were also a number of other bold proposals for developing the whole site. Architecture student Mathias Hennig (b. 1964), who had come from East Germany and declared himself unable to believe how the Rally Grounds were being used 'as though nothing had happened between 1933 and 1945', produced detailed and carefully theorised plans for a spectacular reworking into what he called a 'documentation park'. The proposal included marking out the whole site with 220 six-metre high posts, each to stand for 250,000 deaths; indicating the location of previous structures with massive steel nails; disrupting the current paths and Great Road with a new 'contradictory' set of routes, fences and ditches; and building an architecturally striking documentation centre.[84]. Central concepts employed by Hennig were *aufspüren* – tracking down or marking traces; *sichtbarmachen* – making visible or transparent; and *durchdringen* – penetrating or cutting through. These were notions used by others, too, in works that also sought to signal the site's history and at the same time to break up or deconstruct the existing architecture and layout. Julius Mihm, for example, did so in a 'decomposition' which used what he called 'non-architecture' (*Nicht-Architektur*) to attempt to 'make transparent the structural logic of the object-space' and 'transform' it.[85] Like Hennig's proposal, this also included 'fragmenting' strategies such as erecting fences and digging ditches to break up the existing spatial layout, as well as a documentation centre located at the site of the never built Great German Stadium.

These proposals excited discussion among some of the more radical history workers in Nuremberg for they offered thoughtful strategies that did not rely on the more longstanding ideas of profanation through trivialisation, or of 'healing' through nature or religion.[86] But, as emerged in a debate in which Hennig and Mihm participated, a range of history workers both from organisations such as the Pedagogical Institute and also the city's buildings department, they were deemed too far away from what was called the 'standpoint of real politics'. As the buildings minister Walter Anderle emphasised, 'the current uses – for leisure, parking and so forth – cannot be abolished'. Indeed, not long before, Anderle had cautiously expressed himself keen on a proposal from the Bavarian Sport Association for the Zeppelin Field to be turned into a sports area that might surpass the facilities in Munich;[87] and like the Mayor, Peter Schönlein, he had been furious when their plans to demolish the former SS-Barracks and replace it with a business park were prevented by the Bavarian Conservation Department (see previous chapter).

Nevertheless, although the city authorities were not willing to adopt proposals that would reorder and re-present the whole site, they did finally commit themselves to creating a documentation centre containing a new public exhibition. It became a symbol of what many were to claim was a new era – an era in which Nuremberg would, moreover, take on a new kind of role and status as City of Freedom and Human Rights (Chapter 6).

* * * * *

The flood of educational and artistic activities from the late 1970s dedicated to negotiating the Nazi past in Nuremberg were part of a wider move in West Germany to interrogate the Nazi past of localities. In some places this led to highly uncomfortable facts being unearthed about the wartime activities of people still living, or their descendants, who perhaps held significant local office or still profited from gains made by dubious means (e.g. the acquisition of Jewish properties or businesses). This kind of turn to the past has been most famously told in Michael Verhoeven's film *The Nasty Girl* (*Das schreckliche Mädchen*) (1989), based on the real-life story of Anja Rosmus from Passau who uncovered many unsavoury facts about her neighbours while doing a school project, and who was subsequently threatened, even with her life. In Nuremberg, however, as indeed in many places, this was not the direction that the new emphasis on the past took. There were, surely, many varied reasons for this, not least the kinds of difficulties in which Rosmus had found herself. But, arguably, another reason was the presence of such a large, visible Nazi blot on the landscape as the Nazi Party Rally Grounds that had also seemed to have been ignored. Doing something about this became the first task to which the city's engaged and often radical history workers addressed themselves. Certainly, it was important and worthwhile to do so. But it was only one way of concentrating energies; and paying attention to this highly symbolic example could mean that less visible dimensions of the local Nazi past and its legacy were given less attention than they might have been. An indicative example of what might fall outside the scope of a focus on such a conspicuously difficult heritage – as indeed of my own here – is given in the following chapter.

More broadly, what we have seen in this chapter are some of the particular dilemmas faced in trying to negotiate difficult heritage through art and education. These are difficulties faced in other contexts too, as evident in numerous debates throughout the world about the form and adequacy of various museological and memorial treatments of atrocity, and of the Holocaust in particular. Characteristic of these debates is not only that so many struggle to find criteria on which to make judgements but also that they are so often carried out in terms of cross-national comparisons – Rachel Whiteread's Holocaust Memorial in Vienna being compared with the Gerz's disappearing 'counter-monument' in Harburg for example, or Yad Vashem with the Holocaust Memorial Museum in Washington DC. This is part of an increasing 'cosmopolitanisation' that has implications for public memory – and for those engaged in the work of producing public history – in many places. So too in Nuremberg, as we see in the following chapter, where I turn to an educational and an artistic development that together have been seen as marking a new phase in the city's dealing with its Nazi past: the Documentation Centre of the Nazi Party Rally Grounds and sculptor Dani Karavan's *Straße der Menschenrechte* – or *Way of Human Rights*, as it is called in English.

6

COSMOPOLITAN MEMORY IN THE CITY OF HUMAN RIGHTS

According to a book by Nuremberg authors, the city has recently undergone 'a miraculous transformation of Saul into Paul'.[1] What has converted the city from pariah to saintly status, they claim, is its embracing of an identity as City of Peace and Human Rights and, as the most significant indication of this, its creation of a major new Documentation Centre, opened in late 2001, containing a substantial permanent exhibition, at the former Nazi Party Rally Grounds.

In this chapter, I look at the making of the Documentation Centre – or Dokuzentrum as it is usually called by those who work there and as I shall use henceforth – and some of the particular challenges that staff involved faced in deciding how to display the difficult heritage of the Nazi site. I also look at the wider transformations of public memory and moral commitment that the Dokuzentrum was seen to be part of, and indeed to exemplify. I do so in part in relation to arguments by Daniel Levy and Natan Sznaider, which I outline in more detail below, that a major shift in public memory, towards what they call 'cosmopolitan memory', is underway. In some ways, as we will see, Nuremberg's self-presentation as City of Peace and Human Rights, and many aspects of the way that the Nazi past is articulated to this, illustrates their arguments very well. At the same time, however, there are aspects of the Nuremberg case that raise questions about some of the impetus for, and implications of, a 'cosmopolitanisation' of memory. No less than with the other kinds of negotiating frames that have been highlighted in previous chapters of this book, a cosmopolitan framing brings some things to the fore and allows others to slip out of view.

Below, I begin with an outline of some of the events that led up to the Dokuzentrum finally getting the go-ahead and being built after so many years of prevarication. I then turn to the background to presenting Nuremberg in terms of human rights – an idea that, in these specific terms, was introduced by an art work, Dani Karavan's *Way of Human Rights* that opened in 1993. The uptake of this idea, and some of the further city politics in which it, and the planned Dokuzentrum became entangled – as well as the 'cosmopolitan memory' that it helped articulate – follow. The final part of the chapter then turns to the Dokuzentrum itself to explore its particular negotiations of public memory.

Not a museum

It is not unusual for local people and those elsewhere in Germany to refer to the Dokuzentrum as a museum. Some even give it the shorthand of 'the Nazi Museum'. Once, when it was still in planning, I referred to it as a museum as I chatted with Eckart Dietzfelbinger, the senior researcher on the project. He was quick to correct me, explaining that it would not collect artefacts of the period but would focus on documentation – hence its name. In one of the rooms in the Meistersingerhalle where the project team was then working I noticed various beer mugs from Nazi Party rallies. Would they be on show, I asked him. He laughed and said that they would not, dismissing them as 'kitsch', though observing that local people had been coming to donate such things, knowing that the Dokuzentrum was in the making. Instead, he directed my attention to some original plans of the site. These, he said, certainly would be part of the exhibition.

Later I thought more about the difference – so clear to this experienced history worker – between these two kinds of artefacts. Both were original objects from the period; and both were Nazi productions. But what made the plans 'documentation', unlike the beer mugs? It seemed that why the plans could be more straightforwardly and transparently be read as providing information was that they were regarded as a value-free report on reality. The beer mugs, by contrast, were part of what in English, rather suitably in this case, might be called the 'trappings' of the event – that is, those extras that can allure people without them really thinking about it. Kitsch was light stuff, not serious, with a danger to be misleading.

This insistence on not being a museum reminded me of Hermann Glaser's earlier warning about how opening a museum at the site might contribute to an 'Auratisierung' of the place, a making of it seem more worthy – in other words, creating a 'heritage effect'. It reminded me too of the words of Leibl Rosenberg in a discussion after I had visited the exhibition, *Traces and Fragments: Jewish Books, Jewish Fates in Nuremberg* (*Spuren und Fragmente. Jüdische Bücher, Jüdische Schicksale in Nürnberg*), held in 2000. 'We don't want a Jewish museum here', he said forcefully, 'because we are still here'.

Permanence at last?

The idea to have some kind of permanent museum on the Nazi Rally Grounds site was far from new. History workers had long been campaigning for such a museum; and in 1978, for example, there had been proposals for an institute of research on fascism, together with an exhibition and documentation centre to be based in the Congress Hall.[2] But it was only in the second half of the 1990s, prompted by post-Unification dissatisfaction with the inadequate exhibition on site, resignation to the fact that the Nazi past was not going to slip quietly away, the continued lobbying by history activists, and a reorganisation of city governance that the commitment was finally made. Crucial to this decision too was the fact that the city did not have to foot the whole bill – Bavaria and the federal government, as well as a private foundation, also made substantial contributions.

In 1993 the city's museum and education structure was reorganised, bringing the existing *Fascination and Terror* exhibition in the Zeppelin Building under the remit of the director of the City Museums, Franz Sonnenberger (b. 1951). An ambitious director, with wide-ranging plans for Nuremberg, including building a leading new art gallery, he was clearly embarrassed by the poor physical state of the existing exhibition. He had also acted as the Mayor's personal assistant with responsibility for the inaugural programme of events of the Way of Human Rights (see below). As he saw it, the time was also ripe for a new development and he personally was attracted by the idea of building a whole new museum on the site, perhaps along the lines of some of the spectacular designs by those such as Hennig and Mihm discussed in the previous chapter.[3] Also lobbying hard, though from a different position, were a set of history activists – some of whom were also involved in other history activities in the city, such as the Pedagogical Institute and History for All. In 1991, Carlo Jahn brought these together into the 'Congress Hall Initiative Group', later re-named as 'Group for the Information Centre of the former Nazi Party Rally Grounds'. The group pressed, in particular, for a permanent exhibition and archive to be housed in the Congress Hall, and they also organised tours of the building, partly in order to promote and demonstrate wider interest in order to bolster their case. While these history activists and Sonnenberger agreed that an improved exhibition was necessary, there were differences between their ambitions. Sonnenberger was not at all enamoured with the idea of an exhibition in the Congress Hall. This would make him feel, he commented, like he was renting space from Albert Speer.[4] He also wanted a highly professionalised exhibition and, as he put it, not just 'a space to collect photocopies and newspapers'.[5] This was important not least, he argued, so that people would not say that all that Nuremberg had done was something 'provisional'. In addition, having spent time in the US, he was, as he explained to me, keen on an approach that conceived of museums 'as historical theatre' rather than as 'something that might be in a university'. This, he believed, was also more attractive to visitors; a fact that, as well as being important in itself, was vital as the city expected entrance fees to constitute part of the museum service's budget. The Initiative Group, by contrast, feared that the big plans would lead to nothing once again and preferred to make use of a space that was already available in the Congress Hall.[6] In the end, something in between the two emerged – a new structure that would also make use of the existing space, and an emphasis on research and documentation as well as a professional display.

Securing the finance for the project entailed considerable politically astute lobbying by Sonnenberger. He gathered support, beginning with representatives of the Protestant and Catholic churches, who were both very supportive. Arno Hamburger, head of the Jewish community, wanted longer to think it over, Sonnenberger explained, 'because from the Jewish point of view it is clear that the Nazi Party Rally Grounds are a manifestation of that force that wanted to destroy these people in Germany. So he needed to think it over for a long time. But then he said, "OK,

I'm with you"'. Having his support, as representative of the Jewish community, was extremely important symbolically. Sonnenberger also invited important national representatives, such as Christoph Stölzl, Director of the German National Museum in Berlin and CDU politician and Oscar Schneider, the CDU's parliamentary speaker on culture and former chair of the Nuremberg-Fürth CSU, to Nuremberg to visit the Rally Grounds. All were reported as recognising the importance of the site and the need for some kind of development there.[7] While representatives of all parties in the council said that they agreed that there was a need for an improved exhibition, they also agreed – as did Sonnenberger – that the city alone could not, and should not have to, foot the whole bill. By the end of 1996, after the council elections in which the CSU gained power, there were agreements in principle from the Bavarian and federal governments, and also from the new city council, that they would contribute something towards the planned museum – which by this stage was calculated as likely to cost about 9 million DM.[8] There was, however, nothing fixed.

Then in June 1997 Bruno Schnell, the owner of the publishers that produced the *Nürnberger Nachrichten* (among other publications), pledged to contribute 250,000 DM;[9] and the council agreed to contribute 500,000 DM to the construction plus the running costs of 700,000 DM per year.[10] A board of trustees (*Kuratorium*), consisting of powerful national as well as local figures, was set up to lobby for the project. Its members were: Mayor Ludwig Scholz; Arno Hamburger, Head of Nuremberg's Jewish Community; Bruno Schnell; Dr Karl Braun, Archbishop of Bamberg; Hermann von Loewenich, bishop of the Protestant churches in Bavaria; Dr Gunther Beckstein, Bavarian Minister of the Interior; Monika Hohlmeier, Bavarian Minister for Education and Culture; Dr Hans Jochen Vogel, Federal Minister and representative of the organisation 'Against Forgetting – for Democracy'; Oscar Schneider, former Federal Minister; and Ignatz Bubis, Head of the Central Council of Jews in Germany. Later that year the federal government agreed to contribute 500,000 DM and early the following year Bavaria agreed to contribute 4 million DM.[11] The council then established committees of academics and experts, from Germany and overseas, and planning began in earnest for a proposed opening in 2000 – a year with added significance in Nuremberg as it was the city's 950th anniversary.

There was, however, growing criticism from architectural practices of the planned design that had been produced by the council buildings department and of the fact that there had been no architectural competition. The council design consisted of a glass lighthouse – modelled on one that the Nazis had removed from the area and thus symbolising the idea of shedding light on the Nazi past – linking into rooms in an upper storey of the Congress Hall.[12] In response, an invited architectural competition was held and won by Graz architect Günther Domenig (b. 1934) with a design that met widespread approval in the wider architectural world as well as locally. Consisting of a glass and steel 'stake' (*Pfahl*) through the Congress Hall, Domenig explained that his 'deconstructive' design was intended to 'break the power of the violence' (*brechen die Macht der Gewalt*) of the building.[13] The idea that this was a 'spear' into 'Speer' took off in popular accounts.[14] The problem with the design, however, was that it was projected to cost twice as much as the amount that had been

Figure 6.1 A spear into Speer: Documentation Centre of the former Nazi Party Rally Grounds, exterior and interior, 2007

originally budgeted and it soon became evident that completing the building and exhibition by 2000 would not be possible.[15] Yet by now the momentum seemed to be unstoppable. All of the three main contributors – the federal government, Bavaria and Nuremberg – agreed to contribute 6 million DM each, and so by mid-1999 the funding was secure for the project to go ahead.[16]

The future of the past

In November 1999 Sonnenberger organised a conference entitled 'The future of the past: How should the history of the Third Reich be transmitted in museums and memorial sites in the twenty-first century?'[17] A thoroughly cosmopolitan gathering, it brought together representatives from a wide range of such sites from many countries, including, for example, from the Centre de la Mémoire in Oradour, the Imperial War Museum in London, Auschwitz, the United States Holocaust Museum, and

Yad Vashem. Hans-Christian Täubrich (b. 1949), who was appointed director of the Dokuzentrum project, told me how surprised and pleased he and his colleagues were that everybody invited came: it showed that they regarded this as a significant venture and that they welcomed the opportunity to exchange ideas. This was a recognition of the significance of the Nuremberg site for a wider development, stretching across international borders; and it was part of a process through which the Dokuzentrum project was incorporated into a wider, transnational, network. It helped those in Nuremberg to learn from experiences elsewhere and, as Täubrich explained, to 'make very strong links with those places', such that rather than seeking to explain the whole of National Socialism in this one place, it should be understood 'always in combination' with those others.

In his greeting to the delegates, Mayor Ludwig Scholz (b. 1937, d. 2005; period of office 1996–2002) also welcomed the cosmopolitanism of the project. Expressing his pleasure about the fact that Nuremberg was now committed to building the Documentation Centre, he explained how he saw this as historically rooted but also future-oriented:

> Nuremberg stands, on the one hand, for the tradition of an open-minded cosmopolitan city of traders and merchants, who achieved success through their international contacts and their readiness to absorb the widest possible spectrum of ideas. Yet, on the other hand, Nuremberg became a backdrop, a stage on which the National Socialists paraded their inhuman ideology and racial madness. Humanism at its finest is juxtaposed in our city's history with the vilest manifestations of intellectual and political barbarity.
>
> We have attempted to set new accents and move forward in new directions by acknowledging our entire history. This explains why the opening events of the anniversary year … were dedicated to the issue of 'Peace and Human Rights'… . These events were to date the major achievements in Nuremberg's efforts to forge itself a new profile, to provide a broad platform for the issue of human rights, humanism, democracy and understanding amongst all peoples. The architectural expression of these efforts is the Way of Human Rights, designed by Dani Karavan, as the entrance to the Germanic National Museum – a modern architectural highlight for our city.[18]

Like others, Scholz was keen to show how 'acknowledging our entire history', including National Socialism, could provide a means of 'moving forward' – and doing so in what was seen as a 'new direction'. History, in other words, was seen as a resource through which futures could be moulded. To this purpose he also cleverly identified an older historical precedent for articulating this new future: that of the cosmopolitan – literally 'world open' (*weltoffen*) in the original German – merchants. Simultaneously, as so often in the past, Nazism by contrast, was not acknowledged as an integral part of the city's history but depicted as something imposed, for which the city acted only 'a stage'. Nevertheless, through this kind of presentation of history, the city could be seen as both directly concerning itself with its Nazi past and also moving away from it; creating a new image – a 'new profile' – focused on human rights.

As noted in the previous chapter, the idea that Nuremberg should take on a role to provide wider education about fascism or to become a 'watcher city' had been voiced earlier. But the idea of the city as one of human rights, or peace and human rights, managed to take off in a way that none of these earlier suggestions had done. This was partly a consequence of the widespread realisation, described above, that Nuremberg's image would be more damaged by ignoring the past rather than publicly acknowledging it. Just as, if not more, significant, however, was the particular history of the way that the idea was interjected into Nuremberg and the way that it enabled a universal and future-oriented – or what Levy and Sznaider would call a 'cosmopolitan' – stepping off from a located history.[19]

City of Human Rights

The specific terminology of human rights – and the attractive idea that the former city of the Nazi Party Rallies could transform itself into City of Human Rights – was introduced by Israeli artist Dani Karavan, in his proposal for a new art work and entrance for the Germanic National Museum. In many ways this is a remarkable example of the agency of an art or architectural work. Certainly, many individual art works might prompt individuals to reflection, or they might cause controversy; and art works are frequently used as part of urban, and also rural, impression-management, to help to transform images of a place. But for an art or architectural work to interject a new discourse into a place, which then becomes part of a major 're-profiling' that circulates independently of the work itself, is surely highly unusual. Pieces such as Anthony Gormley's *Angel of the North* may have become iconic images of a region, works such as Horst Hoheisel's 'inverted fountain' (*Aschrott Brunnen*) in Kassel may make many think differently about the place than they might otherwise, or buildings such as Frank Gehry's Guggenheim Museum in Bilbao may have been crucial to the regeneration of that city and its image, but they do not set up a new language for the imagining of those places in quite the same way. Not coincidentally, the Rally Grounds themselves are an example of an architectural interjection that prompts a transformation of a place's image with ramifications well beyond it, and independently of, it. Perhaps partly for this reason, an artistic-architectural intervention was an especially powerful technique for a 're-profiling' of Nuremberg. It was not, however, initially produced to meet such an ambitious goal – this was, as journalist Siegfried Zelnhefer described it, a 'stroke of luck' for the city.[20]

The original tender for this project for which Karavan's art work came to be created was released in February 1988, and it contained no mention of human rights. The task was to create a new entrance for the refurbished and extended Germanic National Museum and to link together its old and new buildings in a way that recognised 'the cultural historical status of the museum'.[21] Nine artists, whose common feature was only that they had produced significant large-scale architectural public sculpture, were invited to compete for the tender, of whom four did so.[22] Karavan's proposal, which met all of the practical requirements, won unanimously. To deal with the fact that there were two buildings of different ages separated by an alleyway he decided to create a row of pillars – a form that won much praise from the jury; the director of the

129

Museum, Gerhard Bott, writing a whole essay on the historical resonance of this form in a collection about Karavan's work.[23] What seemed to be judged especially attractive about the pillar proposal was that it made a 'historical citation' to the nineteenth-century romantic nationalism within which the museum had been founded (in 1852).[24] It was only in the second stage of the tender process, when Karavan came back with more detailed proposals, that he specified that there would be 30 pillars and that this would represent the 30 articles of the Universal Declaration of Human Rights.[25] It was at this stage that he proposed that the piece be called *Way of Human Rights* (as it was called in English; *Straße der Menschenrechte* in German).

That Nuremberg might even go beyond this artwork and present itself more generally as City of Human Rights was a further suggestion made by Karavan. Initially, some in Nuremberg were nervous that this might seem to be too much of a presumption, and might be judged cynically by the wider world.[26] However, by the time that the *Way of Human Rights* was opened, he had been won round and at the opening of the sculpture and new entrance to the museum in October 1993, he announced that the city would found a biennial human rights award. The first such award was made in September 1995, on the sixtieth anniversary of the declaration of the Nuremberg Laws. The first recipient was Sergej Kowaljow, from Russia. Since then, the prize has continued to be awarded every other year, to candidates from numerous different countries.[27] In addition, a raft of other human rights activities has been set up, especially since 2000 when the Mayor's office established a human rights office (as part of the Mayor's office) to develop and oversee further human rights activities. These have included: annual film festivals of human rights, a human

Figure 6.2   Way of Human Rights

rights and peace 'table' (a communal meal in the city), initiatives on fair trade in toys, a mayors for peace meeting and the planting of gingko trees. In 2000 the city was awarded a UNESCO prize for its initiatives.

The idea of Nuremberg as City of Human Rights has become part of the common presentation of the city, as, for example, in the recent guide to the city produced by the council.[28] Transforming the City of the Nazi Party Rallies into the City of Human Rights could, surely, be regarded as a thoroughly redemptive move; and, no doubt, this made it more palatable and attractive to some. However, Karavan's piece itself never refers explicitly to Nuremberg but just transforms the narrow pedestrianised street in which it is situated into a place for contemplating human rights. It hints not only at the terrible as well as honourable events that have led to the declaration but is also a reminder that human rights are not always honoured – here historically, as elsewhere.

The *Way* was not intended to be a memorial – a point made explicitly by Karavan at the inauguration.[29] Nevertheless, despite his claim that neither is it a monument, it certainly has monumentality. A three-entrance archway wall leads onto a row of twenty-seven 8.5m tall pillars, all in white concrete. In addition, there are two apparently sunken pillars and an oak tree. On each pillar is engraved one of the 30 articles of the Convention on Human Rights, in German and one other language. The thirtieth article is inscribed on a plaque near to the tree.

Karavan has used the pillar form in other art works, and as critics have noted it makes allusions to the classical motif of the victory column – an idea especially clear here in the company of the archway.[30] Here, however, it also seems to echo the white facades and repeating pillars of the Zeppelin Building; and perhaps also makes reference to the rows of columns that had been planned for the entrance to the Mars Field.[31] Whether or not these references are evident to visitors, the statements on human rights are entirely lucid; and it does seem to be a work that draws people to stop and pay closer attention.

Cosmopolitan memory

Karavan's casting of his artwork in terms of human rights picked up on, as well as further propelled, a discourse of human rights that has been increasingly, and ever more widely, invoked since the Nuremberg trials and the Universal Declaration that emerged in part as a consequence in 1948. According to Levy and Sznaider this spreading discourse of human rights is bound up with the development of 'cosmopolitan memory'.[32] Their argument, in brief, is that there is a spread of forms of commemoration which are participated in by people who do not have direct connection to the events being remembered. Less and less, they argue, does the nation act as the 'container', or frame, for public memory. Instead, memory is becoming 'deterritorialised', 'transcending ethnic and national boundaries', as people orient themselves in relation to events and histories – and interpretations of them – that are 'transnational' and 'global'.[33]

In their detailed exposition, Levy and Sznaider compare Germany, Israel and the US order to document the common shifts that they argue can be seen in all three, while

from respected historian Wolfgang Benz. This was completed two years later. As the property of the Diehl company, only the conclusion was made public. This was no endorsement of company behaviour but contained enough interpretive leeway to be claimed as an exoneration by Diehl and the CSU.

Interesting for consideration of arguments about cosmopolitanism and displacement, however, is the way in which 'the Diehl affair' became interwoven in city politics with the promotion of the city as one of Peace and Human Rights. Mayor Scholz frequently referred to these developments in his public statements about the affair, including in his letters to the press about why Diehl should retain his award, and why Dani Karavan should not dismantle his sculpture or resign from the Human Rights Prize jury. Nuremberg's commitment to addressing the Nazi past was, Scholz claimed, evident in these new developments, and especially in the commitment to create a new Documentation Centre – a development that was given official endorsement, and the commitment of at least some city money, in June/July 1997, between the controversial announcement of the Diehl award and its conferring.[50] The Office of Human Rights was also established by the Mayor, as a branch of his own office, during this same period. Although it would not be right to see these developments only in relation to their potential to provide an alibi for other local activities – not least, there were other groups involved who had other motives – it was undoubtedly the case that a 'cosmopolitan' emphasis could provide an apparently morally justifiable form of 'displacement'. That is, a cosmopolitan emphasis on human rights could also be the basis for a rather useful oscillation – a means of negotiating a way out of a troublesome heritage.

Making the Dokuzentrum

Whatever the displacements involved, many in Nuremberg, not least the history activists who had been pressing for a more permanent exhibition for so long, were certainly pleased that at last something would be built. Not surprisingly, there were some in the city who did not think it appropriate or necessary – I met several such people during the course of my work and there were also some who later scrawled their disapproval across the pages of the Dokuzentrum's visitor books.[51] But these voices were virtually absent in the public domain, where, across the political spectrum, there was consensus that creating such an exhibition was a good and overdue development.

Because it was seen as an important and challenging task, considerable care went into the making of the Dokuzentrum and exhibition – even though the time to do so was 'phenomenally short' as Sonnenberger put it. The original plan to open in 2000, as part of the city's 950th celebrations, was shelved after the architectural competition; and in the end it opened in November 2001, which was still a remarkably rapid achievement. It was only possible because masses of relevant research had already been undertaken, especially by Dietzfelbinger who had earlier worked on the Zeppelin Building exhibition; and the basic principles for the exhibition had been set out back in July 1997 in document produced by a high-powered academic advisory board (*wissenschaftlicher Beirat*) that was established by the city council and museum service to oversee and guide the project. A high-powered group, with considerable historical and comparative museological expertise, its chair was Gregor Schöllgen, professor of History at Erlangen-Nürnberg University; and its other members were: Dr Judith Belinfante, President of the Association of Jewish Museums in Europe; Professor Wolfgang Benz, Centre for Research on Anti-Semitism, Technical University, Berlin; Dr Peter März, Centre for Political Education, Bavaria; Professor Horst Möller, Institute for Contemporary History, Munich; Professor Reinhard Rürup, The Topography of Terror Foundation and Institute of Contemporary History, Technical University, Berlin; Professor Hermann Schäfer, Director of the House of German History Museum, Bonn; and Professor Christoph Stölzl of the German Historical Museum.

The expert 'basic principles' document was written by Schöllgen on behalf of the advisory board. It acknowledges: 'As with all endeavours of this kind, success depends considerably on the foundations, on which the project rests'.[52] The document in effect lays those foundations with its outline of the areas to be covered by the exhibition – something that was not really opened up for further discussion because, as Sonnenberger explained to me in 2000, time was very pressing and 'we wanted to avoid great big debates right at the beginning – so we were very pleased that it was a concise document'. Neither, as Schöllgen reflected with some surprise (in an interview with me in 2000), did it seem to produce any disagreement, perhaps because by this stage there was so much agreement that the project should go ahead. Written also to persuade potential funders of the need to support the project, the document begins by stressing the importance of not forgetting history; and does so by casting the Rally Grounds history primarily as an example of a product of totalitarianism – a particularly timely framing given the recent and ongoing demise of totalitarian socialist regimes. It begins: 'History does not disappear, certainly not the history of totalitarian regimes'. Such regimes have left 'more or less deep traces' including a wide range of 'stone witnesses' such as vast Stalinist buildings in the East, Fascist architecture in Italy and Spain, or the monumental relics of the Third Reich in Germany.[53] In this way, the project was, from the start, defined as one whose significance lay beyond that of Nuremberg in particular, and even beyond that of the 'container' of the nation.

This did not mean, however, that the specificity of the particular location was to be subsumed to a generalised history. On the contrary, the document also outlines the particular features of the Rally Grounds site, in part in order to argue why it so pressingly deserved a documentation centre. This includes discussion of some of the features that distinguish the site from those such as concentration camps, because, as the document explains, 'Although the Rally Grounds area was also used during the war as a place of forced labour and deportation, it was not for annihilation. Therefore it is neither sensible nor appropriate to conceive and instantiate the exhibition on the former Nazi Party Rally Grounds as a type of memorial site (*Gedenkstätte*)'.[54] Instead it is to be informational or documentary, opening a 'window … with a view onto the history of the "Third Reich"'. This idea of a 'window' – a specific viewing position or framing, rather as in standpoint theory – became very important for defining what would be included in the exhibition. As project director Täubrich explained during the exhibition's making: 'So we always start from the local history and open up historical windows showing what the results were from this place here, or from the events that took place here'. In this way, useful limits were set on what would be covered; and the specificity of the particular 'authentic backdrop' that the Rally Grounds offered was made the focal point.[55]

All of these were surely sensible decisions and akin to those so often made in public historical or even wider touristic representation. The authenticity of a particular site acts as a point of entry into a wider, but inevitably temporally and spatially constrained, account. Here, however, they also came together with other particular concerns. One of these was how to convey the horror – the 'flip-side' as it was often cast – of the rally spectacle. As in the earlier exhibition, the kinds of links that were envisaged were through reference to the slave labourers who were compelled to cut stone for the buildings; or through mention of the railway station from where Jews were deported to extermination camps. But going beyond this, beyond matters that could be linked directly, was seen as inappropriate. For example, when I asked Franz Sonnenberger how much about Nuremberg's Jewish population would be included in the exhibition, he explained that there would be little, partly because this was dealt with elsewhere, at the Jewish Museum in nearby Fürth, but also because it did not fit clearly into the historical narrative of the exhibition. To work well, in his view, history exhibitions – unlike, say, art or natural history – had to have a strong narrative (*Erzählung*) or story (here he emphasised the two senses of *Geschichte* in German – history and story). This meant, he explained, that they needed, like a novel, to be conceptualised as a sequential narrative or 'narrative chain', with links between each. Adding in another topic, such as about Jewish life in the city, would be like trying to add in a chapter that wasn't part of the main story – it would just disrupt visitors' engagement. Instead, what was planned was to show some of the less glossy aspects of the rallies themselves: for example, the vandalism that some of the rally participants caused to local buildings or the hours involved in just hanging around waiting for something to happen at the rallies. Täubrich explained these as what he called 'metaphors' for conveying broader ideas: e.g. vandalism to indicate the unsavoury character of many rally groupies and, more generally, the destructive tendencies behind the façade; or showing long boring bits of original film shot by a television company which could highlight the contrast not just with Riefenstahl's short-clip construction of a lively event but also the fact of that construction itself. Just how to convey that boredom without boring the audience was, though, a difficult matter as Täubrich laughingly pointed out.

Täubrich's emphasis on metaphor was one dimension of Sonnenberger's 'historical theatre'. The dynamic of exhibition making brought these into play with another important emphasis – documentation – that was especially the remit of the project's head academic researcher, Eckart Dietzfelbinger. As he explained, making sure that everything was thoroughly academically sound and properly documented was important not least because there were always people ready to criticise if you didn't get the facts right. This was something that museum workers were especially conscious of at the time due to the criticism of the touring exhibition about Crimes of the Wehrmacht, produced by the Hamburg Institute for Social Research, which had been withdrawn following allegations that some of the images that they showed of atrocities committed by the regular army were not of Wehrmacht soldiers at all.[56] Moreover, as Dietzfelbinger pointed out, this was a highly political topic for which there were people ready to deny 'the truth'; so it was especially important to not give them any grounds to question the legitimacy of the displays. 'Objectivity', as he put it, was crucial. So, while on the one hand the exhibition was conceptualised as a particular 'window' from which to tell a particular story, it was also seen as dealing with objective facts and truth.

In addition, making sure that visitors understood what they were being presented with was seen as a kind of moral duty. In this, an exhibition on such difficult heritage may differ – at least quantitatively – from some other kinds of exhibitions, such as, for example, those about art or even some aspects of science or history. Interpretive leeway – which is sometimes even celebrated in some museological perspectives – was regarded as, for the most part, inappropriate in this kind of representation. Much effort, therefore, also went into ensuring that the exhibition would be read in the kinds of ways in which its makers intended. For example, the project team presented all of their draft texts and exhibition ideas to a class of fifteen and sixteen year-olds at a practically- rather than academically-oriented school (a *Realschule*) in the city to try to ensure that it was all fully understandable.[57]

There was also caution over what was seen as the potentially even more interpretatively 'leaky' matter of other non-verbal media. A telling example of the perceived dangers here concerned a large picture of Hitler's face that designers

Figure 6.3   Hitler image in *Fascination and Terror*

Figure 6.4   Fascination and Terror

proposed to erect at the end of one section of the exhibition, to mark the movement into the next. When this was presented to the advisory board, however, they were concerned that the image might be too 'impressive' (*beeindruckend*), especially given that Hitler's eyes were widely reported as being able to entrance. Even if members of the advisory board might not believe this themselves, they were nevertheless concerned that such an oversized direct-gaze image might risk reproducing that effect. Instead, the designers chose to mark the section with a different image of Hitler, no longer larger than life but instead a full-body shot of him climbing up some stairs towards the camera, a view which positions the viewer as looking down on him rather than being caught in his gaze (Figure 6.3).

These are just some examples of the care and subtlety of the considerations that went into the making of the Dokuzentrum exhibition. Other thoughtful negotiations of history included the approach to the Congress Hall building itself. Its interior spaces were left in their raw brick state; Domenig's glass spear design allowing the visitor to confront this directly. The literal 'window' afforded by his design was extended outside the building too, with an external 'end of the spear' viewing platform which allows the visitor to look out over the ugly raw interior of the building and to other parts of the site beyond. The powerful metaphor of transparency at work here was played through internally too, text being mounted on glass panels so that the building behind them was not obscured. Throughout, the visitor was invited not just to look at a Nazi product but to see through it – to see beyond.

Fascination and Terror

Fascination and Terror is in many ways an excellent exhibition as the majority of visitors and reviewers agree – 'impressive' (and synonyms of it) was the word most often used by visitors whom I interviewed and also those who wrote in the exhibition's visitor books.[59] It is clearly the product of thorough research and careful, and often inspired, decision-making about what to include. It manages to be visually striking in a relatively understated way, without some of the theatrical dramatisations – such as projecting coloured light as flames onto the Reichstag as was contemplated at one early stage; and it does so especially through the use of large black and white images of original photographs and a thoughtful use of film. Covering an area of $1,300m^2$, it manages to pack in a considerable amount of fascinating detail, especially about the rallies and the buildings, including video interviews with eye-witnesses. At the same time, it succeeds in providing a more general background to National Socialism, explaining its rise, how it worked and its consequences.

To what extent, however, can the finished exhibition – a key marker of the city's projection as cosmopolitan – be interpreted as a cosmopolitan form of public memory? To explore this question, I introduce some ideas from Rosmarie Beier-de Haan, of the German Historical Museum, about exhibitionary features that we might identify as 'cosmopolitan'. Drawing on Ulrich Beck's ideas about 'second' or 'cosmopolitan modernity', she identifies a new display mode that she calls (after Beck) 'staging' in which, rather than seeking to 'represent' a particular past, exhibitions are designed to invite individualised reflections on and relations to what is displayed. It is as part of this reorientation that many history museums increasingly present what they are doing in terms of 'memory' rather than 'history'.[59] In staging, the distance between viewer and viewed is shrunk or even collapsed; and what is presented does not claim to be *the* authoritative account. Such exhibitions typically seek to avoid predefined categories of either the nation-state or those standard to social history – especially gender or class – that became widespread in many museum exhibitions during the 1970s and 1980s. Likewise, rather than presenting showcased objects accompanied by learned commentary, or text-heavy panels, such exhibitions are more likely to use mixed media (including objects) to provoke the viewer and make them part of the exhibition itself; and they are more likely to build in possibilities for visitor choice of route or depth of information. Some of these features can be seen, for example, in the United States Holocaust Memorial Museum where the implication of visitors as particular individuals – each visitor is given an identity card of a particular Holocaust victim – allows the account to become more readily de-appropriated as the possession of a specific group and available as a common, though differentially accessed – cosmopolitan – memory.[60]

Considered in relation to this formulation, *Fascination and Terror* seems scarcely cosmopolitan. Certainly, it uses mixed media but this is not so much in order to invite different individual 'takes' on what is displayed but rather to maximise representational effectiveness. Much of the exhibition is presented through conventional media of text panels, that visitors can view with an accompanying audio-guide; and – as Sonnenberger viewed as so crucial for this topic – it is all spatially arranged into a fairly tightly directed semi-chronological account. The account itself is also presented as authoritative – or 'didactic' as some visitors put it. All of this is important for this difficult topic for the reasons that Dietzfelbinger explained above.

While not stylistically cosmopolitan in these ways, the exhibition does nevertheless make a few – significant – cosmopolitan moves. In particular, the main finale of the exhibition is a visually impressive section about the Nuremberg trials – events which did not take place on the Rally Grounds site itself but elsewhere in the city, and that have come to be seen as an iconic and motivating development in human rights discourse. There is also a section that provides examples of the press reaction to the war in different countries – something that establishes the theme as one of concern beyond the nation, though at the same time employs the nation as a frame for policy articulation and difference. For the most part, it is either the nation or more specifically the local site – the Rally Grounds themselves – that are referenced in the exhibition. Throughout, there are many references to 'Germany', in the kind of 'flagging' of the nation – the simple use of its name as a noun or in adjectival constructions, or of symbols of nation, such as the flag – that Michael Billig argues is so important to how we come to take the existence of nations for granted.[61] So the exhibition does refer, for example, to Germany invading Poland. For much of the account, then, the nation does serve as the 'container' of the account – until, towards the end, the exhibition gives attention to the Holocaust, a cosmopolitan category that stretches beyond Germany, followed quickly by the trials, which do so too, though this time anchored to Nuremberg itself. It is, thus, possible to read the exhibition as one in which the nation is finally transcended.

Alongside the flagging of nation is a use of the local to articulate to wider concerns. This is, however, a selective 'local': most often the specific Rally Grounds site itself. This becomes, for example, the basis for wider discussions of the Nazi use of propaganda. Sometimes, however, the city of Nuremberg is the 'window' – as with the trials, though also in sections about the declaring of the Nuremberg Laws, the political context in the city in which the Nazis gained power and sections on Julius Streicher, the city's Nazi Gauleiter and the virulently anti-Semitic newspaper, *Die Stürmer*, which he produced. The section on Streicher is one that many visitors mention, often commenting on what an awful man he was – an impression helpfully aided by the fact that he looked such a thug. However, as Neil Gregor has argued in a discussion of other accounts of the city's past, an emphasis on *Gauleiter* Streicher, the party rallies, and the postwar trials ... embod[ies] a narrative of Nazism in which propaganda is privileged over participation, in which 'fanatical' Nazi leaders are emphasised over everyday Nazi supporters, in which dramatic moments of high politics are foregrounded over issues of acquiescence and consent in everyday life.[62]

What is absent in these accounts is attention to the kind of local politics of the kind that the Diehl affair illustrated; to the actions of local firms or the acquisition of Jewish property, from which some might continue to profit today. Also largely absent are direct links with terror and death, of the sort that would have been more evident had there been inclusion of attention to prisoner of war camps, and also deportation, at the site. Regret over this, together with an account of how it came about, is expressed in the intervention below. Although there are some pictures and brief accounts of the players involved in the construction of the Rally Grounds, these are not used to provide a route into such questions. Nor are the depictions of insidious everyday acts of racism – images of shops with '*Juden Verboten*' (*Jews Forbidden*) signs or schoolbooks with anti-Semitic illustrations for example. Even though these are from the locality they seem to be widely perceived by visitors as largely disconnected from place, and instead to be part of a familiar set of images 'from that time', as some put it. This all contributes to Nuremberg appearing primarily as a reflex of the nation as agent in the early sections, but then emerging more actively as a producer of cosmopolitan discourse – in the trials and in attention to the making of the documentation centre itself – at the end of the exhibition.

Gaps and their making

Interview with Eckart Dietzfelbinger, Head of Scientific Research, Documentation Centre of the former Nazi Party Rally Grounds (2003).

I ask whether he thinks anything is missing in the exhibition. He says that although overall he thinks the exhibition turned out very well, there are also 'serious deficits':

> Fascination predominates and there is no unifying concept, which I regret very much. I was responsible for the area on the history of building, including architects, but also the links with concentration camps and war time. During the course of our research we found eighty pictures that nobody knew about of prisoner of war camps; and we planned to put these together with accounts by prisoners of war, in a whole room. Because that is part of the history. There were at least several thousand people who died out there. But that was thrown out. The reaction of survivors to this is interesting. They don't come here often but when they do the tenor is clearly one of disappointment. Meanwhile, the response from visitors in general ... is very positive ... But my opinion on the exhibition is that there are major deficits.

I ask how it happened that these 'deficits' arose.

Oh, that is quite simple. We had an advisory committee, established in 1997 … And the committee recommended that we made an exhibition that took Nuremberg as its focus, not the whole of the Third Reich. And the Nuremberg focus was on an industrial city of the nineteenth and twentieth century and the idea was to work outwards from that to show how Nuremberg became city of the party rallies. There were many reasons for that focus. But our management wanted to do both. They wanted both an exhibition about Nuremberg and about the Third Reich. And conflict arose over this. That came together with the time plan and more and more being chucked out, as is always the case. It came to a head at the beginning of 2001. Time was running out. And in the hectic time the making of part of the exhibition was taken over by the Institute of Contemporary History, even though we had developed it ourselves. And then everything was thrown out … It could have all happened. The material, the documents, everything was there.

He tells me how he voiced his concerns but to no avail. The room that he had proposed, planned in detail with ten information panels about the links with war prisoners and their exploitation and deaths, was cut in the attempt to squeeze in both the Nuremberg and Third Reich themes, and in the constraints on space and time. Such cutting for reasons of time and space, Dietzfelbinger comments, no doubt 'is a phenomenon that you have seen elsewhere'.

I agree that I have.[63]

Fascination and Terror is not about memory in the way that Beier-de Haan suggests is increasingly characteristic of exhibitions in cosmopolitan modernity. On the contrary, for reasons outlined above, it is historical documentary, mainly focused on 'the past', with little other than the building in which it is housed and a video of young people skateboarding around the site to find out about its history, to connect it to the present. The exhibition is, of course, principally about the historical moment in which the Rally Grounds were built. Nevertheless, it is not only that the exhibition focuses on the past that creates a sense of distance from the present but also that ending the main part of the exhibition at the Nuremberg trials creates a narrative and temporal closure. Here we see specific individuals being judged and usually condemned, metaphorically standing in not for a nation or a city but for Nazi criminals, especially those in positions of significant power and influence. While this makes a good end to the story, it also seals the presentation as 'past': justice has now been done. What it does not do is to raise any questions about the possible continuation of Nazi influence or of the effectiveness of the trials themselves. Instead, the trials stand not only as an end point of the narrative, marking off an end to the Nazi period, but they also act as a temporal switch, pointing to a new kind of future – one in which human rights is, or at least should be, respected.

After the section of the exhibition about the trials, there is one further area, which feels to some extent like a transit area, or even an afterthought, as it opens out to the viewing platform and exit. This is about some of the ways in which the Rally Grounds have been dealt with since 1945. It includes pictures of the blowing up of the side wings of the Zeppelin Building and other changes to the area, and also some of the proposals that there have been over the years, such as the idea to turn the Congress Hall into a shopping centre. Standing in an exhibition that is in many ways a triumph over that history of inadequate treatment of the past, this section confirms a sense of progress, of having at last more properly come to terms with the past. Like the trial room, it seems like a redemptive ending: at last, as we leave the exhibition, we can breathe a sigh of relief that all that long history of failing to deal well with the past is over.

In the old exhibition in the Zeppelin Building there was a different approach at the end of the exhibition. This was a simple noticeboard on which were pinned recent newspaper articles about neo-Nazi activity – desecrations of graveyards, planned marches, attacks on immigrants. It was a simple but also very effective reminder of a link between past and present – a link that is scarcely present in the current exhibition. During the making of the current exhibition I asked the project director whether this strategy in the Zeppelin Building – which I found so effective and which so many visitors had remarked upon positively to me – would be taken in the new exhibition. He explained that it would not but emphasised that making links with the present would permeate 'the whole context of the everyday work of the Dokuzentrum – the exhibition is just one leg but our work will not end here'. The Dokuzentrum would become, he hoped, a site for discussion of topics such as intolerance and racism – a hope also expressed by others, including Sonnenberger. In many ways it has: the Dokuzentrum staff have done a tremendous amount of work with school groups in particular discussing such topics. But many visitors only participate in the exhibition and so for them the links are not made self-evident. This does not mean, of course, that they do not make them themselves – a question to which I return in Chapter 8.

Visitor criticisms of *Fascination and Terror*

As Dokuzentrum staff themselves report, the visitor response to *Fascination and Terror* is very positive, with most visitors saying that they have learnt much more about the Rally Grounds and their history in particular and, more generally, about 'the Nazi time'. Dietzfelbinger is right that few identify what he sees as gaps in the account, which he sees as a consequence of a lack of knowledge of what is missing. It is also a consequence, as one visitor said to me, of the fact that 'there is just so much information to accumulate that it's hard to know what might not be there'; or, as another put it in response to a question about whether they would change anything in the exhibition: 'I didn't really think about it in that way'. Most visitors spent over an hour in the exhibition, generally in the region of two hours; and I met one who had been in there for almost six hours and still felt that he had not seen everything and so intended to come back again the next day for more. (Perhaps not surprisingly, he described his head as being 'too full to separate out any particular parts of it'.) Yet, although visitors did not usually speak of specific items of missing information, several were critical of what they described as 'too little about Nuremberg'. These were visitors who described themselves as having a strong interest in the history of the Nazi period. One (b. 1961) said, for example, that he thought that there could have been more 'just about everyday politics in Nuremberg at the time'; and another (b. 1962) that 'there should be more details – not so crude. There should be more about those who were directly part of it, like the Mayor, like there is about Streicher. I think there is still much that is buried'. And a woman born in 1938, having strongly praised the exhibition, suddenly remarked when asked if she had any further questions, 'I think maybe I missed it, but where do you think that the money came from to build these huge buildings? How did he [Hitler] get it? This – how many hectares of land? – how did he, were they donated and how did he get the money? How could he do that?'

Such observations were sometimes coupled with a criticism from other visitors too who complained that there was 'too much general material' or 'so much of this is what you find in history text books'; with several simply commenting in the following ways: 'it was so much of what I already knew, much of it is very general and familiar' or 'I knew most of it already and so don't have particular impressions'. There were also some comments on what a civil servant born in 1966 described as 'the danger of showing so much about propaganda without much about the outcome – I mean, concentration camps … There are very few bad pictures [i.e. images of the horrors of concentration camps]'. An Irish-American born in 1935 also remarked on the lack 'of images of the Holocaust'.

Characteristic of almost all such comments, however, were acknowledge-ments of the difficulty of the task of creating an exhibition for an audience that would not necessarily have much prior knowledge; and visitors almost always replied to my question about who they thought the audience was intended to be as 'young people'. So, criticisms were often accompanied by comments on the fact that the general material was necessary for those who did not know already. As one man born in 1941 concluded, 'It is mainly for the younger generations, not so much for people like me'; and the woman born 1938 quoted above: 'for young people it is very good'. Visitors are also aware of other constraints of exhibition making, commenting, for example, 'you can only show so much and the exhibition is already long'. Furthermore, almost all comments on the generality of the material were also accompanied by praise of how well it was presented and – most often singled out in visitor responses – the architecture of the Dokuzentrum.

* * * * *

The move in Nuremberg to address aspects of the city's Nazi past in a high-quality permanent exhibition and to present itself as a City of Human Rights is the outcome of long negotiations, including people and groups with diverse motives and politics. In highlighting some of the displacements and exclusions involved in particular ways of framing I do not mean to suggest that the developments are not worthwhile. Neither do I argue that those displacements and exclusions are all necessarily calculated or intended. What is in many ways more interesting is how they can result from a combination of other kinds of decisions, such as those about narrative coherence; about what counts as 'local', how far to extend from it and how to engage audiences from around the world; and about how a strong emphasis on facts and documents, coupled with a tight time-schedule, might mean that some wider questions of framing do not arise. The task of addressing this history – and dealing with a site like the Nazi Party Rally Grounds – is undoubtedly difficult, as we will see further in the following chapter, which looks in more detail at the work of tour guides out on the grounds.

The turn to look at difficult histories is, as I have discussed earlier, often bound up with a moral project of defining the current community in opposition to that of the past. This marking of difference between then and now, between 'them' and 'us', can also have the consequence that the other moral project with which the display of such histories is associated – highlighting the dangers of reoccurrence – is weakened. Difficult heritage can become a fossil of a bad time rather than the indication of need for continued vigilance called for by so many history activists, such as those involved in the making and running of the Dokuzentrum.

The attempt to foster 'cosmopolitan memory' treads a similarly difficult line. As argued here, a cosmopolitan emphasis, as on human rights, can entail displacements from more local, perhaps less dramatic, but nevertheless significant events. My argument here is not that such developments are *necessarily* bound up with such displacements but it does point to this potential in a cosmopolitan discourse. As with other ways of framing heritage debates that I have explored in this book, this too can produce particular kinds of emphases and silences.

7

NEGOTIATING ON
THE GROUND(S)

Guiding tours of Nazi heritage

In their careful theorisation of collective remembrance, Winter and Sivan argue that the work of secondary elites within civil society is crucial both to an understanding of the ways in which processes of remembrance are shaped and to a proper appreciation of the kinds of agency involved in these activities that exist at the interface between the individual and the state.[1] Visits to heritage sites are one such 'interface activity'. Previous chapters have also included attention to the work of secondary elites – people involved in 'managing culture' in the public realm – engaged in the interface activity of assembling Nazi heritage, in the Dokuzentrum and earlier exhibitions, and in other educational and artistic projects. These chapters have highlighted, among other things, some of the areas of negotiation and struggle involved in these different kinds of accompanied witnessing, as well as some of the negotiating frames through which it is conducted. This chapter continues these interests but does so by looking directly at an interface activity – literally 'on the ground' – between history-workers and members of the public: guided walking tours of the Rally Grounds.

Many analyses of tourism have emphasised the importance of tour guide activity, Del Casino and Hanna, for example, arguing that tourism workers are part of the performance of a site.[2] In the case of the Nazi Party Rally Grounds, which is an open public space used for purposes other than tourism too, the site can be engaged with by visitors in ways not mediated by tour guides – some of which we will see in the following chapter. Nevertheless, tours are an important way in which many people come to experience the site and they are of particular interest for how history-workers – guides and their organisations – negotiate a way through the site and through its history. As Christian Gudehus observes in his analysis of a range of tours to different sites connected with the Nazi past – including the Wannsee villa and various concentration camps – tours provide an opportunity to look in detail at what kinds of accounts of this history are presented to the public in practice as well as to understand what may be involved in trying to guide people through heritage and into certain ways of seeing, and relating to, history.[3]

Negotiation as mediation

As a framework for presenting and analysing this negotiation I draw on theorising of mediation, in particular Stuart Hall's classic 'encoding'/'decoding' model.[4]

This entails considering the meanings, or 'preferred readings', which producers attempt to 'encode' into cultural products ('texts') and the meanings that audiences ('readers') extrapolate, or 'decode', from these. Particularly important here is Hall's acknowledgement that there could be a disjuncture between the meanings 'written-in' and those 'read-off', and that this was not simply a matter of 'media effects', that is of readers being 'impacted upon' by the media. Instead, he sets out the following range of processes that can be involved in 'decoding': 'dominant-hegemonic' (identifying with and not questioning 'the message'), 'negotiated' (questioning or reinterpreting what has been presented), or 'oppositional' (rejecting or ignoring the message). This allows more sophisticated understandings of media consumption in which audiences are recognised as an active rather than passive part of the communication process.

More recent media theorising has sought to refine, complicate and to some extent challenge this model. Hall's important recognition that production may implicate imagined or actual audiences, thus creating a feedback loop, has been extended to theorise further the complexities of production.[5] Ethnographic work in particular has highlighted the ways in which cultural products are not necessarily simply the outcomes of producers' intentions, and thus that 'encoding' cannot necessarily be extrapolated from the 'media text' – a point clear from the previous chapter too.[6] There has also been consideration of the implications of different media, genres and their contexts for shaping possible readings.[7] This has included, to a limited extent, recognition of the variable materiality of different forms of media and also of the need to extend the idea of encoding and decoding to include more sensory or embodied processes.[8]

Drawing on these various ideas, I suggest that we see history workers – including the exhibition producers in the previous chapter, as well as the tour guides and those leading the educational game discussed in this chapter – as engaged in trying to encode 'preferred readings' as part of a wider process of mediation. The nature of their engagement, however, may vary: they may subscribe strongly to conveying a particular account, or may be less engaged, or, as has been reported of tour guides in some other contexts, even ironic.[9] Their own *positioning* here is crucial. Equally, 'encoding' needs to be understood not as an automatic and smooth-running process but as *negotiated* and sometimes even *contested*. Any attempt to encode meaning is, then, shaped in part at least by the following:

- conventions and restrictions of the *medium* (the guided tour) and *genre* (e.g. a city tour or a tour of a site of atrocity);
- *audiences* – both those actually encountered on tours and those 'imagined' in the planning of the tour;
- the *materialities* of the tour context – including the place and space of the tour itself, and in particular the way in which, say, buildings, statuary, graffiti or bystanders may suggest readings that are not those that the tour guides might prefer.

It is important to see these as interrelated within a *process* of mediation and the attempt to encode meaning. Below, after a brief background, I look at first at guides' *positioning* in relation to the site and the account that they attempt to encode. Then I look at walking tours, addressing questions of medium and genre, before looking in more detail at guides' attempts to encourage preferred readings – a discussion that focuses especially upon audience and materiality. This is then followed by an intervention about a game – which develops some of these points and highlights especially well a dilemma also faced in the Dokuzentrum and no doubt in many other contexts: that of trying to ensure particular kinds of readings at the same time as engaging the audience as active.

Tours and guides

Walking tours of the site were initiated in 1984, by the city's Kunstpädagogische Zentrum (Centre for Art Pedagogy) and replaced in 1986 by those of *Geschichte für Alle* – GfA (History for All). Today GfA provides most of the tours of the site as well as many more specialised tours and educational activities, including the game discussed below. Begun by a group of history students at the University of Erlangen-Nürnberg, GfA is a registered and non-profit-making organisation that, as its own literature states, focuses upon local and regional history. In addition to running tours (of other places too, though to a lesser extent), it also carries out commissioned historical research and produces publications.

GfA tours are largely organised according to a 'script' that has been collectively produced and revised by various GfA members over the years. This is not a script that aims to set out precisely what guides should say and is not intended for word-for-word memorisation; though much of it could be used in this way. Rather, it sets out the main recommended tour stops and for each gives a list of themes that should be covered and others that might be, together with information on the content to fill in these themes. There are some suggestions for activities or, say, making use of particular information boards, and, in addition, each guide is given a folder of pictures to use to illustrate points. The script also includes several pages of additional information on which guides can draw to expand upon certain themes, a list of relevant literature (it being assumed that they are likely to read up more themselves), and a checklist of useful facts and figures. The content is primarily oriented to telling about the history of the various buildings and site as a whole, within a context of providing some basic background to the 'Third Reich', and explaining the role of propaganda, and the link between fascination and terror, rather as in the Dozuzentrum.

Tours take about two hours. Group size varies, there usually being between about half a dozen and thirty people on each tour, depending on how many happen to turn up (no pre-booking being required for many tours). Generally, groups are taken first to the Luitpold marching ground, which is now grassed over though has remnants of the staged seating still visible. They then walk to the Congress Hall; then part way along the Great Road. Some guides take their groups from here to see the foundation stone of the never-built Great German Stadium, or even around the lake which has formed in the pit dug for its foundations. From the Great Road many guides also talk about the other parts of the larger Rally Grounds site that originally existed. This includes the Mars Field and the extensive areas of barracks for accommodating the hundreds of thousands who attended the rallies. Guides may also mention the municipal stadium, now used by Nuremberg Football Club. Following a pleasant tree-lined walk along a lake, groups reach the Zeppelin Building, where tours usually end. (See Figure 2.5 for a map of the site.)

In line with the framework suggested above, we need to understand the positioning of the guides in relation to the organisation for which they work and the script which is provided. More broadly, however, positioning also needs to take into account the nature of the organisation and its wider social and political position.

As we saw in Chapter 5, GfA was founded (1985) at a time when the idea of 'working through' the Nazi past, and of the importance of doing so in order to have a 'healthy' rather than 'repressed' identity, had become widespread within West Germany. Those on the left of the political spectrum, in particular, promulgated the idea that 'facing up to' the Nazi past was a necessary moral task; and in many places history workshops were established in order to accomplish this political-moral-historical work. Although GfA was broadly part of this movement, it also sought to some extent to differentiate itself from history workshops, partly by emphasising the academic and politically non-aligned character of the organisation's work – something that has been important for its continued funding by the city government under different ruling political parties over the years. This has also meant avoiding presenting tours as part of an active 'anti-fascist' agenda; and trying to present the site factually rather than through moralising statements. As Alexander Schmidt (b. 1963), one of the most active members of the organisation for many years, argues, a moralising presentation 'does not work well, especially with school classes. The current generation of pupils has, as a rule, thoroughly "gone through" Terror and Brutality of the "Third Reich" in school. Whoever tells of it too much and too stridently does not achieve "sorrow" (*Betroffenheit*) but boredom'.[10] Compared with some of the tours discussed by Gudehus, guides here rarely make overtly moral comments but instead, in ways that I discuss below, relate examples that act as allegories.

History students at the university have always been one of the main sources of tour guides for GfA and posters in the university, and word of mouth, are the main ways in which guides are recruited. As several such students explained to me, GfA tour guiding is attractive employment because it relates to your subject more than most other casual work, is interesting, provides useful experience in valued skills such as public speaking, and pays relatively well. While several guides stressed how important it was to appear objective and to 'just tell the facts', as Schmidt had emphasised, some come to such work out of a specific experience of anti-Nazi concern. One former guide, for example, described to me how she had been brought up in Wunsiedel, the town in northern Bavaria where Rudolf Hess's grave is located. Seeing neo-Nazi pilgrims to this site politicised her and fostered her commitment to a different kind of representation of Nazi sites. Others noted that their interest in this topic had been influenced by concern with the ways in which immigrants are treated; and some described broad concern with topics such as racism and sexism. And even those who described their participation in less politicised terms nevertheless expressed a sense of commitment to what they regarded as worthwhile work – 'it's a part of our history that everybody should know, so it's good to tell it', as one guide put it.

All of those who act as GfA guides undergo training to do so. Currently this entails attending a number of training sessions (some of which I attended) and guided tours as an observer during the year and then giving a tour under supervision. The training and the script can be seen as part of the process of encoding by the organisation. In theory there is scope for slippage between the script and the guides' own versions of a tour, which is to some extent encouraged: the script states 'You can amend, expand or shorten this tour: it is your tour'.[11] Nevertheless, the fact that certain themes are listed in bold as 'the most important' and the script's injunctions to repeat or emphasise certain points makes it less open than the idea of the tour belonging to the guide implies. In practice, the main variations made by guides are those flagged up as alternatives in the script itself, such as whether or not to go to the foundation stone of the German Stadium and how much detail to pursue. The training and script thus contribute to a fairly high degree of consistency between tours, as does the fact that the guides mostly come from similar backgrounds and share views on the importance of informing people about the past, especially this particular past. This is a context, then, in which guides are committed to the encoding preferred by the organisation for which they work: I never witnessed any ironic or dissenting comments by guides about the topic that they were addressing or about the organisation itself.

One day, one tour, one guide

It is a hot day in summer and I have just gone on a tour led by Erika, who has been a guide for several years. This was a prearranged tour for a club of firemen and their families from another part of Germany. It is quite common for groups like this to choose to come here as one of their social days out. The men are all wearing matching T-shirts with the club's insignia; the women are more variably, though comfortably, dressed. It has been quite a strenuous tour for Erika, partly on account of the heat, and partly because of the group dynamic. Group members already know each other and so are often engaged in ongoing conversations that have nothing to do with the tour. A couple of the younger men are particularly inattentive to Erika's presentations, and this is not always helped by the way that one older man interrupts to tell them to listen, and then gives his own accounts of what various parts of the site were – some of which Erika has to correct. So after the tour ends and they clap to thank her, she turns to me, sighing with relief and using her folder as a fan to cool herself, and suggests that we go for a drink. She takes me to the boathouse of the yacht club, of which she is a member. This is a members-only club, situated within the Rally Grounds area, on the edge of a lake, with what would be an idyllic view except for the fact that it looks onto the ugly side of the Congress Hall. We sit on the veranda drinking ice-cold apple juice from the club's fridge; and Erika tells me about how she became a tour guide. As a member of the yacht club she often spent time at the Rally Grounds and decided to read more about it, and this got her interested in 'this whole history', though she had 'always been interested to some extent'. Then, as her children grew older, she says, she wanted to do more than being a full-time housewife. So, after going on a tour, she got involved with GfA and trained to be a guide herself. She didn't do it for the money, she explained, but it gave her a sense of self-worth to do something that she regarded as important in this way. While many of the guides are students, Erika is by no means the only guide from a different background. The day (and this intervention) is a reminder of some of the variety among both tour groups and tour guides, as well as the unique event – within the common framework – that is each tour.

The tour script has been produced according to conventions widely shared by walking tours. Each tour involves one guide, who will lead a group for a designated time, moving from one location to another, and providing information along the way. Unlike media such as television, this medium requires that the audience physically moves to the place being represented – and, as such, potentially involving a greater degree of separation from everyday life than some other media, and a fairly concentrated form of attention. The conventions of any medium have implications for both encoding and decoding. Only so much complexity and detail is possible within the constraints of time and the fact that the guide cannot assume much prior knowledge. Furthermore, the audience is in direct contact with the site as well as with the guide's account and this may open up a space for readings that differ from that attempted by the guide. So too does the interaction between guide and audience, and among the visitors themselves. For pedagogic reasons – an argument that people learn better if participant rather than simply having to listen to a monologue – GfA also formally encourages such interaction (and see the Rally Grounds game below). This also means that the guide is not positioned straightforwardly as *Führer* (leader), a potentially particularly uncomfortable role in this particular context given the connotations of this label. ('Are you the Führer?' is a favourite 'amusing' greeting to tour guides from some tour participants.)[12]

The particular context is also part of a wider *genre* of difficult heritage, which is likely to be implicated in a range of quite complex and even conflicting emotions and responses. This is partly a function of its 'double encoding' of meaning: that originally 'written in' to the site and the 'preferred readings' that guides attempt to encourage. A key struggle for guides dealing with this genre of tourism is how to manage this.

Encouraging preferred readings

In trying to lead visitors towards certain readings, guides often attempt to gauge something of group members' prior knowledge, interest and viewpoints early on in the tour. Typically they do so by directly asking the questions that the script suggests that they cover themselves: 'What were the party rallies?' and 'Why did Nuremberg become "City of the Party rallies"?' The first question usefully highlights general knowledge of the history of National Socialism, and the second more specific knowledge of the history of the rallies and of the city, something that can also help to indicate whether visitors are themselves from the local area or not.

Asking questions is, more generally, recommended in the script as a way of engaging the audience for reasons just noted. However, it is also recognised as potentially problematic as it may produce 'wrong' or even politically dubious answers. From the ways in which tour guides handle answers to questions it is clear that they seek quite carefully governed preferred readings. In other words, although they ask questions – a technique which would seem to indicate openness to multiple interpretations – they nevertheless attempt to encode a relatively 'closed' audience interpretation. They want visitors to get it right, and not to continue or go away with what guides regard as misconceptions – a perspective that was also important in the making of the Dokuzentrum as we saw in the previous chapter.[13] The importance to guides of 'closing off' what they see as inappropriate readings was made clear to me on a number of occasions during tours. Often, this involved saying 'No' very firmly after certain answers to questions. One tour guide explained to me that she thought it very important to be absolutely categorical about errors and misconceptions in relation to the Nazi past as this was not a subject on which you wanted to leave people with doubts.

Guides also used other techniques to encourage preferred readings and avoid those that they judged misguided. For example, on seeing the Congress Hall tourists are often impressed by its grandeur and do not see it as particularly ugly or threatening. In other words, the materiality of the building might prompt admiration of Nazi achievements. To deal with this, the script suggests asking groups whether they like the façade. It continues: 'Generally there will be a lively mix of agreement and disagreement, beautiful and ugly. Leave this entirely as it is. Perhaps try to steer it via particular problems, such as "Does it seem friendly to you?', or later "What sort of stone is used for the façade?" '[14], the latter being a question that can lead into discussion of the use of concentration camp workers for quarrying and the Nazi ambition to create lasting monuments. In this way, visitors' own impressions are elicited but the 'reality' behind the façade – in this case rather literally, especially when visitors are later taken into the ugly inner courtyard of the building – is gradually revealed. This 'façade-peeling' is a major feature of a tour such as this and stands in interesting contrast to the 'sight sacralisation' – and indeed 'site sacralisation' – of many other tourist genres.[15]

Revealing reality

'Façade-peeling' is also used on other occasions by guides. On one tour, for example, when a picture of rows of male workers, clutching spades against their naked chests, was shown to the tour group, a woman exclaimed 'Oh, beautiful men!'. The group laughed and the guide went on to explain how although the men in the picture were all attractive, this was a carefully staged image, and those who were not so good-looking were placed behind. Similar stories were also told about, for example, the impressive and famous lighting effects designed by Albert Speer. The spur to creating these, as Speer recounts in *Inside the Third Reich*, was trying to find a way to detract from the rather unimpressive and ugly middle-ranking Nazi officials who were due to appear on the Zeppelin Building stage.[16] Speer's idea, guides explain, was to bring them out in the dark accompanied by a distracting spectacular light show which would leave them in shadow. The preferred reading being encoded through such stories, then, is one of not trusting façades. Impressive and attractive though the Nazi rituals, buildings and bodies might have been, the reality was thoroughly ugly.

Façade-peeling stories like these sometimes elicit laughter or at least wry smiles. Guides encourage this – and indeed it can be seen as part of the way in which they attempt to dissipate emotions such as admiration. Laughing at some of the great efforts expended on the rallies is, like façade-peeling itself, a technique which helps to disenchant them. Examples used by guides include accounts of the organisers' attempts to curb alcohol consumption (some guides ask their groups to imagine how difficult that would be in Bavaria), and descriptions of some of the 'sports', such as swimming with a full military uniform and gas-mask (the pictures are quite comical), that were performed during the rallies. Laughter also helps to encourage a more relaxed approach from the group, something that seems to be valued by guides in itself. One guide showed his group contrasting pictures of the Zeppelin Field, one during a rally and one during a Bob Dylan concert (see Figures 2.1 and 3.7). He pointed out the different body-comportments: the former rigid and uniform; the latter relaxed and individualised. The latter, he implied, was politically preferable. The kind of laughter being encouraged was part of this same, freer, body-politics matrix.

The other kind of façade-peeling, used in careful counterpoint to the examples already given, entails highlighting the atrocity which the façade sought to hide. Thus, facts are related such as that concentration camp inmates were used to quarry the stone for the Congress Hall, that Jews were deported from a railway station on the grounds, and that the 'sports' were part of the preparation for war. The question 'Why Nuremberg?' is used, among other things, and as in the Dokuzentrum, to tell of the anti-Semitism of Streicher and his reprehensible newspaper. In this way connections are made between the two terms in the title of the Rally Grounds exhibition – fascination and terror – and any potential admiration of the buildings, rallies and Nazi regime is undercut.

Seeing past/through

Encouraging these preferred readings entails complex visualisation work. Guides have to negotiate tourists through layers of different ways of seeing the Rally Grounds, beginning with 'seeing past' some of those that they see around them. This includes seeing past the now pleasant grassy lawns occupied by twenty-first century relaxed bodies, sunbathing or playing frisbee. Guides must, thus, first help the tourists to 'see' the grounds as they were in the 1930s and 1940s. They must enable them to see the site in use, during the rallies, and also as it never was but would have been had it been fully completed. The last is needed to help convey the extent of Nazi megalomania, something told through the medium of the planned enormous buildings.

Figure 7.1 Helping visitors visualise history

To help visitors to see the site as it was, guides show pictures, and they point to indicate where, say, the seating at the edge of a marching ground might have been. Tourists look from the pictures to the site, and back again, shielding their eyes with their hands as they gaze into the distance and try to imagine the original extent. Size relative to context can be particularly difficult to convey, and while the size of the marching grounds generally remains impressive to those visiting today, that of the buildings does not so readily. As one guide explained to me, today these buildings don't necessarily seem all that big: we have plenty of skyscrapers that are larger. Also, the surrounding trees have grown, making the visual difference between trees and buildings less marked; and in the case of the Zeppelin Building the removal of the side-wings curtails the long line which magnified the building's extent.

Guides can verbally explain the size of the buildings – and they often quote lots of figures, something that itself seems to convey quantity (see Chapter 2); and they make comparisons and tell stories of Nazi attempts to make things larger than previously. For example, they tell the story of how Hitler sent the architects of the Congress Hall back three times until the plans were for a construction that would be a third higher than its Roman precursor. The story of the never-completed German stadium is also important here: that would have been bigger (for 400,000 spectators) than any stadium in existence today and the idea that it would have been so large that those seated at the rear would not have been able to see properly usually draws a gasp and a smile at the absurdity of Nazi gigantomania. So too does a picture of the planned building, in which visitors typically initially mistake the doorways for ventilation grilles or cellar windows. The quest for enormity in Nazi architecture is explained by guides as part of the Nazi subjugation of the individual.[17] Here guides play on visitors' initial misperceptions, telling them to try to see past their initial impressions and 'see the reality'.

Helping visitors to see architectural enormity and linking this to the ideology of subjugation of the individual is one of the ways in which guides also try to effect another kind of 'seeing beyond' that which they see before them: in this case, seeing beyond the propaganda to the wider brutality that the rallies also contributed to. This is a particular problem at a site of 'difficult heritage' such as this which is not itself directly a site of atrocity. The tourist gaze must be both directed to the site itself but also directed elsewhere, to other sites where the wider violence took place. Double- and sometimes triple-seeing is necessary. Yet, this must not be done in a way that will seem gratuitous or not part of the place, for a key part of visiting a particular site is to see *in situ*, to experience directly and not be related a general account that could be given anywhere.

Nazi poison

The story of the poisonous lake is one that guides always tell. It is also a story that I was told, in various versions, by other people whom I met at the site (Chapter 8). It works best standing next to one of the warning signs, illustrated with a skull and cross-bones, by the edge of what the signs indicate to be a deceptive and dangerous area of water. Without them, or without the stories, this lake, formed in the foundations of what was to have been the Great German Stadium, would simply look attractive, with its reed surrounds and ducks swimming. Called Silbersee – Silver Lake – allegedly after a story by the popular German writer, Karl May (1842–1912), *Der Schatz im Silbersee* (*The Treasure in the Silver Lake*) (1962), the lake has been widely rumoured to conceal Nazi treasure. Over the years, this has attracted divers searching for it. Several of these, however, died in their search, in what were initially mysterious circumstances.

The guides explain that the deaths were caused by the presence of hydrogen sulphide, which can be fatally absorbed by the skin, in the depths of the lake. This toxin in turn, they point out, was caused by run-off from an adjacent small hill built from the city's rubble after the war. Some of the other people who told me the story did so without this hill variation. But even with it, it still has allegorical resonance, which was not lost on its tellers.

All of the attempts to make visitors see Nazi atrocity, then, are thoroughly linked to the site itself: they are 'here-sited'. At the Congress Hall visitors are shown images of emaciated men in striped pyjamas quarrying the stones that they see before them; on the Great Road they are shown photographs of Jews, carrying suitcases, lined up at the railway station that lies further along the road; at the Zeppelin Building they

Figure 7.2   The poisonous lake

are shown the preparations for war that took place directly on the marching ground before them. Of course, such images are hardly unfamiliar, even if these particular ones have not been seen by visitors before. The work of visualising the linked 'elsewhere' of the Rally Grounds is already partly accomplished by the fact that the visitor already knows the image of the concentration camp, deportation and warfare. The pictures are a visual trigger to visitors' memories of that larger set of images and knowledge that they already possess. In this way, guides also draw on existing encodings to help encourage their preferred reading of the site.

Embodied encounters

Guides do not, however, only rely upon recounting or showing pictures. They also sometimes employ various bodily techniques to try, for example, to help visitors 'see' size. In doing so, the guides are consciously working against what they see as the danger of the buildings – their materiality – telling a different story from the orally narrated. They are also attempting to make felt the agency of the architecture – its potential effect on the individual, though not with attendant emotions of 'awe' or admiration. This is quite a difficult task. They want visitors to experience the large scale of the buildings and feel small in relation to them, but without their feeling too enthralled by Nazi power.

The 'bodily experiment' that they use to do this takes place in the gallery of the Congress Hall. What happens is that the guide asks for a volunteer and then

Figure 7.3 Seeing size

tells other members of the group to look at a door at the end of the gallery. Group members are asked to guess how tall the individual would be against the door. The volunteer is then instructed to walk towards the door and stand against it. What is supposed to happen is that the group substantially overestimates the height of the volunteer relative to the door, so realising that the building is much bigger than they had assumed. They are also supposed to become aware of the 'shrinkage effect' – the way that individuals are dwarfed by the architecture – as the volunteer walks towards it. This, in turn, is intended to confirm Nazi 'gigantomania', deception and techniques of 'shrinking' the individual.

When it works well, the audience members laugh at their own mistaken overestimate, they shake their heads at how they were tricked, they may persuade someone with them to walk back towards the door to witness the effect again, and they mutter agreement with the guide's comments about how small the individual was made. Sometimes, however, the performance doesn't work. The first dilemma is that members of the tour group may estimate that the door is indeed large and so the denouement falls flat – like when somebody calls out the punch-line of the joke in a stand-up comedian's performance. It also sometimes goes wrong because the tour group members can't quite figure out what they are supposed to be seeing. This tends to happen especially if the volunteer walks quite quickly – this somehow lessens the 'shrinkage effect'. In this circumstance, it is quite common for the guide to ask them to do it again, more slowly. This repeat performance is more likely to succeed, not only, it seemed to me, because the slower walking actually makes the effect more pronounced, but also because of what we might call 'audience complicity' – in general, audiences want the effect to work. They do so because, for the most part, they want to subscribe to the messages about Nazism that are being acted out here.

The possibility of performance failure is, however, significant; and it may be the case that the attempt to tell or inscribe meanings via the bodily carries a greater possibility of failure than does saying through words, even while at the same time there is a greater chance of making a significant 'felt' impact. Bodily performance is, in other words, potentially a more high-risk approach than is the textual or purely verbal. We might indeed venture that in general bodily performances have a greater range of effect (and indeed affect), being both potentially *more* powerful than the verbal/textual and also *more* likely to be misinterpreted or not felt at all.

This is shown too in a second example, in which tour guides try to get tourists to participate in a physical activity beyond that of merely walking the tour, listening and talking. In this activity, tourists are encouraged to impersonate Nazi soldiers. How it goes is like this. On the Great Road, the guide explains that each of the granite slabs was designed to be the size of two Prussian officer's steps and proceeds to demonstrate this by goose-stepping along the road and encouraging the members of the tour group to do likewise.

I always found it interesting to watch this particular part in the tour. It was almost always the case that tourists would initially be hesitant, nervous of the impersonation involved – perhaps fearing that the characters they were acting might rub off on them. Usually only a minority in each group actually tried out the activity. It took me some time to personally stride out. There was, however, also something rather liberating about doing so, and what almost always happened was that those trying to goose-step and those watching would laugh. It was actually very difficult to accomplish – you needed to take very long strides and it was hard to keep them even and not to lose balance. This made it look rather comical (and, to some of us, reminiscent of Basil Fawlty doing a parody of a Nazi stormtrooper in the 1970s British television comedy *Fawlty Towers*).

The guide would explain that the slabs were designed in this way in order to help keep the troops in line – this was important because if the rows upon rows of soldiers got out of step, they might all collide into one another. Evoking an image of a failed Nazi performance is part of a wider strategy employed by the guides in various contexts: conjuring up amusing scenes that would have embarrassed the precision-obsessed Nazi organisers. Encouraging the tourist to play the soldier is to cast the tourist in the role of deficient performer; something that simultaneously depicts the soldiers as potentially incompetent performers. This is choreographed-precision thwarted, performance gone awry.

Involved here was a kind of visual debunking of Nazi pomposity: the performance was a parody that also served to reveal some of the absurdity involved. As with the previous example, this was not an isolated attempt but part of the broader theme of false appearances and of attempts to puncture these, to 'show up' the appearances of nationalist fervour as, in part at least, manufactured acts, appearances which might mask a different reality. One thing about parodic performances is that they create a kind of sense of *communitas* among those who understand what is going on. In the case described, this was almost all participants, as the meaning was explicitly explained by the guide. In some cases, however, stragglers would come along later and initially be baffled, or even look a bit disturbed, by what was going on. Suddenly seeing a member of the tour group, perhaps even one of your own relatives, goose-stepping along the Great Road could be a bit of a shock. And sometimes there would be onlookers, who were not part of the tour, who would look on in puzzlement.

As in the previous example, corporeal performance carried a risk. While it could make the point about potential failure of performance, it also itself risked a failure of a different sort. That is, it might be an activity which some participants engaged in too energetically and enthusiastically, and without perhaps being fully aware of the point that the tour guide was trying to make. On one occasion that I witnessed, it seemed to me that something of this sort was going on: a group of school-boys began to robustly goose-step, taking not just a couple of steps as demonstrated by the guide, but continuing for a long stretch and also stepping out and trying to hone their technique at many later points in the tour. Again, these co-performances by those who were more often positioned as audience might be redirected by the tour guide; in this case, not rerun, but simply moved along, by hurrying forward to the next station on the tour.

Identity complexes

One feature of 'difficult heritage' such as this is its contested place in relation to contemporary identity. The script explains that the tour is not only about the past: 'The time since 1945 is also a theme of our tour: the Party Rally Grounds have remained through to the present an exemplary mirror for "the Germans" and their attitude towards the past'.[18] Guides show this mirror by talking about the ways in which the site has been treated since 1945: the periods of blowing up and grassing over, and some of the ideas for redeveloping and re-using the buildings. In the Congress Hall groups are asked what they think should be done with it. There are sometimes suggestions that it be made into a drive-in cinema or disco, while most usually reply 'leave it as it is' or 'turn it into a museum'. Guides then explain some of the plans over time, including the 1980s shopping and leisure complex plans, and give a brief history culminating in the opening of the Dokuzentrum. As in the exhibition in the Dokuzentrum itself, this factual account is simultaneously a progress narrative, and an allegory in which reflection on the past emerges as a proper part of contemporary identity.

This is not to say, however, that guides emphatically try to drive such a message home or that they present critical reflection as the only acceptable way of relating to the past. Quite often they mobilise profanation-type positions. When visitors suggest that the Congress Hall would make a good disco, some guides agree; and in one case, when a visitor expressed disapproval of the fact that a fairground was set up next to the building, the guide said that he thought that it was fine and that it helped to 'trivialise' the Nazi grandiosity. The guide who showed the picture of the Bob Dylan concert did so approvingly, implying that these kinds of uses were resistant readings and thus appropriate responses to the Nazi past. This does not mean that guides were expressing ambivalence to Nazism or that they were saying that 'anything goes'. Rather, they were pointing to the acceptability of a range of responses, provided that there was also some reflection on the Nazi atrocity and an attempt to understand the mechanisms that made it possible. The kind of historical consciousness that their tour was encouraging was one in which addressing the Nazi past has an acknowledged but not necessarily highly emotive, guilt-ridden or overwhelming presence.

While for most visitors the Nazi past acts as a dreadful period against which contemporary identity is defined (see following chapter) – a process that simultaneously
entails acknowledging it as part of their nation's heritage – there are others for whom
it has more positive connotations and who visit the former Nazi Party Rally Grounds
in order to admire the Nazi achievement and identify with its ambitions. There have
only been rare instances of tour groups openly expressing pro-Nazi views, partly
because since a tour in the late 1980s by a neo-Nazi group, that ended up needing a
police escort, GfA have attempted to avoid accepting requests to lead tours of such
groups.[19] In some groups there can, nevertheless, sometimes be quite open fascination
with the militaristic, or comments that tour guides referred to as 'the "But, of course,
Hitler also built the motorways" type'. On one occasion that I witnessed, when a
large photograph of ranked soldiers was unfurled, some boys in a visiting school
group exclaimed 'Cool!' The guide dealt with this by asking the boys how long they
would like to stand there silently like that. All guides know the booklet with answers
to 'But of course Hitler also …' type of statements and so are ready to counter these
(pointing out, for example, that motorway building was already underway in the
Weimar republic).[20] Through such strategies guides also discourage or at least unsettle
positive evaluations and identifications. They also contain such responses by moving
swiftly on, avoiding being drawn into longer discussions.

Tours are also sometimes attended by older people for whom the past of the Rally
Grounds is also their own lived past. On the two occasions when I witnessed this,
such tour members only shyly, and late on in the tour, revealed their own memories
of being in Hitler youth groups or of waving flags when Hitler visited Nuremberg.
In both cases the interventions that they made were to try to emphasise to the rest
of the group the compulsions that made individuals feel that they had to participate,
that they had little agency to do otherwise. Not surprisingly, the presence of an eye-
witness has a gravitational effect on other tour members who transfer the focus of
their attention away from the guide to this speaker with the authority of having
been there. This could potentially be problematic for guides, partly because of the
shift of attention but also because such apparently authoritative speakers might send
preferred readings off course. For example, guides tried to deflect the suggestion of
a lack of agency by politely pointing out that many people chose to participate and
that not everybody took part. Yet none of the guides with whom I spoke recalled such
experiences as problematic, perhaps because they deal with them so fluently.

Group dynamics and materialities

One move within media theory has been a shift from understanding media 'reception'
as necessarily individual to seeing it as potentially collective. This move is evident in
the replacement of the singular notion of the 'spectator' by the collective one of 'the
audience'[21] and in a tendency to draw less on psychology and more on sociology
and anthropology.[22] Guided tours, collective by nature, highlight the social dynamic
of reception. This is manifest not only in the case of eye-witnesses but also in more
mundane contexts. Lack of interest or attention from some tour members can cause
particular difficulties for guides. On the long walks between stations, members of the

group chat to one another and some continue to do so, perhaps more quietly, as the guide addresses the group. I saw occasions when just a couple of group members had a disruptive effect on the attention of the whole group by making their disinterest evident by talking among themselves or making crude remarks. Several guides told me that school teachers could be the worst offenders for while the school pupils tended to still look to them for leadership, they sometimes regarded themselves as off-duty and on a day out. One guide recounted an occasion when a school teacher, part way into the tour, opened her rucksack and took out her lunch and began to eat it, prompting all of the pupils to reach into their bags for their own snacks. Then she took out a banana and proceeded to pretend to shoot the pupils with it. After that, recalled the guide, it was almost impossible to hold the attention of the group.

Another aspect of collective reception is the speed at which tourists are willing to walk. Trying to make them go sufficiently quickly to cover the site within the available time is a particularly taxing for guides, as I not only witnessed on tours by others but also experienced directly when I gave tours. This can also be understood as part of the materiality of a tour: there is a distance that must be covered. Other materialities include the weather. At the Rally Grounds there is little shelter. Wind and rain leave guides struggling to show the pictures in their folders and to be heard. In the heat, tourists sometimes become increasingly unwilling to keep walking, or to stand and listen in areas lacking shade, and there is a danger of temporarily losing group members – and precious minutes – to drinks stalls. These practical materialities are thoroughly part of the mediatory process, constraining the agency of the guides and what it is possible for them to say and for the group to hear and see.

A Nazi Party Rally Grounds Game

In 2000, GfA devised a 'game' for school groups visiting the Nazi Party Rally Grounds. The idea of this was to encourage pupils to take a more active role in their own learning, rather than replicating hierarchical educational styles. I attended a training session for the game and one of its early trials, led by experienced guide, Max, and new trainee, Anke. What follows is a description of the trial based on my fieldnotes.

The group, consisting of twenty-two 15–16 year olds (of whom eight are girls) from a practically-oriented secondary school (*Realschule*), plus their teacher, is late – perhaps an ominous sign. Max provides a short introduction during which he asks the group lots of questions – such as what 'SS' and 'SA' stand for – partly in order to get them into the spirit of volunteering information, and partly to try to assess how much they already know. The answers suggest that the pupils only have sketchy background knowledge. When he shows a photograph of a marching ground, full of soldiers during a rally, several of the boys sarcastically say – 'so few'. Max splits the pupils into groups of four to six and gives each a file containing information and question sheets – with lists of questions for different parts of the grounds –

and explains that they need to go to the different parts of the grounds and look in the file to find answers to the questions. He says that there are 'no wrong answers' and 'no grades'. As the pupils start leafing through the file, some seem quite excited – 'Stadium – cool!' Max intervenes loudly to say when and where – the Zeppelin Building – we are all to meet up again later. Explaining what and where the Zeppelin Building is proves difficult until the teacher intervenes to say 'Where people play tennis'. They have an hour and a half before regrouping.

Max, Anke and I go for a coffee and Max tells us about some of the previous trials, one of which with an older class had gone OK but others had encountered problems such as pupils wondering off and getting lost, or perhaps asking misinformed members of the public for answers – answers which, despite his message to the pupils, he clearly deemed 'wrong'. Ten minutes before regrouping time we go over to the Zeppelin Building to find some groups already there and the teacher leaning against the wall smoking. Other pupils straggle along, some reporting that others have bunked off on the bus. The teacher tells us that he did something on the subject of 'Jews and Hitler and so forth' yesterday; had they done it any earlier, they would just have forgotten it, he says. In one of the dark, chilly side-rooms inside the Zeppelin Building, Max gives each group a second file, this one containing overhead transparencies, and asks each to prepare a presentation on a particular part of the grounds. A group of girls seems to get on with the task and they call Anke over to assist them. Others tackle it half-heartedly or seem to be doing nothing at all, and several boys repeatedly petition the teacher to let them leave in order to go to football training. Then Max gets each group in turn up to give their presentations, the girls' group first. They speak stiltedly about the Luitpold for no more than one minute. Then Max starts asking them questions in order to keep the discussion going. It is hard work and he ends up answering most of the questions he asks. Then he asks whether they have questions and before he has even finished his question they chant 'No' and dash back to their seats. The same happens with all of the other groups, most of them making no effort at all at a presentation but just waiting for his questions. Despite his promise of 'no wrong answers', he ends up correcting them several times. For example, when they answer one of his questions by saying that the Roman Colosseum was bigger than the Congress Hall, he tells them that the Nazi building was the larger. Occasionally the teacher intervenes to try to remind the pupils of things that they were supposed to have learnt the day before. The pupils become increasingly fidgety and Max draws things to a close. He asks them what they thought of it: 'boring' is the chanted response. He says that they could have made their presentations more interesting.

Afterwards, poor Max is exhausted. Anke offers some insightful criticisms. There is too much material and detail, she says; and that once the groups knew that Max would step in and ask, and answer, questions, it just let them off the hook of doing anything. He agrees that he fell into his usual tour-guide routine, just spouting all the information as he would in that context. Anke is doubtful about whether this is the right approach for this theme. Despite his earlier enthusiasm for this pedagogical approach, so too, today, is Max.

* * * * *

In this chapter I have given examples of some of the struggles involved in practical pedagogical work of accompanied witnessing of difficult heritage. Some of these struggles are common to most heritage tours: difficulties of keeping a group's attention, getting them to keep up or not wander off, being heard, helping them to 'see' or 'experience' the past. Others, however, are more specific to dealing with difficult heritage: making links between past and present; conveying moral values without, perhaps, appearing too overtly to do so; creating the 'right' kinds of identifications and interpretations. In the case discussed here – a site created to have 'eye impact', to speak directly to the emotions, to enlist those who encounter it to the Nazi project – the difficulties are sometimes especially complex. History-workers seek to enable visitors to perceive, or even directly feel, the material suggestivity of the site and at the same time to avoid its perceived agency.

History-workers also work with, and around, the preconceptions, dispositions and behaviour of the groups whom they accompany. This can be very hard, especially if the participants are resistant to taking part or if they are uninterested or at least feel compelled to perform that they are. Even in less extreme cases, however, history-workers face the challenge of trying to guess where those they are guiding might be coming from, sometimes literally as well as metaphorically.

In the following chapter, I turn directly to those who come to the site. What draws them to such a place? And what do they make of it?

8

VISITING DIFFICULT
HERITAGE

The number of sites of difficult heritage, especially those of atrocity, has grown massively during the second half of the twentieth century and into the twenty-first.[1] In part, as I noted in the introduction, this is a dimension of a wider expansion of heritage in general. But it is also a development in its own right, showing particularly high levels of increase both in the number of such sites and the number of people visiting them. Hundreds of thousands of visitors from across the globe make their way to former concentration camps such as Auschwitz and Dachau, or to other sites of terror, such as the House of Slaves on Gorée Island, Senegal or the House of Terror in Budapest; or to museums of Holocaust, slavery or genocide. Since the Documentation Centre at the former Nazi Party Rally Grounds opened in 2001 it has received over 1.2 million visitors.[2]

Why do people visit such sites? This chapter addresses this question on the basis of empirical research carried out at the Rally Grounds and Dokuzentrum.[3] It is concerned not only with stated motivations but also with the ways in which people negotiate their visits, both in terms of how they talk about and frame them and what they actually do while there. It is also concerned with questions raised in earlier chapters about the negotiation of the materiality – the architectural monumentality – of the site, and interpretations of the *Fascination and Terror* exhibition, especially insofar as these may give wider insights into negotiations of difficult heritage.

My research was not only carried out at the Dokuzentrum but also involved participant-observation and interviewing of people present at other parts of the site, engaged in activities such as sitting on benches, playing tennis or roller-blading, as well as on guided tours. This is dissimilar from many other sites of difficult heritage, which typically are more bounded and single-purpose than the Rally Grounds. Nevertheless, the boundaries and seepage between a heritage site – and the interlude of a heritage visit – and the rest of life are a consideration in all kinds of heritage sites both for those managing and for those visiting them.[4] Here, where there is what some visitors perceive as a peculiar, and even objectionable, mixing of activities, these questions of boundaries, seepage and 'appropriateness' are more evident, especially in the moralised commentary by some of those who come to the place.

Researching visiting

My account is partly informed by participant-observation – walking around the area, alone or with others, sitting on the benches, drinking coffee in the cafés, going to the fair and other events held at the site, attending tours and visiting the Dokuzentrum and, earlier, the exhibition in the Zeppelin Building. As well as people who I met at the site, there are many who came to visit it with me – friends and relatives, and also a group of students from the Institute of Sociology at the University of Erlangen-Nuremberg, who also answered a questionnaire for me and participated in group discussions. In addition, I read through thousands of entries in the visitor comment books held by the Dokuzentrum and the earlier exhibition in the Zeppelin Building; and have talked to tour-guides and staff at the Dokuzentrum about their experiences (see also Chapter 7) and research.[5] The main source of the discussion that follows, however, are 60 semi-structured interviews that I carried out with people who I met for the first time at the Rally Grounds. These were conducted either with groups or individuals, depending on how they were visiting. In total this comprised about 110 people.[6]

Twenty of my interviews were carried out in the summer of 2000, before the opening of the Dokuzentrum. Of these, three were with people who had just visited the *Fascination and Terror* exhibition in the Zeppelin Building and another with a woman who was about to go and visit it. The remaining16 were conducted in many different parts of the main area of the Rally Grounds, my aim simply being to try to interview as broad a range of people as possible. Some of those I interviewed were sunbathing, some were walking dogs, some were playing tennis and so on. As I was approaching people 'cold' I knew little about them in advance: only the activity in which they were engaged, their gender and, roughly, their age. I could also sometimes identify tourists by cameras and guidebooks. Of these people, just under half had visited the exhibition at some point. Thirty of the thirty-eight people interviewed lived in Nuremberg or its immediate surrounding, four elsewhere in Germany, and four – of whom three were in one family – in other countries, England and France.

In the summer of 2003 I carried out another 40 interviews. Twenty of these (about 40 people) were conducted in the Dokuzentrum, with people who had just visited the exhibition. Perhaps surprisingly, only one of these was from Nuremberg, and he was currently living elsewhere, and one other a student in the nearby town of Erlangen. Ten were from other countries – Switzerland, the USA, Australia and Namibia – and the rest from other parts of Germany, ranging from Hamburg to Karlsruhe.[7] The remaining 20 interviews were conducted, as in 2000, across the Rally Grounds and I tried to loosely match the sites where I had interviewed previously. Half of these interviewees were from Nuremberg or the immediate area, a quarter from elsewhere in Germany and a quarter from other countries. Just under a third had visited the Dokuzentrum, with two of these and one other having also visited the earlier exhibition in the Zeppelin Building; and I later met one couple again who I had interviewed earlier, before they had visited, and talked with them briefly about it.

My interviews began with a brief explanation that I was a university researcher interested in asking them about 'this place' (in German I said '*dieses Gelände*'). I began with general questions about where they had come from, where they lived, how often they came and for what reasons; and then continued with more questions about whatever activities they engaged in there, including which areas they had visited, their views on whether anything should be altered at the site and what it meant to them. I asked visitors who had visited the Dokuzentrum or earlier exhibition about these, including aspects that they especially remembered and how long they had spent there. I also asked what other similar places people had visited – a question that I purposefully left open in order to try to access the kinds of comparisons that they would make. And I asked about what they knew about the history of the site and where they had learnt about 'this history'. In addition, I gathered basic socio-demographic data – age, occupation, place of residence – and invited participants to make further comments and to ask me questions; and generally used prompts and supplementary questions to allow interviewees to take our conversation wherever they chose. The aim of this kind of qualitative research is not to try to determine frequencies of different kinds of responses but instead to indicate and explore the range and kinds of ways in which people talk about particular themes. One feature of such research is that it typically produces rich material, which is hard to do justice to without presenting extensive quotations. The longer visitor interventions that I include here (and in some earlier chapters) provide an indicative glimpse.[8]

A first interview

It is mid-morning on a warm, clear day in August. A woman is sitting on a bench, looking out over the Dutzend lake, in which the Congress Hall is reflected. I have seen her before and we've nodded and smiled. She is one of the 'regulars' at the Rally Grounds, as I have noticed in my days of walking the terrain, while I have been trying to build up the courage to interview people. Fortunately, she is amenable to being interviewed – something which I continue to be surprised is the case with almost all those I approach. During the course of our conversation I learn, among other things, that she lives nearby, on a main street, and has been coming to walk here and enjoy the air for over 30 years, and that for the last 10 years, since she retired at age 60, she has generally spent about three to four hours per day here. She knows the people and even the dogs. For her, this is a social space, a place to encounter friends and acquaintances.

Nevertheless, she – I will call her Frau Müller – is also well aware of the site's history and has previously reflected on what should be done about the buildings like the Congress Hall, which, she tells me, the 'Amis' (US forces) had wanted to blow up but it was too expensive, too large and too difficult. Her view now, she says, is that it should be left. She didn't think this previously but then a Romanian woman told her that Germans have, not culture (*Kultur*) but 'what was it? Yes, past' (*Ja, Vergangenheit*); to which she added 'and we should not forget'.

After asking me about where I am from and why I came here, she tells me about all sorts of changes that have happened to the site over the years and about her experiences with Americans who she came to know because her brother had a car-washing business just over the back-wall from where many of them were stationed in Fürth. She then begins on a story about how one day when she was near here in her car, a '*Schwarzer*', a black man, waved to her and she waved back. Then the police pulled her over and asked 'Did you wave to the Negro (*Neger*)?' She said yes and they asked if she knew him. Alerted by their use of the word '*Neger*' she concocted a tale of how he had helped her with her car when it was broken down one day. They query whether this is a reason to wave to him and she retorts that if they (i.e. the policemen) had helped her she would have waved back to them likewise. They then suggest that she has been drinking – it is 11 a.m. – and she tells them that she would be happy to blow into the bag. 'What can I say?', she comments, 'they must have been racist'. She doesn't like to say this about Germans (*Deutsche*) but this is the only explanation. Her own view is that people are people ('*Menschen sind Menschen*'). I ask: 'could this have happened anywhere or was it especially likely here?' She thinks anywhere but that things are even worse since the Wall came down because lots more neo-Nazis from the East have come over. Even the parents of her nephew's wife, who is from the East, say that the Wall should have been built higher rather than pulled down.

Why people come

Not surprisingly for such a mixed site, people's motivations for being there could be very various.[9] For many, such as Frau Müller in the intervention above, they were visiting a pleasant leafy space, where they could walk, take the air, sit and meet friends. For people living in the surrounding area, the site is the only large park nearby; though many people also travel some considerable distance to use it for leisure purposes. For example, two teenage girls told me that they travel about 40 minutes every other week to play tennis, and sometimes other sports, here; and a man in his late sixties told me he travels for about an hour once per week just to spend time walking in what he regards as an especially amenable green area. Among those who I interviewed who were not there to visit Nazi heritage, the most common replies to my question of why they were there were either 'relaxation' (*Entspannung*) or specific activities such as 'to sunbathe' or 'to roller-blade'; and to my question of 'What does this place mean to you?' the most frequent replies were 'fresh air' and 'peace and quiet'. One local woman born in 1938 told me, for example, that she comes 'to recover my nerves, against stress'; and a man who lives nearby, born 1941, said: 'I am at home here. I come to recover from everyday stress'. Moreover, many people who I met elsewhere on other occasions, including students in the university, told me that they had visited the grounds but only to park their cars there while visiting the city's Christmas market, to go to a football match, rock concert or the fair.

Despite the fact that the great majority of visits to the site are not undertaken as part of visiting Nazi heritage, this does not mean that people are unaware of the site's history. On the contrary, every person whom I interviewed – whether lying sunbathing or having a barbecue – knew that this was the site of the Nuremberg rallies, and many spontaneously told me facts about the buildings' history. Their motivations to be there, however, were other; and the site's heritage was, in this context, irrelevant. This did not mean that it was necessarily irrelevant in all contexts: almost half of those who were there for leisure purposes had on previous occasions visited an exhibition or attended a tour about the site's history, and the majority of others said that they intended to do so at some point. I return to this below.

But what of those who were there to visit a Nazi site? Why did they choose to do so? The most common reply to my question was 'history' – an interest in history in general, and often more specifically in the history of the Third Reich or Nazi period. For those visitors for whom this was part of a more generalised historical interest, they typically replied to my question about other 'similar' places that they had been with examples of other historical sites such as castles or Nuremberg's Old Town. The latter was also part of a visiting of this site as one of the places to visit as part of a visit to Nuremberg.[10] Although my sample is too small to draw any general conclusions, there was a greater proportion of people visiting the site as part of visiting Nuremberg subsequent to the building of the Dokuzentrum than was the case beforehand, suggesting that this had put the Rally Grounds onto the Nuremberg tourist itinerary to an extent that was not the case previously. As part of this general 'visiting Nuremberg', a visit to the Rally Grounds and Dokuzentrum was typically sandwiched between activities such as visiting the castle, Dürer's house and eating *Lebkuchen* or Nuremberg sausages; and can be seen as part of a more general touristic 'doing of place' that seeks to experience a location through engagement in what are presented as the significant 'to dos' of its tourist offer.

Among people who come specifically to see the architectural remains of the site of the Nuremberg rallies, some surely do so as part of an appreciation of what they regard as the achievements of the Third Reich. However, I only met one person in the course of my interviews who was almost unequivocally appreciative: Mr Smith, who I described in an intervention in Chapter 2. Coming to this place was, for him, another realisation of his collecting of Nazi memorabilia and historical information. As he explains: 'I am absolutely fascinated. I have been studying it for years. I studied it before you were born! I probably know more than the locals ... I have been reading books, I have watched videos.' Actual visiting, he maintains, goes beyond this second-hand knowledge. Here, at 'the place itself', he tells me, he can 'hear the crowds' and 'feel the energy'. He is particularly thrilled to have stood in the same place as Hitler ('it was incredible'). What he describes is a physical impulse from the place and buildings: a high level of material suggestivity that is experienced corporeally as well as intellectually. Gaining these in-site experiences is something that he has also done elsewhere: he tells me that he has also been to the Eagle's nest and 'I stood on the Führer bunker in Berlin'. Quite where the motivation for such an interest came from in the first place is not something that I properly pursued, though his comment that 'the Luftwaffe dropped bombs on me, the buggers', when he lived in Portsmouth as a child, suggests that the place of wartime as significant in his own lifetime was partly what prompted his interest in the period.

The majority of those visiting this Nazi site as part of a historical interest share the idea that being physically present at a heritage site is significantly different from learning about it through books or other sources, even if they do not claim to experience the 'power' of it quite as forcefully as Mr Smith does. For example, a man from East Germany now living in Bayreuth, who describes himself as of 'the generation that did not experience it directly' (he was born in 1962), explains that 'to see it with your own eyes is more important than what you learn in school. It helps you really grasp it'. He was bringing his fourteen-year-old daughter to visit partly for this reason and because he believed it important that 'young people should not forget' and because, he claimed, she learnt virtually nothing about it at school, even though 'Bayreuth was an especially brown city'. Many others also contrasted making an actual visit with book learning, saying that the embodied encounter, in the words of one of them, 'makes it more real and memorable'. This is a familiar theme in tourism research – that, as Jack Kugelmass nicely puts it, what is involved in a 'sensualiz[ation of] history', and one that is made more evocative and memorable through being embodied practice.[11] Moreover, what seems to be involved is that visitors conceptualise a scale of meaningfulness of sources, some describing how still more significant – and 'real' – for them were eye-witness accounts from their grandparents.[12]

Those who are visiting the Dokuzentrum or going on tours frame their physical encounter as part of an educational event. They are there, they say, in order to learn more about the Nazi past. This learning itself, however, is cast as what seems to be the most important motivation of many to visit. This is as a kind of moral duty to bear witness to an atrocious past; this being expressed by some simply as something that one 'should do'. As such, attendance becomes as much an act of commemoration as of education. When asked about other 'similar' places that they had visited, such visitors typically listed concentration camps or perhaps Jewish museums or the Anne Frank house in Amsterdam. And in response to a question about what should happen to the site in future, they emphasised that it should be retained and, frequently, that it should be retained as a memorial, or, more specifically, as a *Gedenkstätte* – a memorial-educational complex – or a *Mahnmal* – a warning memorial.[13] Almost all such visitors, at some point during our discussions, expressed the idea that remembering the horrors of the past was especially important in order to avoid repeating it. Two Jehovah's Witnesses, for example, recall how Jehovah's Witnesses too were persecuted by the Nazis and tell me that it is important 'that it is all remembered, in order to avoid making the same mistakes again'; and a man in his late thirties tells me that an exhibition is useful 'if it is directed at young people to help prevent hate and violence'. *Nie wieder!*, *Never again!*, was the most frequently inscribed statement in the Dokuzentrum visitor books.[14]

Making visits to sites associated with atrocity is, then, for many people a means through which they can perform their own commitment to remembering and, thus, to helping to avoid bad history being repeated. It is almost a talismanic activity that can contribute towards warding off a bad future. Many such visitors spontaneously emphasised that they thought it especially important that young people make such visits in order to avoid the past 'falling into forgottenness', as one older woman put it. Despite the fact that the Rally Grounds was a site of perpetration rather than primarily directly of suffering, it is perceived by many of those engaged in moral witnessing as one element within a network of sites connected with Nazi atrocity. This is not to say that they all necessarily think that it is quite the same kind of site as sites of suffering, neither that it should be presented or treated in quite the same way. The intervention below, which reports the discussion about it by two women, is one of several examples of visitors discussing this. Others also made contrasts between the Rally Grounds and concentration camps, saying, for example, that they found visits to places such as Dachau made more of an emotional impression upon them, some describing them as more 'authentic' than the Dokuzentrum exhibition. A German woman born in 1938 (speaking in English) put it this way: 'But another thing is to walk on the ground in a concentration camp. It is awful. The ground began to speak. But I still think here it is very good'. Nevertheless, despite its different historical role, the Rally Grounds has come to be seen by many as a place for bearing witness not just to Nazi power but also of the atrocity of Holocaust. For some visitors, as I discuss further below, this has consequences for their perception, and moral evaluation, of how the site is maintained and used.

If these are the main motivations to visit, I should also note that not all visitors were there of their own accord and that motivation should not be seen as only a matter of individual decision-making. Visiting is almost always co-visiting; and even people who attend alone may have made their decision in relation to others (e.g. a friend who advised them to come). Moreover, a significant feature of visiting heritage sites and exhibitions is that other people are also present and that this affords the possibility of viewing and judging how others also behave. This is another dimension of moral witnessing: a witnessing of others and opening of oneself up to be viewed in public. Moral witnessing is always, in some sense, accompanied witnessing (see Chapter 5). More specifically, school children, youth groups and soldiers in particular were typically attending the Dokuzentrum as part of organised tours, arranged as part of a moral education. Soldiers – members of the Bundeswehr – explained to me that their visits (which often also involved spending time undertaking activities in the study forum) were part of a wider, national, educational programme which also involved trips to other sites, such as concentration camps. Making such visits has been on the curriculum in most German schools for at least the past decade.[15]

Historical consciousness

The idea that the past can provide lessons for the present and future is, then, pervasive among those visiting this heritage site and widely socially institutionalised. In most cases, how this lesson provision might work more specifically or what kinds of precise content it might provide are not spelled out. What is involved, rather, is a more general assumption that history teaches and that knowing about it is in itself a way of making sure that there is less chance of bad events being repeated. This talismanic-pedagogical historical consciousness is, I suggest, widespread and itself implicated in the expansion of heritage visiting. It involves a particular temporal orientation – or way of relating to history – as historical theorist Jörn Rüsen has put it.[16] More specifically, it entails an understanding of the past as to some degree separate from the present – and generally as parcelled into specific episodes – but also as open to analogical interpretation.[17] That is, it is an orientation in which we can legitimately make comparisons between 'then' and 'now'; and can think through the present via historical information. This may sometimes play out, especially in the repeated invocation of 'never again', as a 'subject[ion] of history to trauma theory which makes all presents and futures into mere repetitions'.[18] Involved here too is a democratisation: such thinking of the present through the past belongs not only in the realm of experts but is something in which lay-people may also engage.

In the case of the Nazi past, its separateness and distance from the present was not uniformly conceptualised by visitors, and this in turn seemed to be related to differentials in the extent to which they made analogies between past and present. In what I have elsewhere called a 'present orientation', but that might better be discussed as 'cosmopolitan memory' in Levy and Sznaider's terms (see Chapter 6), there was much evidence of drawing on the past to comment on the present.[19] Respondents might, for example, move spontaneously from discussing the Nazi period to talking about the war in Iraq or what they saw as a dangerous rise in neo-Nazism in Germany following reunification. Such visitors were also especially likely to identify specific features of the Nazi regime and then to generalise out from these into actions that they could see in operation in the present, engaging in a disconnection from the specific case even while beginning from it. They might talk of 'racism', the term most often used in German being *Ausländerfeindlichkeit*, literally animosity to foreigners. This could encapsulate both the anti-Semitism of the Nazi period and other kinds of racism evident in the present – exemplifying a move to a more capacious and less place-bound category in just the way suggested in arguments about cosmopolitan memory. Visitors making such links with the present were also likely to talk of the site as acting as a *Mahnmal* and to comment upon the importance of its persistence into the future as such, especially for younger generations. That is, they also expressed the future-orientation characteristic of a cosmopolitan memory formation.

Lessons for today

The following is taken from an interview with an Irish-born American, born 1935, who had just come out of *Fascination and Terror*.

> To go through it [the exhibition] and to see what happened in those years, it makes one aware that certain things like that are happening. Also, that we must be as alert today about the horror that is taking place all over the world, as we are made aware by the horror that was here. So I was very touched and moved – and challenged – by the presentation … The remark that came to me was 'Peace to All, Peace be with all of Creation' …

We need to be reminded not just of what has happened in the past but what could happen now and in the future, when one person or a few people – whether they are charismatic or not, and obviously it's a bit more dangerous if they are charismatic – or what can happen, or what manipulation can take place, and how symbols can be used and abused for another purpose. It's happening today just as much as it was happening in the 1930s and 1940s. But we turn a blind eye to it and we don't have exhibitions in the free world to indicate today that it is not just people in the past who can abuse power. People in the present can abuse power; leaders in the present day abuse power and manipulate justice. And war and control of economies is just as real today as it was back then. It can be conditioned for life or for use. Maybe it's happening today. Because none of the world powers today will examine themselves publicly. We only examine ourselves in the past. But that's not the point.

People younger than about twenty only infrequently mobilised such a present-oriented or cosmopolitan historical consciousness but instead were more likely to articulate the past as a relatively self-contained episode. As such, it was cast as more temporally distant from their current concerns, as an example of an atrocity of a different, perhaps even more thoroughly foreign, period. In both visitor books and interviews this kind of historical consciousness was evident in more frequent use of terms such as 'damals'/'then' and 'die Nazizeit'/'the Nazi period'.[20] Expressing this particularly strongly was the following comment about the *Fascination and Terror* exhibition in a visitor book: 'An impressive journey into an incomprehensible time'; or the comment of a teenage girl that the exhibition helped to tell you about 'how terrible things were in that time'. Also characteristic of many of these accounts was a focus on Hitler, evident, for example, in the younger visitors described below who wanted to know what had happened to Hitler, in their reference to the period as 'the Hitler time' or to the content of the exhibition or significance of the place as 'all about Hitler and so forth'. A group of younger teenage skateboarders in 2000 told me that they wouldn't mind what was in the new exhibition as long as it was interesting; and to my probe about what that might be, they replied 'stuff about Hitler'. (A thirteen-year-old girl also told me how the site had 'been built by Hitler'.) Such a focus on Hitler has the effect of turning the past events into a singularity, propelled primarily by an atypical individual. This is a very different way of relating to the Nazi past from one in which the past is understood primarily in terms of potentially 'transferable' lessons and concepts. Whether younger people will later in their lives come to develop a more cosmopolitan orientation to the past, or whether the Nazi past is for them more detached from the present than it is for older people, is difficult to determine. However, as university students – whose lives were also several generations removed from the direct experience of the war – were more likely to show cosmopolitan orientations than were those younger, it seems that engaging in such analogies may increase with age.

What happened to Hitler?

I interview a group of Pathfinders (*Pfadfinder* – a group rather like Scouts or Guides), aged between 13 and 17, who have just visited the exhibition. When I ask whether they have any further comments or questions, one girl pipes up 'What happened to Hitler?' It takes me a moment to realise what she is asking by which time a debate has broken out over whether he was one of the ones hanged in Nuremberg or did he escape to Russia. One of the older boys explains that he committed suicide in his bunker in Berlin, an account I confirm. 'He did die then?' she checks, it clearly being important to her to know that he did. Later, when I read through numerous comments in visitor books I notice that the question of what happened to Hitler comes up there too – not often, but now and then. It makes me realise that so much of the first part of the exhibition is focused on Hitler, especially visually. One consequence of this is that, for a sense of narrative satisfaction, visitors want to know what happened to him later – something that is not covered due to the narrative focus on Nuremberg. It also reminds me that visitors may construct narratives that pick up on exhibitionary cues in ways not anticipated by exhibition makers.

In my discussion of *Fascination and Terror* in Chapter 6 I noted that the exhibition avoids making links with the present, and that its account finishes with the Nuremberg trials. It may be that this contained account of the past helps to sustain the temporal orientation of past separateness that is exhibited by some of the younger visitors. Nevertheless, as I have described, it does not prevent many, especially older, visitors from talking analogically, often at length and with great eloquence, about the present and even future. Despite the fact that the exhibition itself can only be understood as cosmopolitan to a limited extent, such visitor accounts surely are. In Hall's terms, they are thoroughly 'negotiated' – partly taking on the 'encoding' of the exhibition but then moving on from it to range broadly across different parts of the world, referring not only to political events but also to other exhibitions or sites visited elsewhere.[21]

Not all of those visiting the Rally Grounds and making links between past and present did so, however, in approval of the Dokuzentrum or of broader attempts to educate about the Nazi past. Sitting on benches in the sunshine I met several groups of older people, all from the local area, who expressed annoyance at time and money being spent in this way. The majority of these had not visited the Dokuzentrum and one woman born in 1934 told me that she thought few of her generation would do so as they had experienced events first-hand. Such individuals argued in favour of severing past and present: typically this was expressed through the idea that a line – a *Schlussstrich* – should be drawn under the Nazi past, so that it was no longer 'for ever and ever something with which to beat us', as one local woman in her sixties put it. 'There has been', she said, 'enough stirring up [*Hetzerei*]. What is past is past'. Likewise, the electrician quoted at more length in an intervention below argued that there was 'much too much about the Nazis. We should look to the future and not to the past'. Nevertheless, those calling for a line to be drawn under the past, themselves often also engaged in other kinds of linking of this past and the present. In a conversation between two local women in their sixties, for example, they recalled the hardship that their mothers had endured in the years during and after the war and continued on from this to talk about the lack of social assistance at that time, compared with now, when, they claimed, all kinds of undeserving people – especially from Eastern Europe – manage to trick the system to acquire money from the state. From this they went on to talk of reparations to Jews, which they felt should no longer be continued (a theme which also arose in some other interviews with older local people). Theirs was, then, a mode of relating to the past in which they recognised continuities and themselves engaged in past–present analogies but at the same time argued for the selective making of particular temporal breaks.

Expressed here was also a resentment (and awareness) of what they saw as the capacity of certain other people to make or break what counted as publicly acceptable historical linkages. This was evident in a different way in the words of the local worker below who argued that Germany was being treated differently from other nations. Other respondents too, sometimes to different effect, pointed out the selective nature of historical accounts. In one interview, a man born in 1938 became angry when I raised the topic of the Dokuzentrum, arguing that history is written by the victors and reminding me forcefully of 'your Bomber Harris who destroyed Dresden' and who would, he argued, have been seen as a war criminal had Germany won the war.[22]

These various orientations to the Nazi past exemplified by interviewees were also part of their self-positioning and reflection on others. This was not just talking *about* the past and history but, as I discuss further in the following sections, also a way of drawing on it to negotiate identities and moral standpoints.

Ascribing heritage and identity

In Chapter 1 I suggested that some heritage posed particular identity difficulties, a history of perpetration being potentially especially unsettling. As we have seen in previous chapters, this was often perceived to be the case by those involved in publicly representing Nuremberg's Nazi heritage. But to what extent is this so for visitors too? And given that heritage is typically conceptualised as property, to whom is it seen to belong? That is, of whose identity is this heritage considered to be indicative?

As the discussion above suggests, many people, especially younger ones, may avoid identification with the heritage exhibited by seeing it as the product of a thoroughly other and past social collective: the Nazis. Self is defined contra 'the Nazis' in the 'then'/'now' temporal constructions employed by such visitors. For example, one teenager explained to me that 'then, in Nazi-times, you had to join in but now you are freer to decide what to do'. Rather than casting self-identity versus contemporary others, then, what is involved here is doing so via those of the past. While especially prevalent among younger visitors such a means of negotiating self was by no means restricted to them but might be employed by others too, sometimes alongside other kinds of differentiations and identifications. So while talking about Nuremberg, a respondent might effectively do so contra 'the Nazis'. One local man, for example, told me how 'the Nazis came to Nuremberg and made it the City of the Party Rallies'. He also talked of the 'destruction of Nuremberg' and its rebuilding postwar, and how the latter was still in process today. Nuremberg – the city and its inhabitants – was thus seen as still dealing with the aftermath of wrongs done to it.

Temporal differentiation was not only restricted to the Nazi period. Some visitors, particularly those in their forties and fifties, invoked generational differences. This was often itself reflexively expressed in terms of how their own approach to the past differed from that of the previous generation. Those who were from 'the generation of the time', explained a man in his fifties, tended to prefer to 'keep silent'. This was in contrast to what he regarded as a preferable willingness to address the past among those 'who came after'. Such 'generational talk' is common in Germany, frequently being invoked in newspapers, for example; and many people simply talk about themselves as being one of 'those born after' – the implicit reference point is the Third Reich and, thus, the potential to have been a perpetrator. An interviewee born in 1941, for example, described himself as *'quasi Nachkrieggebohren'* – 'practically born after the war'. Such comments illustrate too the embeddedness of 'the war' as a reference point in continuing self-identification.

But what of national and local identifications? Visitors from outside Germany, who were nearly always visiting the site specifically in order to see the Nazi heritage, almost invariably talked about Germany and Germans. This was German heritage and the way in which it had been treated was evidence of a German 'mentality', as one Swiss visitor put it – though he also acknowledged that it was 'part of European history'. Another Swiss visitor, when asked his impressions of the place, replied simply *'ratlose Deutsche'* – meaning Germans at a loss to know what to do. Despite such references to 'Germans', however, this is not to say that 'Germans' were necessarily considered to be a homogeneous and unchanging mass. Rather, what was taken-for-granted – in the way that Michael Billig regards as typical of banal nationalism[23] – was that the Nazi heritage was German. As such, foreign visitors might talk about the neglect of parts of the site as evidence of 'Germans wanting to forget about their past', as some Canadian visitors did; or they might equally praise Germans or Germany in terms like the following by a US visitor commenting on the Dokuzentrum:

> it just struck me that this can be here in this country in which this horror grew up at the time. That's a great tribute. In America, in the US, I wish [laughs] we could do something about some of the horrors that continue to be. It's a brave thing to do. And a great thing for the present generation to have for the future.

If the heritage was self-evidently 'German' to visitors from other countries, it was only partially so to visitors from Germany. The majority from places outside Nuremberg talked about the site and how it was being treated more specifically in terms of 'Nuremberg' rather than Germany. The city was usually invoked as the taken-for-granted agent; though occasionally respondents might specify the city council or authorities, or, in relation to the Dokuzentrum, its 'makers' or 'managers'.[24] Only infrequently did non-Nuremberg German visitors talk about the Rally Grounds as 'German' or see what was happening in Nuremberg as directly connected to their own lives. One eloquent exception was a science professor from the Rhineland, born in 1938, who told me that he had wanted to come to the Rally Grounds precisely 'because there is so much silence about it in Germany'. 'Our government believes', he explained, 'that a temptation [*Verführung*] comes out from it, like a sweet poison or something, that one is no longer allowed to show the Germans'. This, he said, was analogous to the way that 'you are also not allowed to buy *Mein Kampf* in Germany – either because it is too poisonous, or because the Germans are so immature'. The result was 'that one isn't allowed to experience anything at all'. I must not, though, take him in any way as a typical respondent, he concluded: 'I am not the majority; I am never the majority'.

Among many, though not all, visitors, then, whether German or not, the tendency was to see the difficult heritage as belonging to others. Such an attribution of ownership could exist alongside making comparisons with other cases. So, for example, two black Americans talked of how they admired how Germany was looking at its own past and contrasted this with what they saw as the much more reluctant and limited addressing of slavery in their own country – 'if only back home would take such an enlightened view on its history, *our* history. You have to admire the Germans for how they are looking at theirs so head on'. Visitors from other parts of Germany likewise, while seeing the site as particularly the product of 'Nuremberg', simultaneously talked about how in their own localities there had been similar, sometimes earlier, moves to somehow marking or commemorating the atrocities of Nazism. While they engaged in cosmopolitan analogy-making, then, they simultaneously ascribed 'ownership' – and effectively responsibility for – the Nazi Party Rally Grounds to others than themselves.

So what of those from Nuremberg? Only very few used deictic linguistic forms such as 'we' or 'our' that implied a sense of ownership or identity with this heritage.[25] Frequently, they used passive forms that avoided needing an agent. So, for example, they might talk of how it was good that there was now a documentation centre or they might refer to an event such as the renovation of the Great Road, but without mentioning who had undertaken this. It might be the case, as Michael Billig's discussion of deixis suggests, that such forms can be evidence of taking an identity category (he talks of the nation) for granted. However, given such respondents' tendency in other parts of their talk to refer to, say, the Nazis, as mentioned above, or to the city authorities, it seems more likely that these agent-less constructions are more reflective of a sense of events happening beyond respondents' control and perhaps even without their knowing who was involved.

While there is a clear tendency, then, for all of those confronted by difficult heritage to engage in a kind of identity-partitioning that results in the heritage being seen as not belonging to them, this is not to say that they do not recognise the identity problems involved in negotiating such heritage. Visitors from outside Germany discussed, often with great sensitivity and sophistication, the dilemmas for Germans of addressing this history and of whether they might end up 'always having to keep thinking about it', as a woman from Britain put it. So too did visitors from other parts of Germany in relation to Nuremberg. And many of those from Nuremberg, even if they tended not to see themselves as in any way responsible for the developments at the Rally Grounds site, talked about questions of how the city would be seen in relation to either addressing or appearing to hide this aspect of its history. Here, with the exception of the minority which voiced the view that too much attention was given to the Nazi past, visitors agreed that it was right that this history was being acknowledged and education provided about it. Many gave descriptions of how the Nazi past had been less acknowledged in earlier years – some remarking, for example, on the fact that the earlier exhibition was only open for part of the year or that visitors often couldn't even find the site – and approved a change towards what they regarded as a greater openness on the part of Germany/Nuremberg. 'I think it is right that we should talk about these things more', said one man who had been a member of the Hitler Youth, 'and I think it is right that we should make sure that the young people know about it all. Yes, it is a good thing that there is this museum [i.e. the Dokuzentrum]'. Some talked about the shift as a consequence of generational change – 'We probably had to wait until the perpetrator generation was gone' said a doctor in his fifties; and the science professor quoted above commented that the silence which he observed 'might change now that Leni Riefenstahl has died'. Many also talked about it in terms of recognising a need to ensure that a younger generation would know about the events – that they would 'never forget' – 'even when all of the eye-witnesses have gone, as they almost have already', as the doctor noted. The shift was sometimes also characterised simply as evidence of 'a more mature approach', as a South African teacher put it. This was an approach in which the country/city was seen as having attained a more advanced identity, capable of acknowledging and reflecting upon their own dreadful heritage.

A kind of cosmopolitanism?

An electrician born in 1966 is sitting on a bench smoking a cigarette and reading the *Bild*, a tabloid newspaper, during his lunch break from his workplace nearby. He comes very often because it is near and he likes to get a bit of peace and relaxation during his lunch break; and he has come to know the whole area quite well, though has not visited the exhibition in the Zeppelin Building and the Dokuzentrum is not yet open. He thinks it's making a good development, he says, as it will attract tourists and bring money to the city. But he hopes that there won't be anything about Nazis in it as there is already far too much about them.

> We should look to the future instead of the past. Other countries also have bad things in their pasts. OK, Germany's was especially brutal but it is now fifty years ago. France was as bad, and England with the colonies was too in the past. People shouldn't just go on about Germany. The exhibition should be about criminal humanity and not just about criminal

Germans. Maybe [he pauses] it should not just be about humanity but perhaps animal welfare or the environment ... There is just far too much about the Nazis, it's always on TV and in the newspapers. It's all to do with the media. A few weeks ago everything was about ferocious dogs and strangely a child seemed to be being attacked every day. Now it's all about neo-Nazis. Next week perhaps it will be child abuse or pornography. So I don't take the media too seriously.

Material suggestivity

In making moral commentaries about how history had been addressed – either by Germans or Nuremberg – visitors frequently did so through observations about the physical site itself. That is, its state and what had been done with it were talked about as evidence of how Germans or Nuremberg had negotiated their past. Thus, the Spanish student quoted in Chapter 1 talked of the weeds growing on the Zeppelin Building as indicating a neglecting of the past. So too did other visitors. Both Mr Smith and a man in his thirties from the former East said that the neglect of the Zeppelin Building in particular showed that 'they' wanted to 'bury' this past. The buildings were thus regarded as both metaphors for, and tangible evidence of, the historical consciousness of those responsible for this heritage.[26] More vociferously, a group of Canadians in their early thirties expressed shock at the way that the Zeppelin marching ground had been grassed over and turned into football pitches – something that one of them described as 'gentrification'. One said 'This place sends a message: let's forget about it'; and another expanded, 'It's like Germany's black mark – they want to hide this history and forget about it'. They made comparisons with the US 'where there's plaques everywhere and you have, like, the Holocaust Museum in Washington'. People playing tennis or skateboarding were described as 'just ignoring history, and Jews, who were the ones who really suffered because of all of this'. The place should instead be redeveloped as a location in which 'to learn about history' and as 'a shrine to Jews and the Holocaust'.

Other visitors, however, were less disapproving. A woman from London, born in 1946, thought for a while about the mixed uses of the place and the fact that many parts seemed to be falling into disrepair and concluded that she thought that this was 'right – there shouldn't be a special effort to look after it or treat it as special. Just leaving it to crumble gives a certain feeling. No, they shouldn't do anything differently – they should just leave it to decay'. And a couple of women from Frankfurt, taking a stroll out across the area during their lunch-break while on a work-related visit nearby, talked through arguments for and against different approaches to such heritage as they pondered the question of what should be done. Their discussion, which also ranges into other key themes, is reproduced below as an example too of the ways in which visitors may collectively negotiate complexities of the site as they jointly reflect upon it.

Negotiating a difficult site

Two women, born 1964 and 1974, who I will call Frau A and Frau B respectively, are sitting on the steps of the Zeppelin Building. They are from Frankfurt and are in Nuremberg, a city that they have never been to previously, for work reasons. It is their first day and, as they are working nearby, they have come to look around the former Nazi Party Rally Grounds during their lunch break. The following is an excerpt from our discussion, held in September 2003.

SHARON: What do you think of this place?

FRAU A: Disappointing!

SHARON: Why?

FRAU A: Well, because it is all torn apart. I mean, I can understand it, but I had somehow thought that there would be more left. I saw a report on television and it was ..., it showed around here and somehow I had the impression that it was more or less maintained as it was. But you have to really search and here you've got the rows to the right [she gesticulates to where the seating of the Zeppelin field would have been] and, there, to the left, and so you can see the boundaries. But it is all totally destroyed; and there behind, behind the stands. So in principle you could take it all away given how it now is.

FRAU B: Yes, one simply imagined it otherwise. One naturally knows it from all those Nazi films, and, yes, here it now is ...

FRAU A: Even with the fences and the trees it now is ...

FRAU B: But despite that I find it somehow strange, because you imagine what once happened here.

FRAU A: Only unfortunately you don't experience it fully ... though you are also impressed by ... even the building style, I find it so ugly. I think it is ... well, does it remain impressive? Only for what it was once used. That is then another matter; but that has been lost.

SHARON: Have you seen other buildings here?

FRAU A: No. We came straight here. There are hardly any signs and it isn't easy to find. And the Nurembergers don't really know. We asked about it ...

SHARON: And they didn't know where? [Agreement] What does this place mean to you?

FRAU B: Well, I have no personal feelings about it. I am too young for that.

FRAU A: It simply interested me. It interested me and it also belongs, I think, to that which one just knows about. It would also have interested me if it had all been beautiful here.

SHARON: Should anything be changed here?

FRAU B: Everything costs a lot of money to maintain. So, I think, there is surely no longer anything else like here. So it would be good if this here could be kept. But then you would need to tear it all down again and bring it back to condition, just in order to give the impression of its enormous size, or, I don't know how to say it … I think another function is … a warning-memorial [*Mahnmal*] function or some such. There are, I think, other things. There are, for example, plenty of concentration camps in Germany that have been renovated. I think those are more effective as warning-memorials than here, because if you were to renovate here, that would only result in something beautiful. That [gesticulating to Zeppelin Building] would look like a lovely, impressive grandstand but not like a warning-memorial. And so I also think that it should surely somehow be maintained … and surely they are also doing that in a way … But whether it is worth it, or what can be achieved by it … Maybe one should also call a halt.

FRAU A: That is the question. Because it would also become difficult again, if one actually held events here, if these were offered, then … if it was actually … then it would be the question here again; well, OK, there weren't actually people killed here in that sense but despite that it is then naturally very difficult.

FRAU B: That is perhaps the reason why nothing was done here for so long.

[…]

FRAU A: If you wanted to renovate it, say, then you shouldn't, as already said, hold fun events here. Or if you have to use it for something completely different, and forget what happened here … but you can't do that either …

FRAU B: Or, on the contrary, you could now say, we'll celebrate here against the opinion of what the Nazis thought or did. You could take it as a counter-event [*Gegenveranstaltung*], which would also make it profane, without question.

FRAU A: You can interpret it in so many ways and… over the years that also gets forgotten, that's clear … Why not use it for something else? Then probably it will just get used for that. I know from old photographs that it was very impressive. So it is difficult, yes, without question.

FRAU B: I don't know for sure what should be done here, and what not. It is not so burdened as a concentration camp, certainly …

FRAU A: But it naturally presents something from a regime that one does not want anymore […] I am very ambivalent about what should be done … It is difficult.

Unusual in this interview, and partly a function of the lengthy working through of possibilities, is the idea of profaning the site through particular kinds of activities. As we have seen in earlier chapters this is an idea promoted by some of those involved in the management of the site, though generally in relation to existing casual uses for leisure activities, and for the physical neglect of the site, rather than the more active 'counter-events' that Frau B suggests here. No other visitors using the site in ways that some of the history workers might count as profanation used this or related language to describe their activities. Instead, they simply reported what they did or, if prompted to comment, casually remarked that they thought it acceptable that the place be used in such ways. As justification, some of them pointed out that it was a park before it was taken over by the National Socialists. They did not, however, express themselves as engaged in some kind of active profanation or countering of Nazi poison. This, I suggest, is partly because they did not load the site with such symbolic significance in the first place: it was simply a place at which a range of activities takes place, which they did not regard as incompatible with one another. A man born in 1934, playing tennis against the Zeppelin Building, put it this way: 'You get used to it. And then you don't think about it any more. It is a piece of history – nothing more'. As a 'piece of history' it should be kept, but, he laughed, it should also be resurfaced to improve its quality for playing tennis.

As I have noted above, any one individual may engage in a range of diverse activities at the site. For example, another man (b. 1956) who I talked to in 2000 as he took a break from playing tennis up the side of the Zeppelin Building, an activity that he came to the site for about once per month, had also visited the exhibition three times with youth groups, though had stopped doing so as they found it too 'intellectual' and 'worthy', and insufficiently 'direct'. He nevertheless talked at length about how important he considered education about the Nazi past to be and of the necessity to retain this particular place 'for future generations'. Carefully differentiating what he called the 'history function' and the 'sport function' of the grounds in his replies, he argued that more could be made of the place in both respects – these not in his view being at all incompatible.

Figure 8.1   Football fans at Nazi Party Rally Grounds for World Cup 2006

181

People may also engage in the 'history function' and 'sport function' on a single visit. When in 2006 Germany hosted the football World Cup, numerous visitors to football matches at Nuremberg's stadium on the Rally Grounds – where some of the matches were held – also went to visit the Dokuzentrum exhibition and other parts of the Rally Grounds site. In preparation for this event, new and more extensive information panels were also set up around the grounds, meaning that in future there would also be more chance of the history and sport functions overlapping to some extent.

The fact that people do not seem troubled by the idea of using the place in various ways – that others (such as the Canadians quoted above) might think incompatible or at least in bad taste – does not mean that they do not engage in any kind of symbolic interpretation of the site's materiality. On the contrary, this was widespread among all kinds of interviewees. As I noted in the previous chapter, many people told me, often with great relish, the story of the Silbersee – the poisonous lake. That the Nazis had left behind physical poison – either directly or indirectly as war rubble – that could continue to attract but that would only result in death was a compelling allegory. Some visitors remarked on the trees growing around the site in ways that seemed to imply that the Nazi presence on the site, and by analogy in the country, was declining. 'It is good that nature is coming back', said one local woman, 'that is what we need more of'. At the same time, however, it was not only the Spanish student who saw weeds growing on the Zeppelin Building as an indication of Germans or Nuremberg trying to ignore the past; and many people complained about litter, some of them attributing this to 'people today who don't show awareness' – a comment that sometimes seemed to have historical as well as environmental resonance.

How far the materiality of the site is suggestive directly to the senses or emotions, rather than being actively interpreted by visitors, is more difficult to determine. Certainly, physical qualities make practical differences to how people use it. The walls of the Zeppelin Building making for such good tennis practice, or the outer corridors of the Congress Hall providing quiet shelter in which to sleep rough, are just a couple of examples of uses of the site that were never originally intended but to which its material qualities lend themselves. But what of the intended Nazi effects? How far are the buildings and former marching grounds still able to impact and enchant in the ways that Hitler and Speer had hoped? Watching people using the place and hearing them talk about it, it seemed to me that there was little to indicate much of this. Certainly, some would stand where Hitler would have stood on the Zeppelin Building, and they might even give a Nazi salute, but this was typically accompanied by joking and parody. And, certainly, some visitors talked of the chilling nature of the site, prompting them to quiet reflection. The woman from London quoted above described the site as 'eerie' and giving her 'a funny feeling'. But in all of their accounts it seemed that what was involved was not so much being directly affected by particular calculated features of the architecture as by their own pre-formed visions of it. They accounted for their senses of disquiet by, for example, knowing that this was where Hitler stood or by imagining vast fervent National Socialist crowds chanting in unison on the marching fields. The London woman explained to me that she had seen the place on newsreels and photographs; as did Frau A and B from Frankfurt. Even Mr Smith, who claimed to 'feel the power' of the buildings went on to talk – in very specific visual detail – about how he was mapping his visual memories of Leni Riefenstahl's films onto what he could see in front of him.

The relative material ineloquence of this site, however, should not necessarily be taken to conclude that this is so for all buildings or places. On the contrary, in its original state the site would undoubtedly have been better – though never unequivocally – able to make particular affective suggestions. Now, however, broken up, grassed over, amputated, skated and cycled upon, it needs considerable assistance from other media, and from pictures held in visitors' imaginations, to do much affective work at all.

Future visions

In previous chapters we have seen how this site of difficult heritage has been negotiated primarily by history workers and others involved in its management and presentation over the years, and I have presented plans for the site to be, variously, destroyed, restored or altered. Plans, I have suggested, however apparently practical, are also indicative of other kinds of cultural assumptions and hopes.[27] In this chapter too we have seen how visitors' various ways of thinking about history and the past, and about materiality, may be reflected in their comments about what should happen in the future. As these have been discussed only partially and in passing, here I provide a brief overview of their speculations on the future of the Nazi Party Rally Grounds.

None of the visitors – even those who wanted a line to be drawn under the Nazi past – argued that any of the original buildings or grounds should be destroyed or removed. Overwhelmingly the most common response to my question about what should be done in the future was to keep what was there. This was often expanded to 'for future generations', 'as a place to learn history' or 'as a warning-memorial'. One woman, born in 1930, spoke for many when she emphatically replied: 'I think that it really must be preserved here in this place and it must for ever more be shown to people. It must never fall into forgottenness'.

On the extent to which such preservation should be accompanied by restoration, visitors were much more divided, with visitors from outside Germany generally arguing more frequently and strongly for at least some attempt to return the buildings or marching grounds to their original state. A man (b.1943) from Britain, for example, argued that 'it should be reconstructed to how it appeared in the 1930s – it was such a defining moment in German history'; and a marine engineer from Australia (b. 1968) argued not just for restoration but for completing the unfinished buildings. (He was especially keen on completing the vast glass roof planned for the Congress Hall.) That German respondents were much less likely to suggest any kind of restoration was surely related to their own greater discomfort over the idea of appearing to reconstruct anything from the Nazi period, physical reconstruction being seen as potentially a reconstruction of other Nazi qualities and agency. I have already discussed above some views on the mixed uses of the site. Several respondents also argued that it was important that the site – including the interiors of buildings such as the Congress Hall – be used for a range of purposes because this could bring a wider audience, who might then come into contact 'with the history by chance', as one woman put it. Even though many accepted that it was used in multiple ways, however, most were against any further building developments, especially, for 'commercial purposes'. This latter was also part of a more general opposing of commerce and making money with what were envisioned as higher aims of commemoration and history pedagogy – as we have seen in previous chapters too.

While many visitors, from Germany and elsewhere, argued for the importance of preservation of the physical structures as a means of preventing forgetting, there was some variation in how a memorial function was conceived. So while Canadian visitors stated that the site 'should be a shrine for Jews and the Holocaust', a student from Hamburg (b. 1978) argued that there should not be more information panels provided as this would 'turn it into a *Mahnmal*'. For him, a historical site was 'more objective', as he put it, if not marked in this way. Many more visitors, however, called for better signposting and more information panels (both of which have now been provided) – that is, for technologies to accompany people to learn and remember as part of their moral witnessing.

* * * * *

Perhaps more than anything, what talking to people at this site of difficult heritage made evident to me was how varied and sophisticated were the ways in which they talked both directly about it and used it as a prompt for reflecting on many connected matters. These included reflections on the past, present and future; on their own biographies and families as well as on the actions of governments, leaders, nations, members of the resistance and neo-Nazis.

A good deal of this talk, even among those visiting for leisure, was morally-inflected. (Recall Frau Müller's self-positioning reminiscences of racism, described in the first intervention in this chapter.) Difficult heritage prompts such ethical reflection. And this, I have suggested, is partly what draws many people to make educational visits to such sites. It provides an opportunity not only to learn about the particular histories that such places present but also to engage in broader moral consideration and self-positioning. Many interviewees did this spontaneously, without any direct prompting from me; and some commented on how they had already been discussing such matters among themselves. While all acknowledged that there were other information sources about the same topics, they regarded coming to an actual site – 'the place where history happened' – to nevertheless be distinctive and more effective in helping them 'grasp' it. The rather physical expression so often employed here – to 'grasp' (*greifen*, or to make *greifbar*) seems significant. One feature of physically attending an actual heritage site or exhibition is that, compared with many other kinds of sources, you are more forcefully pushed into paying attention. Many visitors commented on how the exhibition 'keeps you in there', some expressing a degree of irritation about this but several commenting that they thought this somehow right.[28] Moreover, making a visit typically entails a good deal of effort, many people having travelled considerable distances, which also increases their commitment to a relatively concentrated experience.

This relatively concentrated and collective experience is a dimension of what I have called moral witnessing. Attending a site of difficult heritage is also a performance of a wider commitment to remembering atrocity and evil, and, thus, to guarding against them. Although inherent in this understanding is the idea that what happens during the time-space of a heritage visit somehow seeps out beyond it, into everyday life, visitors nevertheless simultaneously regard such attention as something that they only need to attend to sometimes, almost like periodic inoculations. The woman who I quoted in Chapter 1, who doubted whether it was a good thing to spend too much time looking back at this history, put this idea well when she explained that nevertheless she thought it good to go back to it every 'now and then'. The Swiss visitor who had spent almost six hours in the exhibition told me that he was thinking of going to the fair later in the evening. I felt bad to disappoint him by telling him that it was not open on that particular day.

9

UNSETTLING DIFFICULT
HERITAGE

In this book I have followed the negotiations of one particular difficult heritage – Nazi heritage in Germany, and more specifically the largest site of remaining Nazi architecture, the former Nazi Party Rally Grounds in Nuremberg. Through this, I have attempted to identify different possible negotiating strategies – demolition, amputation, profanation, reconstruction, looking elsewhere, commemoration, art, education and moral witnessing – that might be used in relation to heritage, and especially awkward heritage, of various kinds. In doing so, I have sought to show some of the complications and implications of these approaches in practice.

I have also highlighted assumptions that the different forms of negotiation may involve – assumptions about, for example, the nature of investment, of material agency, the dangers of forgetting or repressing, or the imperative to avoid historical repetition. Such assumptions act as cultural 'givens', not necessarily for all those involved but for many of them. As such, they play a part in shaping actions in ways that may seem obvious or inevitable to those concerned – but that might be otherwise. As the account here has shown, the kinds of assumptions made – and the ways of negotiating that they inform – may alter over time. Likewise, those made in relation to other heritages, difficult and relatively comfortable, will not necessarily be identical. Part of my argument here is that attention should be given to exploring specific cases and also the untidiness of practice. Local specificities, actors and contingencies are ingredients in the shaping not only of the kinds of approaches that *are* taken but also those that are even contemplated, as well a what is ruled out. While recognising this specificity, however, nevertheless, at the same time, I expect that many of the assumptions – which act as partial negotiating frames – that I identify here will be found elsewhere. This is because heritage operates as what Collier and Ong call a 'global assemblage' – a globally recognised cultural form, made up of heterogeneous practices, technologies and ideas.[1] Like any global assemblage it is always, inevitably, locally realised, despite its prevalence; and in its local realisation it will be unique, even while it is simultaneously widespread. As I have attempted to chart here, what happens locally does so in multiple interactions with various elsewheres – embodied in people, practices and technologies (e.g. visitors, exhibition advisory committees, books read and visits made by history workers, legislation and funding opportunities). How heritage is negotiated in Nuremberg is always, though to varying extents, conducted in relation to how heritage is done in other places. This is so in cases of conscious avoidance of doing likewise as well as in cases of emulation. And it is so not only when city officials respect the spirit as well as the letter of the conservation regulations but also when they seek to flout or get round them. Because of the inevitability of local specification – or territorialisation – and its working out in practice, we need local studies; and we cannot conclude that they tell us about all other realisations. But they tell us about some. They alert us to possibilities. And they give us starting points for identifying patterns, and gathering analogies and differences to work beyond the case at hand.

My use of the term 'negotiation', as explained in the introduction, is intended to recognise the ongoing and often contested nature of the processes involved. Negotiation isn't a smooth process but entails friction – an encounter with a position that is different from our own.[2] The physical negotiation of a landscape involves trying to find your way around what is there, perhaps carving a route past obstacles or at least moving in acknowledgement and accommodation of what is there. But, as I have also emphasised, negotiation is not only about finding a way around what seems fixed. It is also constitutive. Through negotiations new entities – signposts, exhibitions, tours – may come into being. And through negotiations new identifications and alignments – as citizens refusing to allow history to be silenced, as moral witnesses, as those who want to draw a line under the past – may be mobilised. Such negotiation is also a process of positioning and repositioning. Both physically and discursively, we come to know more about where we stand, if only temporarily.

None of this means that what is involved is entirely fluid, shapeless and indeterminate. On the contrary, as I have described here, there are certain kinds of ways of negotiating that we find repeatedly – such as attempts to counter perceived Nazi enchantment – as well as processes such as oscillation, the tacking back and forth between different kinds of approaches that has characterised policy developments in Nuremberg over the years. While there certainly have been some significant shifts in approaches to the Nazi past – such as the increasingly medicalised and psychologised forms of historical consciousness – there have also been continuities as we have seen; and within both cultural policy-making and the wider population, including local people and tourists, a spectrum of approaches and assumptions can be found. Again, while I have charted these through a detailed specific example, there is much of wider resonance, precisely because so much of the local is entangled in material and discursive threads that criss-cross boundaries of multiple kinds.

The turn to difficult heritage

This book has charted the expansion of 'difficult heritage', especially within Germany, a country which has been to the forefront of such developments. As the case of Nuremberg has shown, these have often been highly contested; and some in Germany remain unconvinced about, or even opposed to, the increased and continuing public emphasis on the country's Nazi past.

In the immediate postwar years in Germany, West and East, there was some display of difficult heritage, often instigated by the occupying powers. This was typically undertaken in order to confront local populations with crimes that they might otherwise try to deny or forget. As when the local population of Weimar was taken around the Buchenwald concentration camp – walking in their Sunday best amidst the piles of corpses – the intention of those staging these encounters was to force Germans to acknowledge the horror done in their name. By doing so, it was hoped, they would never forget; and the persistence of such a vivid memory, imprinted through embodied encounter, would help to ensure that they would not allow such horror to be repeated. Many of the same ideas – the mnemonic effect of actual encounter, the moral dimensions of witnessing, history as talisman against future atrocity – were taken up by some Germans themselves, and harnessed to educational and ideological projects, in ways described in earlier chapters. While some such public displays of difficult heritage have been in place since soon after the war, and others established in the decades before German unification, it is since unification that the number of such public presentations has massively escalated. Moreover, it is during this most recent period that many earlier displays have been reworked, usually at least partly with the ostensible aim of making them more fully acknowledge difficulty, and resort less to ideologically comfortable accounts (this is especially so for such sites in the former East). A key part of this development too has been new levels of willingness to acknowledge and display the heritage of perpetration.

As this book has described, there have been many reasons given, and allegations made, over the years for not publicly marking or displaying Nazi architecture in Nuremberg. These include fears of being seen as somehow commemorating or even celebrating Nazism, or of attracting or even generating Nazi support. They have also included concerns that the city would become more demonstrably identified as a perpetrator city, and its Nazi identity 'cemented' more indelibly, perhaps for ever more. Sometimes this has been raised as a concern for business investment, but mostly it has been simply regarded as unjust – as Nuremberg having to carry an unfair burden of the Nazi legacy. For many years, even in a city that prided itself on its 'red' credentials, those arguing that there should be more public acknowledgement of the city's difficult heritage remained a small minority – even if some of them managed to hold high office for considerable periods of time. But while there were significant developments, especially in the years around the fiftieth anniversary of the Nazi seizure of power (as was also the case in many other parts of Germany), widespread political consensus that Nuremberg's image would be harmed more by appearing to be *not* acknowledging its terrible past only emerged in the 1990s.

This change was spurred partly by the spread of the idea that not revealing uncomfortable aspects of the past constituted a form of repression, and that this could lead to further ills. Neo-Nazi activities were identified by some as evidence of the pathologies that might result from such repression; and, more practically, it was argued that attention to unsettling history could be used to provide education to prevent attraction to Nazism. Unification intensified the push towards 'facing up to' awkward pasts, especially as the West confronted the East with its self-serving versions of history, and was in the process confronted by some of its own embarrassing silences or half-hearted attempts to acknowledge its Nazi past. This push to revelation was not only motivated by within-Germany politics, however. Also crucial was the awareness that, as was acknowledged in local debates in Nuremberg (Chapter 5), 'the eyes of the world' were upon the country at this time. What those eyes were looking to see was whether the 'new Germany' really would be thoroughly different from the last unified Germany – that under the Nazi regime. Acknowledging its awful past – showing that it was willing to keep it in gaze – became a way for Germany to show that it was aware of this risk and would prevent it being repeated.

There are also two other features of this turn to the unsettling, which seem to be involved in the turn to difficult heritage more widely. One is an increased willingness by nations and cities – though there seem to be striking parallels at individual level too – to define their ongoing identities through difference from the past rather than through predominantly continuity-seeking temporal narratives. This is not to say that the 'bad bits' of histories were necessarily ignored previously but that they were regarded as unfortunate interruptions that required negotiating by strategies such as the 'temporal skipping' discussed in Chapter 3. And they somehow lay outside the 'real' identity story of the place, in the same way that the Nazi Party Rally Grounds were not included on tourist maps of Nuremberg (Chapter 3). What the turn to difficult heritage allows, however, is for these pasts to be acknowledged as part of an identity-story but simultaneously made the focus of an account of change and difference. Certainly, there may well remain all kinds of partitioning strategies in place that enable individuals, and also cities and countries, to appear to be acknowledging these pasts as their own even while simultaneously allocating responsibility elsewhere (as in the concentration on Nazis discussed in earlier chapters). But whether this is the case or not, what is enabled here is a greater sense of difference between contemporary selves and past 'other selves'. This, I suggest, has become ever more compelling in a world in which differentiation from contemporary others – long argued by various social and cultural theorists and commentators to be the predominant means of self-definition – has become ever more politically unacceptable (though, of course, it continues).[3]

The second feature of the wider turn to difficult heritage is that this has come to be understood as a sign of openness and honesty – towards the past but also, by association, in the present. Like the spread of glass architecture and metaphors of political transparency, exemplified in Norman Foster's new dome on the Reichstag in Berlin as well as in Günter Domenig's design for the Dokuzentrum in Nuremberg, demonstrations of attention to difficult heritage are means of appearing to be hiding nothing, to be avoiding any form of dissemblance. They are performative acts, on a par with official apologies: acknowledgements of the past that imply a willingness to be self-critical.

Heritage dilemmas, effects and potentials

As we have seen, however, performed openness can involve displacements of its own. Attention to certain areas may deflect attention from areas of remaining silence and avoidance. So, in Nuremberg, there has undoubtedly been much acknowledged publicly that was not earlier. But equally, there remain areas of silence. And as we have seen, the claim that difficult heritage *is* being publicly addressed can be entangled in the maintenance of such silences. Furthermore, as the detailed account here has also suggested, even well-intentioned attempts to openly face the past can end up telling redemptive stories

There is a reflexive point to be made here about my own focus too. It has been predominantly concerned with the negotiating of the Nazi Party Rally Grounds – the most visible aspect of the city's Nazi legacy. Does focusing attention here give it undue significance – or downplay the significance of other areas of life and history? Certainly, my intention has not been to imply that this is the only or necessarily most important area of possible attention: work needs to be done on multiple aspects of life. Understanding the variations between different spheres – public and private, centre-stage or in the wings – as well as their connections, remains one of the most important historical and ethnographic tasks to be done. Moreover, looking at the complexities and entanglements over time has produced an account that does not reproduce a redemptive allegory and one which, I hope, contributes to the understanding of official, visible heritage – which, after all, does matter too.

Official, visible heritage has certain qualities that make it suggestible in particular ways. That is, put otherwise, there is a 'heritage effect'.[4] One aspect of this that has been troublesome for the difficult history discussed here is that designating it as heritage seems to accord it value and, unless carefully countered, to imply that it is being seen positively and even treasured. In other contexts it has been argued that heritage risks effecting a lulling, soporific, complacency.[5]

The 'pastness' of heritage, coupled with redemptive forms of apprehension, might produce such effects even in relation to difficult topics. We might simply categorise them as of a time gone by; or favourably relativise the present by contrasting it with a much more awful past. As we have seen in the visitor study here, this does happen sometimes. Much more frequently, however, visiting difficult heritage becomes an occasion for prompting reflection. Indeed, many people use it as a starting point for contemporary critique – even though this is not actively attempted by the site or exhibition that they have visited. Why they do so is perhaps related to a broader feature of the global assemblage. As Collier and Ong write: ' "global assemblages" are ... domains in which the forms and values of individual and collective existence are problematised or at stake, in the sense that they are subject to technological, political, and ethical reflection and intervention'.[6] In the case of heritage, and especially difficult heritage, this is undoubtedly the case. It has prompted multiple kinds of reflection and intervention. How the Nazi Party Rally Grounds have been negotiated has raised wider questions about the identity of those living in Nuremberg and in Germany more generally. Moreover, because this is a form that people recognise as similar in some ways to others elsewhere – but at the same time as distinctive – it prompts them to make comparisons and ask questions about it.

The Nazi Party Rally Grounds is not a well-packaged and presented heritage site. Instead, as I have described, it is a space of mixed uses, with buildings and grounds in varying states of disrepair. It is not a space which is frozen into any single particular time, nor even into two – then and now. Rather, it is – like Anselm Kiefer's painting *Nuremberg* – a space of many layers, with fragments and traces from different pasts showing through into the present. It is a palimpsest. This lessens some of the potential heritage effect. The incompleteness of the site as heritage – its untidiness to classification as well as literally – can, as the previous chapter described, be unsettling for some visitors, who are unsure quite what is going on here, and who may condemn the neglect or trivial uses of the site. But that very unsettlement also prompts them to reflection; and to thinking not only about 'the past' but also about how it has been variously negotiated since.

What to do

In the introduction, I offered my account as a democratic anthropology, concerned not only with reflecting on the case at hand but also in being prompted by what I have learnt from history-workers and visitors among others, and on this basis making my own suggestions about how a site such as this might be presented. Here I should first note that discussions have continued since the opening of the Dokuzentrum about the future of the Nazi Party Rally Grounds. In 2001 a competition was held for ideas about how to develop the whole site.[7] This was not, as we have seen in previous chapters, the first time that such a competition had been held. And it was not the first time that no solution was reached – and no prize awarded. This repeated process is itself telling. Instead of being able to fix on a 'single' solution – the 'whole conception' (Chapter 5) – the place is instead locked into continuing oscillation (Chapter 4). One suggestion, therefore, might be to simply acknowledge this and allow it to flourish. This would have its parallels to the 'now and then' relationship to this kind of heritage that some visitors argued to be the way to approach it.

Yet, although I suspect that such oscillation will characterise the future of this site, I do not choose to advocate this – at least, not in a *laisser-faire* manner that, as was the case with 'profanation' in the 1980s, became an excuse for letting almost anything happen. What oscillation will mean in the long term is that the site will be likely to shrink further as new developments are built upon it. My alternative suggestion would be for a more structured oscillation, which allows different kinds of uses and events, without further reducing the space. The mixed uses of the site bring an expanded audience into tangential encounter with this history. As we have seen, even those who come for other reasons than to visit a heritage site are not closed off to considering its history and engaging in moral reflection about it. This can be further enabled. A move in this direction, for example, was the installation of new information stations around the site in the lead up to the World Cup in 2006. England football fans visiting Nuremberg for the England versus Trinidad and Tobago match were thus able to learn some history of the stadium in which the match was being played, as well as about other parts of the site, some fans even visiting the Dokuzentrum.[8] Structured oscillation allows for these different uses – but making sure that the means are readily available to allow 'accompanied witnessing', to help open up reflection and understanding.

In James Young's analysis of Holocaust memorials, he praises especially those that manage to avoid being redemptive (or that are 'anti-redemptory') and those that incorporate a reflexive critique of their own history or memory. As he puts it: 'part of what a post-Holocaust generation must ethically represent is the experience of the memory-act itself'.[9] His strictures can be extended, I suggest, to negotiating other kinds of history and heritage too – including the case discussed here. In the account above, I have argued that there are certain kinds of temporal structurings that emerge both in cultural policy and visitor accounts. In particular, there are the tendencies to make clear-cut divisions between past and present (temporal disjuncture), and to construct progressive narratives (chronologies of progress); and that these can play into redemptive accounts that also fail to pay attention to their own situation and history. These kinds of temporal structurings, or forms of historical consciousness, and their effects are common at many other heritage sites and in popular understandings elsewhere too. The challenge is to open up other possibilities. Playing these historical consciousnesses one against the other is one way of doing this – though as we have seen they easily remain as alternatives, rather than unsettling each other. Better, I suggest, is to take inspiration from some of the examples provided by Young and to try to enable awareness not just of 'the past' but of history and memory – in this case including post-1945 history and its revisions – in ways that recognise ongoing change and developments, rather than reaching closure. That is, even in relation to heritage, the aim should be towards the anti-redemptory, the anti-monumental and even anti-heritage.

In other words, the call here is for continual unsettlement. It is for opening up heritage – which, as we have seen, always risks settlement into a single frozen past – with what we might call the palimpsest effect. That is, as in Kiefer's *Nuremberg*, we seek to allow different layers of the past to appear, variably, through their later accretions, and in so doing to disturb, prod, and raise questions – that is, to unsettle fixity and heritage. To some extent, the Nazi Party Rally Grounds at Nuremberg do this even with fairly minimal managed intervention. Through the eclectic mix of activities at the site and the evident marks of neglect or revision, questions are raised among visitors about how the site has been negotiated, and this in turn prompts wider moral reflection and commentary. My argument, however, is that this could be the basis for providing more (artistic and educational) 'accompaniment' to help visitors to reflect further – to consider, among other things, the background to some of the neglect or revision, or to be provided with alternative imagined fates, perhaps via art works – rather than leaving this to potentially slip into ready-formed, or even misinformed, accounts.

My call here for unsettling heritage is not intended to be restricted to Nuremberg. Difficult heritage has, as we have seen, the potential to unsettle. While this is sometimes seen as one of its disturbing features, and even as something to be managed into more comfortable experiences, it is also what makes these sites potentially so good to think with critically and ethically. It also gives them the potential to unsettle heritage, and some of the settlement effects of heritage, more generally. So too does an account of such difficult heritage, by highlighting changing and ongoing negotiating frames, the various settlements and continuing movements involved – and also to potential future alternative directions. It is to such reflexive unsettlement that I hope that this book can make a contribution.

NOTES

These notes use the following abbreviations:

FAZ – *Frankfurter Allgemeine Zeitung*
GfA – *Geschichte für Alle*, History for All
NN – *Nürnberger Nachrichten*, Nuremberg News
NAnz – *Nürnberger Anzeiger*, Nuremberg Reporter
NZ – *Nürnberger Zeitung*, Nuremberg Newspaper
StAN – *StadtArchiv Nürnberg*, Nuremberg City Archive
TZ – *Tageszeitung*, Daily Newspaper
All translations are mine unless otherwise stated.
All websites listed were checked in January 2008.

1 Introduction

1 In using the term 'story' I give recognition to the fact that this is, inevitably, a selective and crafted account (Clifford 1997). It is shaped by a narrative drive to explore wider questions and tell about these, rather than to provide a full documentation. Nevertheless, I have striven for empirical accuracy and the account has been constrained by the research findings and a consideration of much more 'data' than can be presented here.

2 See, for example, Buruma 2002: 112–35; Yoshida 2006; Duffy 2001 and http://humanum. arts.cuhk.edu.hk/NanjingMassacre/NMGP.html. Note: Nanking is also sometimes spelt Nanjing.

3 The dispute over the display of the *Enola Gay* at the US National Air and Space Museum is the classical example; see Linenthal and Engelhardt 1996. See Grayling 2006 and Niven 2006a on Dresden; and on a recent dispute at the Canadian War Museum, see Dean F. Oliver, 'A Museum of History, a History of Remembrance', Canadian War Museum, 27.03.2007 at www.warmuseum.ca/cwm/media/bg_history_e.html.

4 And also individuals. Handler 1988; Macdonald 1997a; the notion of 'expressive individuation' is derived from Taylor 1989.

5 Buruma 2002: 114.

6 See, for example, Bevan 2006, which includes further examples, such as the obliteration of Turkish-Muslim heritage, especially the Bridge of Mostar, by Croats.

7 The term 'memorial entrepreneur' is from Jordan 2006.

8 Graham *et al.* 2000: 24; and also Tunbridge and Ashworth 1996: 21; the following quote is also from Tunbridge and Ashworth 1996: 21.

9 Tunbridge and Ashworth 1996: Chapter 5.

10 Tunbridge and Ashworth 1996: 21.

11 In German this distinction between 'places of perpetrators' (*Orte der Täter*) and 'places of victims' (*Orte der Opfer*) is widely used in commentary on the treatment of such sites.

12 See Law 1986 on the notion of 'action at a distance'.

13 Macdonald 2005a.

14 This is adapted from what Alpers 1991 and Kirshenblatt-Gimblett 1998: 51–4 have called 'the museum effect'; see also Macdonald 2006a.

15 Porombka and Schmundt 2006 includes this and other German examples.

16 A focus on 'assemblage' entails looking at the heterogeneous elements – material and discursive – involved in constituting a particular entity. Key theorists are Latour (e.g. 2005) and Deleuze and Guattari (e.g. 1987); see also de Landa 2006, Bennett 2007 and Collier and Ong 2005, who develop the notion of 'global assemblage', which I discuss in the final chapter of this book. I have discussed assemblage theorising, in relation to heritage, in Macdonald forthcoming.

17 Key theorists include Jeismann (e.g. 1985) and Rüsen (e.g. 1990, 2001, 2005). See also Macdonald 2000, Straub 2005 and Berger 1997.

18 Olick 2003: 8. See also Crane 2004; Macdonald 2006a.

19 Bevan 2006; and on destruction and forgetting more generally see Forty 1999, Küchler 1999.

20 See, for example, Kaschuba 2002; Williams 2007 on the related development of the memorial museum; and Beck-Gernsheim 1999 and Bodemann 2002 on the turn to Jewish culture in Germany.

21 Hughes 2004.

22 Coombes 2003; Dubin 2006a; Karp *et al.* 2006.

23 See the museum's website: www.terrorhaza.hu/index3.html. Jewish groups have criticised the fact that the building's earlier use by the Nazis is played down and the fact that some of the Communist interrogators were Jewish is played up. See: www.jewishsf.com/bk020809/i42.shtml.

24 See *Sites of Conscience* website (which also lists other examples): www.sitesofconscience. org/eng/gulag.htm.

25 Arditti 1999; and for the continuing campaign: www.madres.org.

26 Huyssen 2003: 102; for more information about the development see the site's official website: www.parquedelamemoria.org.ar/parque-ing/motivacion.htm.

27 Discussed further in Macdonald 2007. For the museum's official website see: www. usnationalslaverymuseum. See also Graham *et al.* 2001.

28 See the project's website at: http://nmaahc.si.edu/.

29 Novick 1999.

30 Hochschild 1998, 2005.

31 Horton and Kardux 2004.

32 The museums' official websites are, respectively: www.empiremuseum.co.uk/ and www. internationalslaverymuseum.org.uk/.

33 Dubin 2006b: 482.

34 See Zimmerer 2006; Olick 2007; Nobles 2003; Hayner 2001; Edkins 2003.

35 Cf. Huyssen 2003, Hoelscher 2006, Kirshenblatt-Gimblett 1998.

36 Huyssen 2003: 14.

37 See Levy and Sznaider 2001, 2002; Novick 1999.

38 Maier 1997; Dudek 1992; Weber 1990.

39 Glaeser 2000: 326.

40 Neumann 2000: 10.

41 Hoelscher 2006: 202.

42 *Collins German Dictionary,* 1980. See Macdonald 2006a for further discussion. Interestingly, my more recent dictionary, *Collins German Dictionary*, 1997 has a different example: that of colonialism.

43 Rosenfeld 2000: 2.

44 Koshar 1998, 2000; Lynch 1976; Lowenthal 1998; Smith 2006; Barthel 1996; Littler and Naidoo 2005; Graham *et al.* 2000; and see Lowenthal 1985 for a discussion of changing conceptions of time and their implications for heritage. Soane 2002 is an interesting

account of differences between English and German conservation practices that, he argues, have roots in the different histories of industrialisation and urbanisation in the two countries. In Britain, he argues, industrialisation was early and fairly rapid, leading to a sense of a 'more radical break from the past' (2002: 269) than in Germany, which industrialised later and maintained more sense of historic continuity. In consequence, he argues, in Britain 'the significance of "heritage" is considered as being something quite distinct from the normal experience of the modern world' whereas in Germany to a greater extent 'the contemplation and interpretation of the built past is considered a relevant and integrated element within the contemporary lifestyle of the country' (2002: 268).

45 Lowenthal 1998: 5; Pickard 2002; see also Herzfeld 1991.
46 Pickard 2002; 'Germans were to the forefront of this worldwide [preservation] movement, and by 1975 West Germans were convinced that one of every twelve buildings had historical value', Koshar 1998: 5.
47 Boswell and Evans 1999; Littler 2005.
48 Niven 2002; Reichel 2001; Koshar 1998; Maier 1997.
49 Moeller 2001: 18.
50 Reichel 1999; Niven 2002: Chapter 1; Neumann 2000: Chapter 8.
51 Moeller 2001: 15.
52 See, for example, Moeller 2001; Gregor 2003a and 2009; Koshar 1998; Frei 1999; and on pre-1949, Olick 2005.
53 Moeller 2001: 18.
54 Ibid.: 19.
55 Rüsen 2005: 200.
56 Generationalist arguments also need a word of caution. First, generations are not the 'naturally occurring' phenomena that they are sometimes conceived as being in such perspectives – rather, they have to be defined in relation to some chosen 'starting point' and decisions have to be made about how to map generation onto particular time-stretches (Davis 1989; Misztal 2003: 83–91). More importantly, however, generationalist arguments tend to depict history in terms of clearly distinguishable periods, 'presuppose a determining set of experiences and values common to a specific social age group' (Carrier 2000: 45), deploy the notion of generation change itself as sufficient explanation and erase differences within a 'generation'.
57 E.g. Maier 1997.
58 E.g. Niven 2002; Thiele 1997; Macdonald 2007.
59 E.g. Carrier 2005; Young 2000 Chapter 7; Niven 2002: Chapter 8; Jeismann 1999; Brumlik et al. 2000.
60 See Clifford 1988: 2 on 'redemptive modes of textualization'.
61 Geertz 1973: 448.
62 For example, Knischewski and Spittler 1997 suggest that the 1980s constitutes a distinct phase of 'conservative backlash'; this is followed by a post-unification stage. Kansteiner 2006a and b sees the period since 1990s as one of 'routinisation, professionalisation and fragmentation'.
63 E.g. König 2003.
64 Rüsen 2005: 201.
65 Assmann 2006: Chapter 7; Niven 2006b.
66 Levy and Sznaider 2001, 2002; and see Chapter six below; see also Jeismann 2001; and Kansteiner 2006a, Chapter 12, who suggests that a 'Europeanisation of ... political memory' may be underway since the 1990s.
67 Levy and Sznaider 2002: 98.
68 Interview with the author in 2000.
69 In the Nuremberg metropolitan region, with a population of about 2.5 million, 18 per cent of the population is recorded as constituted by foreign nationals, which the city council website points out is higher than the average in Bavaria or Germany (www. nuernberg.de/internet/portal_e/buerger/city_portrait.html).

70 With the exception of the early months postwar when the occupying US forces imposed a temporary mayor; see Chapter 3. The CSU is the Bavarian wing of the Christian Democratic Union (CDU).

71 Kosfeld 2001: 69; GfA 2002b: 246.

72 E.g. Ladd 1997; Till 2005; Rosenfeld 2000; Dietzfelbinger and Liedtke 2004; Sereny 2000; Carrier 2005. For discussion and critique see Kauders 2003 and Kansteiner 2002.

73 See Nash 1995: 93–3; Huyssen 1995 Chapter 11; Simons 1997; Saltzman 1999. I have discussed these ideas further in relation to what I call a 'multi-temporal' anthropological approach: Macdonald 2002a.

74 E.g. Macfarlane 2007.

2 Building heritage

1 Gerstenblith 2006; Kirshenblatt-Gimblett 2006.

2 See Gieryn 2002 on the theorisation of 'what buildings do'; see also Parker Pearson and Richards 1994; Markus 1993. For other accounts of the multiple interpretation, presentation and use of buildings see, for example, Bender 1998; Edensor 1998; Buchli 1999 and Breglia 2006.

3 Littler 2005: 13.

4 Tilley 2004: 31.

5 See Miller 2005 for a helpful overview. Key references are Gell 1998 and work by Bruno Latour, e.g. 1993; and Gibson 1986 on 'affordance'. I have discussed some of this further in relation to this material in Macdonald 2006c.

6 Hertz 2006. See also Needham1974; Kress and van Leeuwen 2006.

7 Speer 1995: 61.

8 Speer 1978: 8.

9 Kershaw 1998: 156; Scobie 1990.

10 Schmidt 1995.

11 Petsch 1992: 199.

12 Petsch 1992: 199; Koch 1995.

13 Benton 1999: 211; Hughes, Robert 2003.

14 Petsch 1992: 198.

15 Jaskot 2000: 50.

16 Sontag 1990: 208.

17 Sturken and Cartwright 2001: 163.

18 For an account of his arguments see Speer 1978; Jaskot 2000: Chapter 6; and also Sereny 1996 (e.g. p.153). As Grasskamp (1990) and Jaskot (2000) observe, there has been a tendency among art historians (and also in the Nuremberg trials) to separate off Speer's role as an architect from his position from 1942 as head of the Ministry of Armaments and Munitions, and to regard only the latter as political, thereby 'ignor[ing] the essential political interests served by his actions as the most powerful architect in National Socialist Germany' (Jaskot 2000: 140).

19 Speer 1978: 8.

20 He says 'property relations'. Benjamin 1992: 234.

21 Hewitt 1993: 166; cf. 'Monumental buildings mask the will to power and the arbitrariness of power beneath signs and surfaces which claim to express collective will and collective thought' Lefebvre 1991: 143.

22 Speer 1978, 1995; Burden 1967; Jaskot 2000; Doosry 2002.

23 Dietzfelbinger and Liedtke 2004: 36.

24 Gunther Kress has developed a sensitive analytical approach – 'social semiotics' – to these kinds of questions. E.g. Kress and van Leeuwen 2006, 2001.

25 Petsch 1992, Nerdinger 1995, Jaskot 2000, Whyte 1998.

26 Petsch 1992: 199.

27 The fact that Classicism was also used by the Soviets and other communist regimes has been seen as evidence of Classicism being especially associated with totalitarian regimes or even 'that totalitarian systems favoured classicism *of necessity*, no matter whether they were Fascist or Communist in doctrine' (Grasskamp 1990: 233).

28 Petsch 1992: 234. The idea that Nazi art and architecture are mystifications masking the real nature of the regime is sometimes seen as an alternative to the view that they are expressions of ideology (ibid.). This is not necessarily an either/or matter, however, for we can surely see, say, Nazi architecture as both an expression of some aspects of ideology and a deflection of attention from others.

29 Jaskot 2000: 2.

30 Ibid.

31 Jaskot 2000; Doosry 2002; quotations from Doosry 2002: 384.

32 Jaskot 2000: 58.

33 Doosry 2002: 379.

34 For further information about the site see Nürnberg Kultur 'Information about the former Nazi Party Rally Grounds' website: www.kubiss.de/kulturreferat/reichsparteitags gelaende/.

35 For an account of the earlier history see Dietzfelbinger and Liedtke 2004. In brief, the damp and swampy area had become popular for leisure activities, such as boating and skating, even in the nineteenth century. This expanded in the early twentieth, when it was used for a major exhibition of Bavarian business, industry and craft to commemorate the centenary of Franken becoming part of Bavaria. Organised under the auspices of Bavarian Prince-Regent Luitpold, the area took its name from him. The exhibition was visited by 2.5 million people (ibid.: 17).

36 GfA 2002b: 17.

37 Zelnhefer 2002: 48–9; Connerton 1989: 41–3.

38 Burden 1967: 166.

39 Zelnhefer 2002: 82.

40 GfA 2002b: 201–2.

41 Dietzfelbinger and Liedtke 2004: 63.

42 For a history of the SS-Kaserne see Bundesamt für die Anerkennung ausländischer Flüchtlinge 1999. The SS-Kaserne was also characterised in newspapers at the time as a 'gateway' to the party rally grounds, though it was probably not originally intended and did not act as such (ibid.: 9, 18, 19).

43 See Speer 1995: 112–16 for an account of how so many of the buildings were planned to outstrip existing or classical buildings. 'I found Hitler's excitement rising whenever I could show him that at least in size we had "beaten" the other great buildings of history' (ibid.: 115).

44 Speer 1995: 204.

45 Zelnhefer 1992: 89.

46 I am grateful to Michaela Giebelhausen for pointing this out and more generally for casting her art-historian's eye over the Nazi Party Rally Grounds on a visit there with me in 2007.

47 Burden 1967.

48 Ibid.: 119.

49 Ogan 1992: 19.

50 Scobie 1990: 72.

51 Jaskot 2000: 36.

52 Kershaw 1998: 147.

53 Berlin and Kay 1969; Turner 1967: 89, 88–9.

54 Hitler on laying foundation stone for the Rally Grounds, Reither 2000: 6.

55 This was articulated by Himmler too (who as Head of the SS was responsible for commissioning various buildings) in an article in 1941: 'When people are silent, the

stones speak. By means of the stone, great epochs speak to the present'. Quoted in Jaskot 2000: 114.

56 This theory may have been dreamt up by Speer postwar rather than really having motivated the construction of his buildings as he claimed. The theory is explained in Speer 1978 and 1995 (especially p. 97). In the latter he also describes showing Hitler a picture that he had made of the Zeppelin Building as a ruin, covered in ivy. While other party members were horrified by this, he says, as they saw it as a sign of the future demise of Nazi power, Hitler himself was delighted, understanding the classical allusion. Dietzfelbinger and Liedtke 2004: 147, fn. 22 report an investigation of the claims that such ideas were actually deployed in the construction of the buildings which concludes that they did not.

57 Speer 1995: 97.

58 Scobie 1990: 87.

59 Reichel 1992.

60 Zelnhefer 2002.

61 Jaskot 2000: 52; referring to Scobie 1990.

62 Roche 2000.

63 Connerton 1989: 42 says a million participated at the rally peak. It is, as ever, difficult to be sure about numbers. According to Dietzfelbinger and Liedtke 2004: 68, the Reichsbahn (railway system) recorded 1, 270,500 people being transported to the new rally grounds station, Bahnhof Märzfeld, in 1938. For accounts of the rallies see especially Burden 1967, Reichel 1992 and Zelnhefer 1992 and 2002.

64 Connerton 1989: 43.

65 Durkheim 1965.

66 See Handelman 1998.

67 Handelman 1998: 41.

68 Ibid.

69 Ibid.; Burden 1967: 119.

70 Connerton 1989: 103–4.

71 Ibid.: 43. Connerton is here writing specifically of the annual Munich Bürgerbräukeller ceremonies commemorating the putsch What he says, however, applies equally to the blood flag ritual during the party rallies.

72 Reichel 1992: 162.

73 Winckler 1992: 130.

74 Gregor 2003b; see also Neumann 2000, especially on Weimar (Chapter 8). More generally on 'organic' analogies of the city, see David Harvey 2003. Such analogies are, he argues, very widespread and can be 'beguiling and dangerous' (2003: 27) because they can obscure considerations of social differences within the city and can sometimes serve to naturalise developments or states of affairs rather than locate them in specific histories and contexts.

75 Gregor 2003b.

76 GfA 2002b: 213.

77 Glaser 2000 interview with author. See also Glaser 1992.

78 Gregor 2003b.

79 Dietzfelbinger and Liedtke 2004: 23.

80 Ibid.: 25.

81 Ibid.

82 Such that Hambrecht 1976: 110 argues that 'by the middle of the 1920s North Bavaria's industrial metropolis and her surroundings were "*the* national socialist centre of the Reich"'.

83 See Jaskot 2000: 51 and Zelnhefer 2002: 64; also for the points immediately below.

84 Doosry 2002 and Jaskot 2000 also describe the establishment and workings of an organisation specially established to deal with the construction of the grounds, the Zweckverband Reichsparteitag Nürnberg.

85 It has also been suggested that this was originally accidental – this was simply the road from Regensburg to Nuremberg – though was nevertheless later made much of. Reichel 1992: 139. Sometimes this 'accident' is described today within the framework noted above of a tendency to play down Nuremberg's distinctiveness – a tendency that also prefers to play down Nuremberg's history and instead emphasise the practical.
86 Fein 2002: 19.
87 Kosfeld 2001: 71.
88 Fein 2002: 19.
89 Kershaw 1989: 184.
90 A version of Kusz's poem, written in 1979, is reproduced in Reither 2000: 11–12, though this one, in local dialect, was provided by the poet, to whom I am very grateful for permission to reprint it here. I provide the translation.
91 Beer *et al.* 1995.
92 Jaskot 2000: 62.
93 Ibid.: 63, 68; Dietzfelbinger and Liedtke 2004: 85.
94 Puvogel *et al.* 1995: 180; Dietzfelbinger and Liedtke 2004: 86.
95 Schramm 1993: 202.
96 Ibid.: 195; Schramm 1988: 7.
97 Schramm 1988:7; 1993: 199.
98 Heigl 2003: 10.
99 Schramm 1993: 199.
100 Schramm 1988: 46, 114, 150.
101 Dietzfelbinger and Liedtke 2004: 87.
102 Benton 1999: 201.

3 Demolition, cleaninsing and moving on

1 See Bevan 2006; Kaplan 2006.
2 Koshar 2000: 157–62 outlines some of the debates; and see the website by those promoting the rebuilding of the Schloss: www.berliner-schloss.de.
3 Koshar : 1998: 206; Rosenfeld 2000: 97.
4 Rosenfeld 2000: 97, 150.
5 Rosenfeld 2000: 100–5.
6 Tour guides held in StAN Verkehrsverein Miscellaneous documents; e.g. AV 3139.8. In some cases even the stadium is only included in the German-language version and not those in other languages.
7 Visitors quoted in *NN* 'Hinter den Kulissen der NS-Architektur', 11.08.86; many people have likewise told me of their difficulties of trying to find the site – and often failing.
8 Heigl 2003: 22.
9 Ibid.: 18.
10 Virilio 1989: 54; Quinn 1994: 14, 15.
11 Paul Wood 'The day Saddam's statue fell', BBC News, 9.04.2004 http://news.bbc.co.uk/1/hi/world/middle_east/3611869.stm.
12 Wachter 1999: 336.
13 Sontag 1979: 14.
14 Olick writes that the tribunal decided that the latter could be covered under War Crimes, 2005: 337.
15 Ketternacker 1997: 16.
16 Douglas 1966: 2.
17 Kettenacker 1997: 16.
18 E.g. Niethammer 1982; see also, Frei 1999; Reichel 2001.
19 Reichel 2001: 52; a tendency that was also pointed out by Mitscherlich and Mitscherlich 1967 in their famous account of Germans' relationship to the Nazi past.
20 Kettenacker 1997: 17.

21 E.g. Frei 1999: 14; Marcuse 2001: 88–118; Niethammer 1982 on Bavaria.

22 Niethammer 1982.

23 E.g. Bloch 1989.

24 The case of Schmeissner, which has not been fully investigated, nevertheless indicates how complicated some of these cases could be. He had worked in Nuremberg's building department since 1936, having previously worked in Munich until pressed out due to his support for a (Jewish?) architecture professor who had been removed from post by the Nazis. He took up post in Nuremberg before becoming a member of the NSDAP. The crime with which he was sentenced for five years by the military government was that of 'concealing the hiding place of the national treasures', presumably from the US forces, presumably out of concern with what they might do with them (StAN E10/59 miscellaneous documents).

25 Kettenacker 1997: 23; Wachter 1999: 12.

26 *NN* 'Konferenz über ein neues US-Übungsgelände', 27.01.1953. Occasionally, though generally more recently, the differences between the US Army and the city council were so great that the Bavarian Staatskanzel had to intervene in negotiations. In 1960 the US wanted to increase the runway on the Great Road against the wishes of the city authorities and local population. A compromise was suggested (*NN* 'Düsen-"Unheil" kaum abzuwenden', 15.09.1960).

27 Dietzfelbinger and Liedtke 2004: 102.

28 Wachter 1999: 304.

29 'Es finden sich nur wenige deutscher Schaulustige ein', *NN* 'Armistice Day', 13.11.1948. The noun 'Schaulustige' (literally: 'those who like shows') seems to have an undertone derogatory of those who chose to attend – *Schaulust*, according to Rudy Koshar, being 'an irresistible desire to look, similar to that felt by individuals attracted to grisly scenes of human suffering at automobile crashes' (Koshar 2000: 185).

30 *NN* 'Amerikanischer Armeetag', 6.4.1949. Parades continue through the 1950s; and the US also held international military sports events – StAN Stadtchronik.

31 Another example of this is the use of the Buchenwald site by the Russian occupying forces and later the German Democratic Government for military ritual, including the building of massive commemorative structures in an aesthetic very like that of the Nazi Party Rally Grounds.

32 Geertz 1983; for an example of such an account, see Weiss 1992.

33 *NN* 'Kongresshalle in den Wogen der Meinungen', 9.5.1958.

34 *NN* 'Kongresshalle soll Gross-Stadion werden', 24.4.1958.

35 Ibid.

36 Because the costs kept increasing, Hitler forbade their exact calculation, though according to Speer they were between 700–800 million Reichsmarks. This is generally judged to be a considerable underestimate (Weiss 1992: 228, 238). On the more general failure postwar to recognise the Nazi regime's victims, including forced labourers, see Gregor 2003b.

37 Hauptamt für Hochbauwesen 1955 *Vorschläge über Verwendungsmöglichkeiten der ehemaligen Kongresshalle* (StAN AV 29992a); the document begins with a figure of 82 Reichsmarks million that it calculates were 'invested' in the building of the Congress Hall.

38 *NN* 'Ein kostspielige Erbschaft', 25.4.1958.

39 E.g. Centrum Industriekultur Nürnberg 1992; Dietzfelbinger and Liedtke 2004.

40 Documents in StAN AV Pe 10, 2253, 2254. See Wachter 1999: 349–52 for further discussion of the exhibition.

41 Which they did partly due to the support of the military government (Wachter 1999: 349).

42 *Ausstellungszeitung* (exhibition newspaper) in StAN AV Pe 10 2°, 4.9.1949.

43 Quoted in Wachter 1999: 336.

44 *Deutsche Bauausstellung Katalog* (German Building Exhibition catalogue) 1949: 12 (StAN AV Pe 10 2°); *Ausstellungszeitung* 10.9.1949.
45 *Ausstellungszeitung* 4.8.1949.
46 *Deutsche Bauausstellung Katalog* 1949: 19.
47 Ibid.: 20.
48 *Ausstellungszeitung* 1.8.1949.
49 *Deutsche Bauausstellung Katalog* 1949: 19, 22–3.
50 Ibid.: 83.
51 *Ausstellungszeitung* 1.9.1949; I 1949: 19.
52 The deputy military governor in *Deutsche Bauausstellung Katalog* 1949: 15.
53 *Ausstellungszeitung* 18.9.1949.
54 *Führer durch die deutsche Bau-Ausstellung Nürnberg 1949* (*Guide through the German Building exhibition in Nuremberg, 1949*), StAN.2254 8°.
55 Wunder 1984.
56 E.g. Koshar 1998, who also notes that in some places, such as Frankfurt, there were arguments against such reconstruction on grounds of Germany not deserving this. Such arguments were, however, absent in Nuremberg, on which, see Wachter 1999, Geschichte für Alle 2002a and Macdonald forthcoming.
57 Wettbewerb über die Wiederaufbau der Altstadt Nürnberg (competition for the reconstruction of Nuremberg's Old Town), minutes of the meeting of the prize committee 16–19.02.1948, StAN E10/59 101.
58 *900 Jahre Nürnberg Stadtjubiläum Ausstellung Katalog* (*900 Years Nuremberg City Jubilee Exhibition Catalogue*) 1950, StAN AV 2387.8°. See also Wachter 1999: 352–69.
59 Dr Wilhelm Schwemmer 1960 *Nürnberg: A Guide through the Old Town*, Nuremberg: Verkehrsverein Nürnberg e.V.: 68–9, StAN Av 3099 8°.
60 As Jeffrey K.Olick writes: 'One peculiarity of the postwar German public discourse … was the co-existence of the zero hour trope with that of the "Other Germany" … The zero hour motif was rooted in the desire to begin again, not to be held accountable for the disasters of the past … The "Other Germany", in seeming contrast, argued that the most propitious way to move ahead was to reconnect with an identity that had been repressed or to return to an original tradition that had been lost' (2005: 331).
61 Whyte 1998: 297.
62 Ibid. Reconstruction was not, however, total reconstruction. In Nuremberg, famous buildings were restored with care and at expense but it was decided that there was insufficient money to restore all housing within the Altstadt in this way and so some fairly bland modern architecture was also allowed (Bruckner 2002: 14–16). Nuremberg had suffered particularly extensive bomb damage, the German Building Exhibition catalogue reporting that 91 per cent of all of its buildings had been damaged, and 36 per cent of housing, 38 per cent of public buildings, and 49 per cent of industrial and commercial buildings having been totally destroyed (*Deutsche Bauausstellung Katalog* 1949: 24).
63 Whyte 1998: 296.
64 Ibid.
65 Knischewski and Spittler 1997 on German memorialisation; see Rowlands 1999 for an anthropological analysis of the form of memorials.
66 Reichel 1999: 10; Marcuse 2001: 122.
67 Winter and Sivan rightly point out that there is a more general tension here: 'Victimhood and agency have always been and remain in problematic juxtaposition; they form a duality with different meanings in different historical settings' (2000: 19). See also Assmann 2006: 72–84.
68 When Volkstrauertag was reintroduced in West Germany it was stated that it was 'to remember all those who gave their lives for the good of humanity [*für die Güter der Menschheit*]' (quoted in Neumann 2000: 233), indicating that the sacrifice notion was also still mobilised. The idea of rituals accommodating different interpretations is especially associated in anthropology with Victor Turner, e.g. 1967. It has been demonstrated

well in Alex King's analysis of the commemoration of the Great War (1999) and Marita Sturken's account of the Vietnam Veterans Memorial in Washington DC (1997). David Lloyd makes the more general point that 'The cultural history of commemorations needs to be sensitive to the variety and ambiguity of individual experience' (1998: 218).

69 Dr Harmut Heller, *Der Nürnberger Volksfest* 1993, Friedrich Alexander Universität Zulassungsarbeit zur Ersten Staatsprüfung für das Lehramt an Grundschulen in Bayern, StAN AV 5699.4. He explains that the Volksfest was held at Deutschherrenwiese in the 1920s before being moved to the Fürther Straße; it was also held there postwar before moving to the new site.

70 Ibid.: 24.

71 Gerhard Liedtke, born 1951, co-author of *Nürnberg – Ort der Massen*, in his singly-authored section (Dietzfelbinger and Liedtke 2004: 133). A survey of 500 visitors to the Volksfest in 1992 found that 'the location … between the built remains of the Nazi past on the one side and the natural romance of the Dutzend lake on the other, that can be indicated as unique, is also undisputed', Harmut Heller, *Der Nürnberger Volksfest* 1993: 99.

72 *NN* 'Schluss mit dem Bauen im Torso!', 23.05.1962.

73 Personal communication.

74 Centrum Industriekultur Nürnberg 1992: 143; Dietzfelbinger and Liedtke 2004: 103.

75 Ibid.: 103.

76 See, for example: Till 1999; Marcuse 2001; Niven 2002; Young 1993: 144–50; Rittnar and Roth 1991; Koselleck 1999.

77 *NN* 'Rocker müssen ins Stadion auswandern', 13.6.1984.

78 Official of the Ordnungsschaftamt, 2003.

79 Bund Deutsche Architekten 1963 *Denkschrift*, StAN AV 3458.4°: 16.

80 Ibid.: 3.

81 Geschichte für Alle 1995.

82 Ibid.: 149.

83 *NN* ' "Pulver" aus Türmen', 21.12.1960.

84 Geschichte für Alle 1995: 176.

85 Ibid.

86 *NN* ' "Pulver" aus Türmen', 21.12.1960.

87 Geschichte für Alle 1995: 177.

88 *NN* 'In 54 Minuten war der Spuk vorbei', 24.4.1960.

89 Benton 1999.

90 See previous chapter and also Parker Pearson and Richards 1994.

91 Weiss 1992: 231.

92 Reported in *NN* 'Alle Embleme entfernt', 4/5.09.1965.

93 Ibid.

94 This swastika key pattern was also used elsewhere, such as on Troost's House of German Art in Munich, on which a similar ceiling behind the frontal colonnade remains in place (Scobie 1990: 89), and the wrought iron railings of the former Luftgaukommando Building, also in Munich (Rosenfeld 2000: 261–2). A similar justification of the swastika design – euphemistically refereed to as a 'noodle design' – on the latter also took place in 1978 (see ibid.).

95 *NN* 'Frost sprengt Decke', 17.5.1967.

96 Ibid.

97 *NN* 'Säulen müssen fallen', 30.05.1967.

98 *NN* 'Immer noch Säulendebatte', 3.6.1967.

99 E.g. Geschichte für Alle 2002b: 101.

100 Neo-Nazi activities in Nuremberg were led by Karl-Heinz Hoffmann, who founded the infamous Wehrsportgruppe in 1973. This group was responsible for weapons trafficking, meetings in Nuremberg in SS uniform, a bomb attack at the Munich *Oktoberfest* and the shooting of the Erlangen Jewish community chairman and his partner in 1980.

101 Quoted in *NN* 'Säulen müssen fallen', 30.5.1967.
102 See, for example, Gregor 2003a; Moeller 2001.
103 See Adorno 1986. For accounts of some of the changes underway see, for example, Kansteiner 2006a; Michman 2002; Fulbrook 1999.
104 Documents on Nuremberg Forum in StAN ref F7/I. 841–3.
105 See also Glaser 1992.

4 Preservation, profanation and image-management

1 Cook 2004: 304.
2 Ibid.; see also Caplan 2007.
3 See Lower Manhattan Development Corporation website about the twin-towers memorial: www.wtcsitememorial.org/ and Williams 2007.
4 Winter and Sivan 1999; Sites of conscience website: www.sitesofconscience.org/eng/index.htm.
5 Williams 2007 – book subtitle.
6 See Memorial Museums in Germany for the Victims of National Socialism website for these and other sites of connected with national Socialist crime: http://141.35.114.211:8080/gfue/de/home/fmpro?-db=kontakte.fp5&-lay=detail&-format=/gfue/en/index.html&-token.5=en&-findany, from which further details below are taken. The site illustrates the classification struggles over sites of Nazi perpetration-at-a-distance, such as the Nazi Party Rally Grounds or Obersalzburg, which are here oddly classified as 'Focus on Jewish victims'. See also Puvogel *et al.* 1995 for a more extensive and detailed list but that only covers West Germany and is not so up-to-date; and see Reichel 1999 for discussion.
7 See Niven 2002 for an overview. Marcuse 2001 provides a very detailed account of Dachau from which details below about Dachau are taken.
8 See also: www.kz-gedenkstaette-dachau.de/.
9 Till 2005, Jordan 2006.
10 www.topographie.de/.
11 www.proradok.de/; www.museen.nuernberg.de/prozesse/.
12 *Denkmalschutz Findbuch* 2004, StAN C20/II. This also notes that there had been an office of care of monuments in Bavaria since the early twentieth century.
13 This is Rosenfeld's translation (2000: 260), from Bayerisches Staatsministerium für Unterricht und Kultur, ed., *Bayerisches Denkmalschutzgesetz: Text und Einführung*, Munich 1974: 7.
14 Rosenfeld 2000: 260.
15 Ibid.: 261.
16 Minutes and other documents 1973–6 of the city council (*Stadtrat*)StAN and Building Committee (*Bauausschuss*), StAN C85/III 479–86 and Monument Protection Authority (*Denkmalschutzbehörde*) StAN C20/II. Information below is drown from these and also helpful conversations with Nuremberg's Denkmalschutzbehörde (monument preservation authorities) and the head of the Building Department, for which I am very grateful. See also Lübbeke 1987.
17 Cf. Herzfeld 1991: 235.
18 31.1.1973 10. Sitzung des Bauauschusses. C85/III 479; 15.1.–9.4.1973; see also *NN* 'Mehr sicherheit für Motorsportfreunde', 13.2.1973.
19 *NN* 'Ein sündhaft teures Denkmal', 13.11.1973.
20 Newspaper reports covering this, and from which the following details are derived, include: *NAnz* 'OB entsetzt: US-Kaserne soll Denkmal werden', 18.2.1992; *NZ* 'Schutz für die Kaserne?', 19.2.1992; *Tageszeitung* 'SS-Kaserne: Abriß oder Baudenkmal?', 21.2.1992; *NN* 'Die Handschrift Hitlers', 8.7.1993. See also Bundesamt für die Anerkennung ausländischer Flüchtlinge 1999.
21 Boyer 2005.
22 Documents relating to the Zeppelin Building StAN C75 985.

23 Interview with Hermann Glaser, 2000.
24 *NN* 'Schützenhilfe von der Staatsregierung', 22.02.83.
25 See especially Fischer 1996. The following account has also drawn on *NA* 'Zehn Millionen Mark für Hitlers "Große Straße" am Dutzendteich', 29.06.1989; *NN* 'Ungeliebtes Denkmal', 13.03.1991 and *NN* 'Nachtarbeit an der Nazi-Ruine: Große Straße muß Beton ersetzt brüchige Granitplatten auf dem Parkplatz', 13.7.1994.
26 Quoted in Dietzfelbinger and Liedtke 2004: 101.
27 Fischer 1996: 443.
28 Quoted in *NN* 'Nachtarbeit an der Nazi-Ruine: Große Straße muß Beton ersetzt brüchige Granitplatten auf dem Parkplatz', 13.7.1994.
29 For example, in Glaser 1989.
30 Glaser 1989: 15.
31 For the debate and quote, see Stadtrat Protokollen, Sitzung des Stadrats 15.07.1987, Office of the Mayor, Nuremberg Town Hall.
32 Ibid.
33 Douglas 1966.
34 Bund Deutsche Architekten 1963 *Denkschrift*, StAN AV 3458.4°: 16.
35 Weiss 1992: 232; Stadtratbeschluss 18.1.1989.
36 *Entsprechend* – in the terms of the heritage protection legislation. See *Deutsche Denkmalschutzgesetze* 1982 Deutsches Nationalkomitee für Denkmalschutz, Bonn, bearbeitet von Wolfgang Brönner, p. 21.
37 These were members of a group calling themselves the 'Feier-Initiative für aktions-pazifistische Gestaltung von Volkstrauertagen', led by Hermann Kraus (b. 1926), *NN* 'Misstöne bei der Feier zum Volkstrauertag', 15.11.1982; *NN* 'Totenehrung am Mahnmal', 14.11.1983.
38 *NN* 'Erstmals zwei Gedenkfeiern', 18.11.1985.
39 *NA* 'Das aktuelle Interview', 14.11.1985.
40 *NN* 'Kritik an CSU Absage', 16.11.1989; *NN* 'Opfer mahnen zum Frieden', 20.11.1989; *NN* 'Trauerspiel um die Feier zum Volkstrauertag', 15.11.1989.
41 Post-unification, Remembrance Day at the war memorial on the Rally Grounds were also sometimes a focus for political disruption – though now mainly from neo-Nazis; e.g. in 1993 *NN* 'Große Empörung über "Schändliche Parolen"', 15.11.1993. There was also some such disruption in subsequent years.
42 Bundesamt für die Anerkennung ausländischer Flüchtlinge 1999: 42.
43 Documents about this, from which the following is drawn, are in StAN E52 177. See also Dietzfelbinger and Liedtke 2004: 112–13.
44 *NN* 'Erbmasse kommt teuer', 10.07.1986.
45 *NN* 'Mahnmal statt Kommerz', 27.06.1987; *NN* 'Kühne Pläne für Kongreßhallen – Torso', 12.03.1987.
46 Quoted in Dietzfelbinger and Liedtke 2004: 112.
47 Ibid. and Pressemappe 'Congress and Partner' StAN E52 177.
48 *NN* 'Konsumtempel im Relikt der Nazizeit?', 24.3.1987.
49 For example, in the *Nuremberg Forum* StAN F7/I 841–3.
50 Mitscherlich and Mitscherlich 1967; *NN* 'Deutsche Pflichten', 6.11.1979.
51 Quoted in *NN* 'Plädoyer für den Verfall', 23.05.1987.
52 Letter from BLfD to StadtNürnberg/Baureferat 16.04.1987.
53 Neumann 2000: 10.
54 Quoted in Dietzfelbinger and Liedtke 2004: 112.
55 Stadtrat Protokollen, Sitzung des Stadrats 15.07.1987, Office of the Mayor, Nuremberg Town Hall; *NN* 'Kein Einkaufszentrum in der Kongresshalle', 15.7.1987.
56 Dietzfelbinger and Liedtke 2004: 113.
57 Neumann 2000: 193.
58 Korrek *et al.* 2001.
59 Conference documents in StAN F7/I 860.

60 *NN* 'Den Nachgeborenen stets zur Mahnung', 11.07.1988.
61 *NN* 'Deutsches Erbe', 11.07.1988; *NN* 'Den Nachgeborenen stets zur Mahnung', 11.07.1988; *NN* 'Die NS-Erblast', 9.07.1988.
62 *NN* 'Ein blosses Stehenlassen genügt nicht', 03.12.1988.
63 SPD *Denkschrift: Über die Nutzung des Bauten des ehemaligen NSDAP-Reichspartei-tagsgeländes*, January 1989, StAN E52 177.
64 *Überlegungen zum Nürnberg-Image: Plädoyer für eine gemeinsame Imagepflege*, Verkehrs-verein Nürnberg 1988: 3. The report was based on discussions with various organisations, including the Tourism Department, the Press Office, the Trade Fair Society, the city bank and city businesses held the previous year.
65 Ibid.: 2.
66 Ibid.

5 Accompanied witnessing

1 Thomas Brons quoted in *NN* 'Stadt soll Stiftung anregen', 09.09.1989.
2 Kirshenblatt-Gimblett 1998: 1.
3 *NN* 'Stadt soll Stiftung anregen', 09.09.1989.
4 Many works have discussed the growth of interest in the Nazi past in Germany – a development in which generational change and the popular television series *Holocaust*, broadcast in 1979, are usually singled out as especially important. See, for example, Frei 2005; Kansteiner 2006a; Fulbrook 1999.
5 See Jordan 2006; Koshar 2000: Chapter 4.
6 *NN* 'Nazi-Ideologie in Stein', 5.12.1981.
7 Harald Lamprecht '"Vielleicht schämen sich die Leute hier …"', *Nürnberg Heute* 34, July 1983, pp. 2–9, 4.
8 Ibid.: 6.
9 See, for example, Niven 2002, Chapter 1; Herf 1997.
10 Dietzfelbinger 1990: 28.
11 Reported in *NN* 'Tonband-Führung zu NS-Relikten', 10.07.1987.
12 Marcuse 2001.
13 *Nürnberg 1922–1945*, 1990: 1. This is taken from the from the English version, as are the following quotations.
14 In 1983 a small exhibition about 1933 was shown elsewhere instead, Dietzfelbinger and Liedtke 2004: 129.
15 *NN* 'Nazi-Ideologie in Stein', 5.12.1981.
16 *NN* 'Scheitert NS-Ausstellung an Geldmangel?', 25.09.1982.
17 Figure from Dietzfelbinger and Liedtke 2004: 121.
18 *NN* 'Kehrseite der NS-Pracht', 19.11.1984.
19 *NN* 'Die Gewalt verharmlost?', 12.02.1985 – which says it attracted 14,000 visitors; Dietzfelbinger and Liedtke 2004: 121 report 8,000 seeing it.
20 *NN* 'Kontrastreiche Schau 19.11.1994.
21 *NN* 'Die Gewalt verharmlost?', 12.02.1985. The following quotations are also from this.
22 *NAnz* 'Briefe an den "Anzeiger"' 31.01.1985; see also the comments by pupils in *NAnz* 'Die Umfrage', 1.12.1984.
23 Quoted in *NAnz* 'Die NS-Schau im Goldenen Saal bedient sich Propaganda-Methoden', 17.01.1985.
24 E.g. Marcuse 2001; Niven 2002.
25 There is a mass of thoughtful literature on this subject. See, for example, van Alphen 1997; Young 1993, 2000; Liss 1998; Köppen and Scherpe 1997.
26 For discussion, see, for example, Clendinnen 1999; Lang 1999.
27 On the discourse of 'just facts' see Handler and Gable 1997; Marcuse 2001 provides interesting discussion of emotion and education in relation to Dachau, e.g. pp. 390–2; see also Landsberg 2004 Chapter 4.

28 *NN* 'Verkümmert NS-Ausstellung?', 1.7.1988.
29 Ibid.
30 *NN* 'Gästerkord und nazistische Umtriebe', 30.10.1989; and figures provided by staff.
31 *NN* 'Gästerkord und nazistische Umtriebe', 30.10.1989.
32 This is also witnessed at other sites, such as Dachau, on which, see Marcuse 2001.
33 *NN* 'Tonband-Führung zu NS-Relikten', 10.07.1987; and personal communication with Michael Weber.
34 *NN* 'Wegweiser zu den Monumenten der Macht', 21.07.1989.
35 *NN* 'Der Schauplatz macht neugierig', 4/5.06.1988; *NN* 'Die Rede eines Selbstgerechten', 8.06.1988; *NN* 'Symbole der Vernichtung', 7.11.1988.
36 *NN* 'Overkill an der Zeppelintribune', 13.7.1988.
37 *NN* 'NS-Fackel und Flächenbrand 17.07.1987.
38 *NN* 'Die meisten Besucher sind für Fortführung', 24.10.1987.
39 *NN* 'Aktion wider den Ungeist', 7.7.1987; to see some of Helnwein's work see http://www.helnwein.com/.
40 Dietzfelbinger and Liedtke 2004: 140.
41 Exhibition catalogue: Karl Prantl *Steine der Großen Straße*, 16.5–9.6.1991, Kunsthalle Nürnberg. Copy of Eckart Dietzfelbinger.
42 Ibid.
43 *NN* 'Der Diskurs ist eröffnet', 27/28.07.1991.
44 Hermann Glaser 'Rolling Histories', *Plärrer* July/Aug 1991.
45 Quoted in *NZ* 'Blinder Gläser? ',Nr 181, 7.08.1991.
46 Ibid.; and see *NN* 'Kongreßhalle für NS-Kunst', 21.11.1987 for the suggestion, which had been made on a radio programme.
47 *NN* 'Zeichen gegen Mißbrauch von Menschen', 20.12.1996.
48 Hermann Glaser 'Rolling Histories', *Plärrer* July/August 1991.
49 Young 2000: 9.
50 Ibid.
51 Quoted in *NN* 'Redende Steine', 16.5.1991.
52 In Dietzfelbinger and Liedtke 2004: 141.
53 These can be viewed at: www.adbk-nuernberg.de/users/munding/g_nbg.htm.
54 In *NAnz* 'Ironisch-warnender Blick auf die Bauten der Nazis', 24.08.1993.
55 Butler 2007.
56 Quoted in *NAnz* 'Ironisch-warnender Blick auf die Bauten der Nazis', 24.08.1993.
57 E.g. *NZ* 'Tod in Bildern', 26.07.1991; *NN* 'Gewalt der Bilder', 26.07.1991.
58 *NN* 'Begrüßungsgeld bald in der Kongreßhalle', 21.11.1989.
59 Glaser 1989.
60 *NAnz* Interview mit Nürnbergs Kulturreferentin Karla Fohrbeck, 8/9 09 1990.
61 Fohrbeck document presented to the council, dated 10.09.1990, copy of Eckart Dietzfelbinger; p. 1. The following quotations are from this.
62 Ibid.: 2, 4.
63 Ibid.: 6.
64 Ibid.: 5.
65 *NAnz* 'Interview mit Nürnbergs Kulturreferentin Karla Fohrbeck', 8/9 09 1990; see also *NN* 'Ideenskizzen zum NS-Gelände', 29.08.1990.
66 *NN* 'Trotz Zustimmung bleibt die Skepsis', 1/2.09.1990.
67 E.g. *NZ* 'Leistner greift die Kulturreferetin scharf an', 13.09.1990; though she later agreed that it could be continued if necessary.
68 *NN* 'Nürnbergs empfindlicher Punkt', 22.08.1990.
69 Ibid.
70 Ibid.
71 Oberth, Matthias 1995 ' "Ich bemühe mich, das Stigma von Nürnberg zu nehmen": Interview mit Arno Hamburger', *Nürnberg Heute*, pp. 34–6, p. 35.
72 Ibid.

73 Ibid.: 36. Bodemann 2005 is a compelling account of the complexities facing Jews living in postwar Germany.
74 *TZ* 'NS-Entsorgungsstätte Nürnberg?', 17.09.1990.
75 Ibid.
76 Ibid.
77 *NN* 'Trotz Zustimmung bleibt die Skepsis', 1/2.09.1990.
78 *TZ* 'NS-Entsorgungsstätte Nürnberg?', 17.09.1990.
79 Fohrbeck document presented to the council, dated 10.09.1990, copy of Eckart Dietzfelbinger; p. 8, p. 3.
80 *NZ* 'Ratlosigkeiten', 15.09.1990.
81 'Der braune Flecke auf Nürnbergs weisser Weste', *PAN*, Feb 1991.
82 Centrum Industriekultur 1992.
83 Ogan and Weiss 1992.
84 Mathias Hennig, *Dokumentationspark Reichsparteitagsgelände* 1994 Diplomarbeit, Nürnberg Fachhochschule (Eckart Dietzfelbinger copy). See also *NN* 'Konzept wider das Vergessen', 4.2.1994; and '… der Schmerz spurbar machen …', interview with Mathias Hennig in *Sign* magazine (date unclear).
85 Julius H. Mihm, *De-Komposition Reichsparteitagsgelände Nürnberg*, Diplomarbeit, Fachbereich Architektur, Universität Hannover, 1993 (Eckart Dietzfelbinger copy).
86 Discussion of 19.05.1994 in Pedagogical Institute, original minutes (Eckart Dietzfelbinger copy). The following quotations are from this.
87 *NAnz* 'Freizeitpark – eine traumhafte Idee', 7.3.1991.

6 Cosmopolitan memory in the City of Human Rights

1   Dietzfelbinger and Liedtke 2004: 8.
2   Weiss 1992: 233.
3   Sonnenberger interview with author in 2000. The plans for the new documentation centre were also set out in various documents and official statements, e.g. Franz Sonnenberger 1998, *Faszination und Gewalt. Leitlinien für der neuen Dauerausstellung des Dokumentationszentrums Reichsparteitagsgelände*, and Museen der Stadt Nürnberg, *Dokumentationszentrum Reichsparteitagsgelände Nürnberg. Denkschrift zur Auseinandersetzung mit dem steinernen Erbe der nationalsozialistischen Gewaltherrschaft*, 1996; documents provided by Franz Sonnenberger. For a wider account of his ideas about the organisation and tasks of Nuremberg museums, see Sonnenberger 1998. See also Probst, Volker 'Was bleibt vom Gedenken?', *Plärrer* July 1995, pp. 32–3.
4   Ibid.: 32.
5   Ibid.: 33.
6   Ibid.; see also *NN* ' "Faszination und Gewalt" in achten Jahr ein Renner', 04.08.1992.
7   *NZ* 'Die Nazi-Zeit als dunkler Hintergrund?', 26.10.1996; *NZ* 'Historische Erbschaften darf man nicht ablehnen', 28.06.1997.
8   *NN* 'Breite Zustimmung', 10.01.1997.
9   *NN* 'Überfälliges Signal', 18.06.1997.
10 *NN* 'Geld für NS-Museum', 15.07.1997.
11 *NN* 'Der Bund zieht mit', 14.11.1997; *NN* 'Freistaat unterstützt nationale Aufgabe', 13.02.1998.
12 *NN* 'Licht in das Dunkel einer Epoche', 14/15.06.1997.
13 *NN* 'Angst vor den rechten Winkeln', 23.12.1998.
14 E.g. Jeismann, Michael *FAZ* 'Wie wir den Drachen töteten', 02.11.2001.
15 *NZ* 'Der Nürnberger Stadtrat setzt markante Zeichen', 10.12.1998.
16 Pressemitteilung 'Neues Dokumentationszentrum Reichsparteitagsgelände Nürnberg – eine nationale Aufgabe', 25.08.1999.
17 *Die Zukunft der Vergangenheit: Wie soll die Geschichte des Nationalsozialismus in Museen und Gedenkstätten im 21. Jahrhundert vermittelt werden?* Proceedings from the conference

were published as Museen der Stadt Nürnberg 2000. All translations from this document, including of the title, are from this book, which contains German and English text.

18 Ibid.: 6–7.

19 Levy and Sznaider 2001, 2002.

20 Zelnhefer, Siegfried 1995 'Nürnberger Glücksfälle: eine Straße und ein Preis', *Nürnberg Heute*, pp. 44–9.

21 Peters 2000: 275.

22 Zelnhefer 1995 'Nürnberger Glücksfälle: eine Straße und ein Preis', *Nürnberg Heute*, pp. 44–9, 44.

23 Bott 1995.

24 Peters 2000: 275–6.

25 Ibid.: 279. See also Schneider 1993; this article, describing Karavan's work and the plan for the *Way of Human Rights*, is published in a first collection outlining the plans for the Germanic National Museum. It is worth noting that none of the four prefaces to the book (Bott and Randa 1993) – written by the country's president, Richard von Weizsäcker, interior minister, Rudolf Seiters, minister-president of Bavaria, Max Streibl, and Nuremberg's mayor, Peter Schönlein – even mentions Karavan's sculpture or its possible significance for the city. I am grateful to Dr Irmtraud von Andrian for providing me with a copy of this book.

26 Personal communication with anonymous source. See also the city's website about its human rights activities, in which Karavan's sculpture is acknowledged as the prompt for the other activities: www.menschenrechte.nuernberg.de/.

27 www.menschenrechte.nuernberg.de.

28 www2.nuernberg.de/internet/pr/best_of.html; pp. 13–14.

29 Karavan's address reproduced in Laub and Scheurmann 1995: 20.

30 Bott 1995; note also that the archway echoes an archway in the old city wall at the other end of the street.

31 Ibid.: 88.

32 Levy and Sznaider 2001, 2002.

33 Levy and Sznaider 2002: 88.

34 Robertson 1995.

35 Levy and Sznaider 2004: 173.

36 Levy and Sznaider 2002: 96.

37 Ibid.: 102.

38 This led among other things to the establishing of Holocaust days in various countries, see Macdonald 2005c.

39 Beck and Grande 2007; Giesen 2003. See also Delanty and Rumford 2005: 95–102.

40 Schlesinger and Foret 2006: 69.

41 Kansteiner 2006b: 138.

42 Gregor 2003b: 596.

43 In the end, however, Mayor Scholz attended the opening – antifaschistische Chronik für Nürnberg: www.loester.net/zeittafel2/htm.

44 Gregor 2003b: 596.

45 Ibid.: 596–7.

46 Ibid.

47 Ibid.: 598

48 Gregor 2003b debunks this claim and provides references to other works to support this. For a more sympathetic interpretation see Schöllgen 2002.

49 Dani Karavan and Daniel Jacoby, head of the jury of the Human Rights prize, were highly critical of the fact that the whole report was not published and made a public statement saying that they regarded the award of honorary citizenship to be a 'serious mistake'. Because they nevertheless viewed the work of human rights to be important and had received many letters from citizens asking them not to resign, they decided to continue in this work. See: http://nuernberg.vvn-bda.de/ehrenbuerger.htm and www.loester.net/erkl.

htm. In May 2007, Diehl's hundredth birthday, he donated a million euros to the city, and was officially feted by Mayor Ulrich Maly in a speech in which the latter commented on the allegations against Diehl by saying 'none of us knows what we ourselves would have done': Stadt Nürnberg press release from the Rathaus, http://www2.nuernberg.de/presse/mitteilungen/presse_08453.html.

50 For example, in the Mayor's letter to a local newspaper, *NAnz* 'Diehl ist keine persönliche Schuld angelastet worden', 11.12.1997; or in his introduction to Museen der Stadt Nürnberg 2000.

51 See following chapter and also Macdonald 2005b.

52 Museen der Stadt Nürnberg 1997 *Reichsparteitagsgelände Nürnberg: Kulissen der Gewalt. Projekt eines Dokumentationszentrums zur NS-Geschichte.*

53 Ibid.

54 Ibid.; and the following quotations.

55 Täubrich 2000 interview with author.

56 Dietzfelbinger interview with author in 2000. On the Wehrmacht exhibition see Niven 2000 and Thiele 1996.

57 On the basis of this, for example, they discovered that terms such as *Gauleiter* (the head of a Nazi region) were not understood and, therefore, provided a glossary or in other cases changed how things were expressed (Sonnenberger 2000 interview with author). Though in the final hectic stages of exhibition making aspects of this were lost.

58 Macdonald 2005b.

59 Beier-de Haan 2006: 187; see also Beier-de Haan 2005.

60 See Liss 1998.

61 Billig 1995.

62 Gregor 2003b: 630

63 Franz Sonnenberger offers a complementary, though slightly different, account for the motivation for cutting. According to him, the academics were asked to write the texts to ensure that they would be sufficiently scholarly; but what they produced were too long and so he had to edit them. The result was the same: that not all of what had been hoped to include could in the end be accommodated.

7 Negotiating on the ground(s)

1 Winter and Sivan 2000; see also Bennett (2007) on the work of managing and assembling 'culture' and what he calls 'the working surfaces on the social'; and Macdonald forthcoming on exploring ideas of assemblage in relation to Nuremberg's Nazi heritage.

2 Del Casino and Hanna 2000: 29. Macdonald 2006b, on which this chapter substantially draws, contains further discussion of tour guide literature.

3 Gudehus 2006. See also Katriel 1997 for an in-depth study of tour guide accounts.

4 Hall 1980.

5 du Gay 1997.

6 Handler and Gable 1997; Macdonald 2002b.

7 Askew and Wilk 2002.

8 Bial 2004.

9 E.g. Dahles 2002; Bruner 2005.

10 Schmidt 2002.

11 The section on the conclusion of the tour also states: 'Geschichte für Alle does not want to present a "lesson" from the Rally Grounds and the dealings with them. How you conclude the tour depends on the group and individual opinions/desires/feelings' (GfA 1999: 42).

12 Schmidt 2002.

13 In Hall's terms, what they are seeking is a 'dominant-hegemonic' reading, though as the tours might themselves be seen as counter-dominant-hegemonic (in that when the tours were first begun they were undertaken against the preference of the city and tourism

authorities at that time to ignore the Party Rally Grounds) the terminology seems less appropriate in this case.

14 GfA 1999: 15.
15 Fine and Speer 1984.
16 Speer 1995.
17 GfA 1999: 23.
18 GfA 1999:6.
19 Schmidt 2002.
20 Ogan and Jahn 1996.
21 Brooker and Jermyn 2003: 127.
22 Askew 2002.

8 Visiting difficult heritage

1 E.g. Lennon and Foley 2000: 3; see also Williams 2007 on 'memorial museums'.
2 Figures provided by Documentation Centre of the Former Nazi Party Rally Grounds.
3 As Lennon and Foley note, 'there is … little research available on the significance that such visits have to those who make them' (2000: 4); though for a couple of excellent exceptions see Kugelmass 1992 on Jewish tourism to Poland and Sandell 2007 on visits to the Anne Frank house. There is, however, a considerable body of scholarship theorising tourist motivation in general, much of it developing the classic accounts of Cohen 1970 and MacCannell 1989 – both of which emphasise, to different degrees, modernist quests for authenticity and escaping of routine. Urry's notion of the 'post-tourist' (1990) is a partial critique of the centrality accorded to authenticity in these accounts. Lennon and Foley draw on this earlier work to suggest that what they call 'dark tourism' involves 'anxiety and doubt about the project of modernity' (2000: 11).
4 See Meethan 2001: 153–6.
5 In addition to extensive observational experience, staff at the Dokuzentrum have been carrying out primarily quantitative research on visitors, from which some information below derives.
6 Especially in larger groups some participants would occasionally join or leave part way through, so figures are to some extent inexact.
7 Dokuzentrum figures are that approximately one-third of visitors are from abroad.
8 In my account below, in order not to make the text too cumbersome, I do not provide details about all respondents, particularly where their comments are representative of others' too.
9 Part of John Urry's argument in *The Tourist Gaze* (1990) is that tourism is increasingly blended into other activities. In this case, however, it is the multiple affordances of the site that are especially significant.
10 In research on visiting of the Science Museum in London, 'doing place' was likewise one of what I there called the 'cultural itineraries' of visiting (Macdonald 2002b: Chapter 8).
11 Kugelmass 1992: 401; his argument draws on Connerton 1989.
12 On the importance of family memorial practices see Welzer *et al.* 2002. What is also evident in the ways in which visitors talk is that a visit to an 'actual site' seems to set up a debate for them about the qualities and affect of different sources.
13 For discussion of *Mahnmal* see Chapter 4. Neumann writes the following about the term *Gedenkstätte:* 'The verb *gedanken* means "to commemorate" or "to remember". A *Gedenkstätte* is a kind of extended *Denkmal*. The term could refer to a larger landscaped complex with several different monuments. In most cases, a *Gedenkstätte* includes the display of information, or a museum … The most prominent *Gedenkstätten* in today's Germany are those at the sites of former concentration camps' (2000: 11).
14 Macdonald 2005b.
15 Reither 1996.
16 Rüsen 2005.

17 Lowenthal 1985 traces the history of this way of thinking about the past.
18 Huyssen 2006: 182.
19 Macdonald 2005b; Levy and Sznaider 2001.
20 Macdonald 2005b: 130. Welzer *et al.* 2002 also provide examples of such historical partitioning – accompanied by a blurring together of different periods of history into a generalised 'past'. The following references to comments in visitor books are also in Macdonald 2005b.
21 Hall 1980; and see previous chapter.
22 The argument about victors writing the history also occurred in various comments in the Dokuzentrum visitor books: Macdonald 2005b.
23 Billig 1995.
24 There is further discussion of this in Macdonald 2005b.
25 The use of such language is discussed in Billig 1995.
26 Cf. Hughes 2003.
27 See also Abram 1998.
28 This has implications for assumptions often made in heritage management about visitors necessarily wanting freedom of choice. I also discuss this in Macdonald 2002b: Chapter 8.

9 Unsettling diffcult heritage

1 Collier and Ong 2005.
2 Tsing 2005: 'Cultures are continually co-produced in the interactions I call "friction": the awkward, unequal, unstable, and creative qualities of interconnection across difference', p. 4.
3 See Elisabeth Beck-Gernsheim 1999 for insightful discussion.
4 See note 14, Chapter 1.
5 This was an argument of Hewison's *The Heritage Industry* (1987); and is part of Walter Benjamin's concern over heritage (Buck-Morss 1987: 331).
6 Collier and Ong 2005: 4.
7 Städtebaulicher Ideenwettbewerb für das ehemalige Reichsparteitagsgelände 2001 *Dokumentation*, Auslober: Stadt Nürnberg. See also Baulust 2004 *Positionen: Zum Umgang mit dem ehemaligen Reichsparteitagsgelände*, Nuremberg: Initiative für Architektur und Öffentlichkeit e.V.
8 'Fans shown the "blue card" on how to behave', *Telegraph* 16.06.2006. The Nuremberg authorities were particularly concerned about the likely behaviour of England fans. For this reason they produced a 'blue card' informing fans of the illegality of Nazi insignia among other things. In the event, there were few arrests and the authorities seem to have been relieved about the general behaviour, if not the joke Nazi helmets worn by some fans. 'Police praise England fans', *Guardian* 16.06.2006. Having a photograph in the Hitler podium on the Zeppelin Building seems to have been almost de rigeur for fans, BBC Sport World Cup 2006 blog 'The old and the new in Nuremberg', 22.06.2006.
9 Young 2000: 1–11; quote on p. 9.

REFERENCES

Abram, Simone 1998 'Introduction: anthropological perspectives on local development', in S. Abram and J. Waldren (eds) *Anthropological Perspectives on Local Development*, London: Routledge, pp. 1–17.

Adorno, Theodor 1986 'What does coming to terms with the past mean?', in Geoffrey H. Hartmann (ed.) *Bitburg in Moral and Political Perspective*, Bloomington, IN: Indiana University Press, pp. 114–30.

Alpers, Svetlana 1991 'The museum as a way of seeing', in I. Karp and S.D. Lavine (eds) *Exhibiting Cultures: The Poetics and Politics of Museum Display*, Washington, DC: Smithsonian Institution, pp. 25–32.

Arditti, Rita 1999 *Searching for Life: The Grandmothers of the Plaza de Mayo and the Disappeared Children of Argentina*, Berkeley, CA: California University Press.

Askew, Kelly 2002 'Introduction', in K. Askew and R.R. Wilk (eds) *The Anthropology of Media*, Oxford: Blackwell, pp. 1–13.

Askew, Kelly and Richard R. Wilk (eds) 2002 *The Anthropology of Media*, Oxford: Blackwell.

Assmann, Aleida 2006 *Der lange Schatten der Vergangenheit. Erinnerungskultur und Geschichtspolitik*, Munich: C.H. Beck.

Barthel, Diane 1996 *Historic Preservation: Collective Memory and Historical Identity*, New Brunswick, NJ: Rutgers University Press.

Beck, Ulrich and Edgar Grande 2007 *Cosmopolitan Europe*, Cambridge: Polity.

Beck-Gernsheim, Elisabeth 1999 *Juden, Deutsche und andere Erinnerungslandschaften*, Frankfurt: Suhrkamp.

Beer, Helmut, Thomas Heyden, Christian Koch, Gerd-Dieter Liedtke, Winfried Nerdinger, and Alexander Schmidt 1995 *Bauen in Nürnberg 1933–1945. Architektur und Bauformen im Nationalsozialismus*, Nuremberg: Tümmels Verlag.

Beier-de Haan, Rosmarie 2005 *Erinnerte Geschichte – inszenierte Geschichte. Ausstellungen und Museen in der Zweiten Moderne*, Frankfurt: Suhrkamp.

Beier-de Haan, Rosmarie 2006 'Re-staging histories and identities', in Sharon Macdonald (ed.) *Companion to Museum Studies*, Oxford: Blackwell, pp. 186–97.

Bender, Barbara (1998) *Stonehenge: Making Space*, Oxford: Berg.

Benjamin, Walter 1992 [1968 trans. H. Zohn] *Illuminations*, London: Fontana.

Bennett, Tony 2007 'The work of culture', *Cultural Sociology* 1(1): 33–47.

Benton, Tim 1999 'From the Arengario to the Lictor's Axe: memories of Italian Fascism', in M. Kwint, C. Breward and J. Aynsley (eds) *Material Memories: Design and Evocation*, Oxford: Berg, pp. 199–218.

Berger, Stefan 1997 *The Search for Normality: National Identity and Historical Consciousness in Germany since 1800*, Oxford: Berghahn.

Berlin, B. and P. Kay 1969 *Basic Colour Terms, their Universality and Evolution*, Los Angeles, CA: University of California Press.

Bernett, Hajo 1992 'Albert Speers "Deutsches Stadion" war eine gigantische Fehlkonstruktion', in B. Ogan and W.W. Weiss (eds) *Faszination und Gewalt. Zur politischen Ästhetik des Nationalsozialismus*, Nuremberg: Tümmels Verlag, pp. 205–10.

Bevan, Robert 2006 *The Destruction of Memory: Architecture at War*, London: Reaktion.

Bial, Henry 2004 'Introduction', in H. Bial (ed.) *The Performance Studies Reader*, London: Routledge, pp. 1–9.

Billig, Michael 1995 *Banal Nationalism*, London: Sage.

Bloch, Maurice 1989 [1979] *Ritual, History and Power: Selected Papers in Anthropology*, London: Athlone.

Bodemann, Y. Michal 1999 *In den Wogen der Erinnerung. Jüdische Existenz in Deutschland*, Munich: DTV.

Bodemann, Y. Michal 2005 *A Jewish Family in Germany Today: An Intimate Portrait*, Durham, NC: Duke University Press.

Boswell, David and Jessica Evans (eds) 1999 *Representing the Nation*, London: Routledge.

Bott, Gerhard 1995 'Some thoughts when looking at Dani Karavan's "Way of Human Rights"', in Peter Laub and Konrad Scheurmann (eds) *Straße der Menschenrechte. Dani Karavan*, Bonn: Arbeitskreis selbständiger Kultur Institute e.V., pp. 84–93.

Bott, Gerhard and Sigrid Randa (eds) 1993 *Aufbruch. Der Kartäuserbau und das Museumsforum des Germanischen Nationalmuseums 1993*, Nuremberg: Germanic National Museum.

Boyer, Dominic 2005 *Spirit and System: Media, Intellectuals, and the Dialectic in Modern German Culture*, Chicago, IL: Chicago University Press.

Breglia, Lisa 2006 *Monumental Ambivalence: The Politics of Heritage*, Austin, TX: University of Texas Press.

Brooker, Will and Deborah Jermyn 2003 'The spectator and the audience: Shifts in screen theory', in W. Brooker and D. Jermyn (eds) *The Audience Studies Reader*, London: Routledge, pp. 126–31.

Bruckner, Dietmar 2002 *Was war los in Nürnberg 1950–2000*, Erfurt: Sutton Verlag.

Brumlik, Micha, Hajo Funke and Lars Rensman (eds) 2000 *Unkämpftes Vergessen. Walser Debatte, Holocaust-Mahnmal und neuere deutsche Geschichtspolitik*, Berlin: Das Arabische Buch.

Bruner, Edward M. 2005 *Culture on Tour*, Chicago, IL: University of Chicago Press.

Buck-Morss, Susan 1987 *The Dialectics of Seeing: Walter Benjamin and the Arcades Project*, Cambridge, MA: MIT Press.

Buchli, Victor 1999 *An Archaeology of Socialism*, Oxford: Berg.

Bund Deutsche Architekten 1963 *Denkschrift*.

Bundesamt für die Anerkennung ausländischer Flüchtlinge (ed.) 1999 *Ein Gebäude – viele Namen. Eine Gebäudegeschichte. SS-Kaserne. Merrell-Narracks. Bundesamt*, Nuremberg: Bundesamt für die Anerkennung ausländischer Flüchtlinge.

Burden, H.T. 1967 *The Nuremberg Party Rallies*, London: Pall Mall Press.

Buruma, Ian 2002 [1994] *The Wages of Guilt: Memories of War in Germany and Japan*, London: Phoenix.

Butler, Shelley Ruth 2007 *Contested Representations: Revisiting 'Into the Heart of Africa'*, Peterborough, Ontario: Broadview.

Caplan, Pat 2007 '"Never again": Genocide Memorials in Rwanda', *Anthropology Today* 23(1): 20–2.

Carrier, Peter 2000 'Places, politics and the archiving of contemporary memory in Pierre Nora's *Les Lieux de Mémoire*', in S. Radstone (ed.) *Memory and Methodology*, Oxford: Berg, pp. 37–57.

Carrier, Peter 2005 *Holocaust Monuments and National Memory: France and Germany since 1989*, Oxford: Berghahn.

Centrum Industriekultur Nürnberg 1992 *Kulissen der Gewalt. Das Reichsparteitagsgelände in Nürnberg*, Nuremberg: Hugendubel.

Clendinnen, Inga 1999 *Reading the Holocaust*, Cambridge: Cambridge University Press.

Clifford, James 1988 *The Predicament of Culture: Twentieth-Century Ethnography, Literature, and Art*, Cambridge, MA: Harvard University Press.

Clifford, James 1997 *Routes: Travel and Translation in the late Twentieth Century*, Cambridge, MA: Harvard University Press.

Cohen, Erik 1970 'A phenomenology of tourist experiences', *Sociology* 13(2): 179–201.

Collier, Stephen J. and Aihwa Ong 2005 'Global assemblages, anthropological problems', in A. Ong and S.J. Collier (eds) *Global Assemblages: Technology, Politics, and Ethics as Anthropological Problems*, Oxford: Blackwell, pp. 3–21.

Connerton, Paul 1989 *How Societies Remember*, Cambridge: Cambridge University Press.

Cook, Susan E. 2004 'The politics of preservation in Rwanda', in S.E. Cook (ed.) *New Perspectives on Genocide: Cambodia and Rwanda*, New Haven, CT: Yale Centre for International Area Studies, pp. 293–311.

Coombes, Annie E. 2003 *History after Apartheid: Visual Culture and Public Memory in a Democratic South Africa*, Durham, NC: Duke University Press.

Crane, Susan A. 2004 'Memory, distortion, and history in the museum', in B. Carbonell (ed.) *Museum Studies: An Anthology of Contexts*, Oxford: Blackwell, pp. 318–34.

Dahles, Heidi 2002 'The politics of tour guiding: Image management in Indonesia', *Annals of Tourism Research* 29(3): 783–800.

Dann, Graham and A. V. Seaton 2001 *Slavery, Contested Heritage and Thanatourism*, New York: Haworth Hospitality Press.

Davidson, M. 2005 'A world of evil and hope amid the dark pines' *The Observer* 13 March.

Davis, John 1989 'The social relations of the production of history', in E.Tonkin, M.McDonald and M.Chapman (eds) *History and Ethnicity*, London: Routledge, pp. 103–20.

DeLanda, Manuel 2006 *A New Philosophy of Society*, London: Continuum.

Delanty, Gerard and Chris Rumford 2005 *Rethinking Europe: Social Theory and the Implications of Europeanization*, London: Routledge.

del Casino Jr, Vincent and Stephen P. Hanna 2000 'Representations and identities in tourism map spaces', *Progress in Human Geography* 24(1): 23–46.

Deleuze, Gilles and Felix Guattari 1987 *A Thousand Plateaus*, Minneapolis, MN: University of Minnesota Press.

Dietzfelbinger, Eckart 1990 *Der Umgang der Stadt Nürnberg mit dem früheren Reichsparteitags-gelände*, Beiträge zur politischen Bildung 9, Nuremberg: Pädagogisches Institut.

Dietzfelbinger, Eckart 1994 'Reichsparteitagsgelände Nürnberg. Restaurieren – Nutzen – Vermitteln', in W. Durth and W. Nerdinger (eds) *Architektur und Städtebau der 30er/40er Jahre. Ergebnisse der Fachtagung in München 1993, des Deutschen Nationalkomitees für Denkmalschutz*, Vol. 48, Bonn: Deutschen Nationalkomitees für Denkmalschutz, pp. 64–73.

Dietzfelbinger, Eckart and Gerhard Liedtke 2004 *Nürnberg – Ort der Massen. Das Reichs-parteitagsgelände. Vorgeschichte und schwieriges Erbe*, Berlin: Ch. Links.

Doosry, Yasmin 2002 *'Wohlauf, laßt uns eine Stadt und einen Turm bauen …'. Studien zum Reichsparteitagsgelände in Nürnberg*, Berlin: Ernst Wasmuth Verlag Tübingen.

Douglas, Mary 1966 *Purity and Danger: An Analysis of the Concepts of Pollution and Taboo*, London: Routledge and Kegan Paul.

Dubin, Steven C. 2006a *Transforming Museums: Mounting Queen Victoria in a Democratic South Africa*, Basingstoke: Palgrave Macmillan.

Dubin, Steven C. 2006b 'Incivilities in civil(-ized) places: "culture wars" in comparative perspective', in Sharon Macdonald (ed.) *Companion to Museum Studies*, Oxford: Blackwell, pp. 477–93.

Dudek, Peter 1992 ' "Vergangenheitsbewältigung" zur Problematik eines umstrittenen Begriffs', *Aus Politik und Zeitgeschichte*, no. 1–2.

Duffy, Terence M. 2001 'Museums of "human suffering" and the struggle for human rights', *Museum International* 53(1): 10–16.

du Gay, Paul (ed.) 1997 *Production of Culture/Cultures of Production*, Milton Keynes: The Open University/London: Sage.

Durkheim, Émile 1965 [orig. 1915] *The Elementary Forms of the Religious Life*, New York: Free Press.

Edensor, Tim 1998 *Tourists at the Taj: Performance and Meaning at a Symbolic Site*, London: Routledge.

Edkins, Jenny 2003 *Trauma and the Memory of Politics*, Cambridge: Cambridge University Press.

Fein, Egon 2002 *Hitlers Weg nach Nürnberg*, Nuremberg: Verlag Nürnberger Press.

Fine, Elisabeth C. and Jean Haskell Speer 1985 'Tour guide performances as sight sacralization', *Annals of Tourism Research* 12: 73–95.

Fine, Gary A. 2001 *Difficult Reputations: Collective Memories of the Evil, Inept and Controversial*, Chicago, IL: Chicago University Press.

Fischer, Bernhard 1996 'Sanierung der Großen Straße in Nürnberg', *Bautechnik* 72(7): 443–6.

Forty, Adrian 1999 'Introduction', in Adrian Forty and Susanne Küchler (eds) *The Art of Forgetting*, Oxford: Berg, pp. 1–18.

Frei, Norbert 1999 [orig. 1996] *Vergangenheitspolitik. Die Anfänge der Bundesrepublik und die NS-Vergangenheit*, Munich: Deutscher Taschenbuch Verlag.

Frei, Norbert 2005 *1945 und Wir*, Munich: C.H. Beck.

Friedrich, Jörg 2002 *Der Brand. Deutschland im Bombenkrieg, 1940–1945*, Munich: Propyläen.

Fulbrook, Mary 1999 *German National Identity after the Holocaust*, Oxford: Blackwell.

Geertz, Clifford 1983 *Local Knowledge*, New York: Basic Books.

Gell, Alfred 1998 *Art and Agency: An Anthropological Theory*, Oxford: Oxford University Press.

Gerstenblith, Patty 2006 'Museum practice: legal issues', in S. Macdonald *Companion to Museum Studies*, Oxford: Blackwell, pp. 442–56.

Geschichte für Alle 1995 *Nürnberg-Langwasser. Geschichte eines Stadtteils*, Nuremberg: Sandberg Verlag.

Geschichte für Alle e.V. 1999 *Das ehemalige Reichsparteitagsgelände in Nürnberg*, 5th version, Nuremberg: Geschichte für Alle.

Geschichte für Alle 2002a *Architektur Nürnberg*, Nuremberg: Sandberg Verlag.

Geschichte für Alle 2002b *Geländebegehung. Das Reichsparteitagsgelände in Nürnberg*, 2nd edition, Nuremberg: Sandberg Verlag.

Gibson, James 1986 *The Ecological Approach to Visual Perception*, Hillsdale, NJ: Lawrence Erlbaum Associates.

Gieryn, Thomas F. 2002 'What buildings do', *Theory and Society* 31(1): 35–74.

Giesen, Bernhard 2003 'The collective identity of Europe: constitutional practice of community memory', in W. Spohn and A. Triandafyllidou (eds) *Europeanisation, National Identities and Migration: Changes in Boundary Constructions between Western and Eastern Europe*, London: Routledge, pp. 21–35.

Giordano, Ralph 1987 *Die zweite Schuld oder von der Last ein Deutscher zu sein*, Munich: Knaur.

Glaeser, Andreas 2000 *Divided in Unity: Identity, Germany, and the Berlin Police*, Chicago, IL: University of Chicago Press.

Glaser, Hermann 1989 'Rumpelkammern im deutschen Kolosseum', *Rheinischer Merkur*, 16 June.

Glaser, Hermann 1992 'Nürnberg: eine Stadt wie jede andere? Die Last, als Symbol des Nationalsozialismus zu gelten', in Bernd Ogan and Wolfgang Weiss (eds) *Faszination und Gewalt. Zur politischen Ästhetik des Nationalsozialismus*, Nuremberg: W. Tümmels Verlag, pp. 39–40.

Goldhagen, Daniel 1996 *Hitler's Willing Executioners: Ordinary Germans and the Holocaust*, London: Little, Brown and Company.

Graham, Brian, Greg Ashworth and John Tunbridge 2000 *A Geography of Heritage: Power, Culture and Economy*, London: Hodder.

Grass, Günther 2004 [orig. 2002] *Im Krebsgang. Eine Novelle*, Munich: Deutscher Taschenbuch Verlag.

Grasskamp, Walter 1990 'The de-nazification of Nazi art: Arno Breker and Albert Speer today', in B. Taylor and W. van der Will (eds) *The Nazification of Art: Art, Design, Music, Architecture and Film in the Third Reich*, Winchester: The Winchester Press, pp. 231–48.

Grayling, A.C. 2006 *Among the Dead Cities: Was the Allied Bombing of Civilians in WWII a Necessity or a Crime?*, London: Bloomsbury.

Gregor, Neil 2003a '"Is he alive, or long since dead?": loss, absence and remembrance in Nuremberg, 1945–1956', *German History*, 21(2): 183–203.

Gregor, Neil 2003b '"The illusion of remembrance": the Karl Diehl affair and the memory of national socialism in Nuremberg, 1945–1999', *The Journal of Modern History* 75(3): 590–633.

Gregor, Neil, 2009, *Haunted City: Nuremberg and the Nazi Past*, Cambridge, MA: Yale University Press.

Gudehus, Christian 2006 *Dem Gedächtnis Zuhören. Erzählungen über NS-Verbrechen und ihre Representation in deutschen Gedenkstätten*, Essen: Klartext.

Hall, Stuart 1980 'Encoding/decoding', in Stuart Hall, Dorothy Hobson, Andrew Lowe and Paul Willis (eds) *Culture, Media and Language*, London: Hutchinson, pp. 128–38.

Hallam, Elizabeth and Jenny Hockey 2001 *Death, Memory and Material Culture*, Oxford: Berg.

Hambrecht, Rainer 1976 *Der Aufstieg der NSDAP in Mittel- und Oberfranken, 1925–1933*, Nuremberg: Nürnberger Werkstücke zur Stadt- und Landesgeschichte.

Handelman, Don 1998 [orig.1990] *Models and Mirrors: Towards an Anthropology of Public Events*, Oxford: Berghahn.

Handler, Richard 1988 *Nationalism and the Politics of Culture in Quebec*, Madison, WI: University of Wisconsin Press.

Handler, Richard and Eric Gable 1997 *The New History in an Old Museum*, Durham, NC: Duke University Press.

Harvey, David 2003 'The city as body politic', in Jane Schneider and Ida Susser (eds) *Wounded Cities: Destruction and Reconstruction in a Globalized World*, Oxford: Berg, pp. 25–44.

Hayner, Priscilla 2001 *Unspeakable Truths: Confronting State Terror and Atrocity*, London: Routledge.

Heigl, Peter 2003 *Die US-Armee in Nürnberg auf Hitlers "Reichsparteitagsgelände"/The U.S. Army in Nuremberg on Hitler's Nazi Party Rally Grounds*, Nuremberg: Documentation Centre of the Nazi Party Rally Grounds.

216

Herf, Jeffrey 1997 *Divided Memory: The Nazi Past in the two Germanys*, Cambridge, MA: Harvard University Press.

Hertz, Robert 2006 [1960] *Death and the Right Hand*, London: Routledge.

Herzfeld, Michael 1991 *A Place in History: Social and Monumental Time in a Cretan Town*, Cambridge, MA: Princeton University Press.

Hewison, Robert 1987 *The Heritage Industry*, London: Methuen.

Hewitt, Andrew 1993 *Fascist Modernism: Aesthetics, Politics and the Avant-Garde*, Stanford, CA: Stanford University Press.

Heyden, Thomas 1995 'Ludwig Ruff (1878–1934): "Des Führers zweiter Baumeister" ', in H. Beer *et al. Bauen in Nürnberg 1933–1945. Architektur und Bauformen im Nationalsozialismus*, Nuremberg: Tümmels Verlag, pp. 180–203.

Hochschild, Adam 1998 *King Leopold's Ghost: A Story of Greed, Terror and Heroism in Colonial Africa*, New York: Mifflin.

Hochschild, Adam 2005 'A monument to denial', *Los Angeles Times*, 2 March.

Hoelscher, Steven 2006 'Heritage', in S. Macdonald *Companion to Museum Studies*, Oxford: Blackwell, pp. 198–218.

Horton, James Oliver and Johanna C. Kardux 2004 'Slavery and the contest for national heritage in the United States and the Netherlands', *American Studies International*, 42(2&3): 51–74.

Hughes, Rachel 2003 'The abject artefacts of memory: photographs from Cambodia's genocide', *Media, Culture and Society* 21(1): 23–44.

Hughes, Rachel 2004 'Memory and sovereignty in post-1979 Cambodia: Choeung Ek and local genocide memorials', in S.E. Cook (ed.) *New Perspectives on Genocide: Cambodia and Rwanda*, New Haven, CT: Yale Centre for International Area Studies, pp. 269–92.

Hughes, Robert 2003 'Albert Speer: size matters', *Visions of Space* [television documentary] BBC2.

Huyssen, Andreas 1995 *Twighlight Memories: Marking Time in a Culture of Amnesia*, London: Routledge.

Huyssen, Andreas 2003 *Present Pasts: Urban Palimpsests and the Politics of Memory*, Stanford, CA: Stanford University Press.

Huyssen, Andreas 2006 'Air war legacies: from Dresden to Baghdad', in Bill Niven (ed.) *Germans as Victims*, Basingstoke: Palgrave, pp. 181–93.

Jaskot, Paul B. 2000 *The Architecture of Oppression: The SS, Forced Labor and the Nazi Monumental Building Economy*, London and New York: Routledge.

Jeismann, Karl-Ernst 1985 *Geschichte als Horizont der Gegenwart. Über den Zusammenhang von Vergangenheitsdeutung, Gegenwartsverständnis und Zukunftsperspektive*, Paderborn: F. Schörnagh.

Jeismann, Michael (ed.) 1999 *Mahnmal Mitte. Eine Kontroverse*, Cologne: DuMont.

Jeismann, Michael 2001 *Auf Wiedersehen Gestern. Die deutsche Vergangenheit und die Politik von Morgen*, Stuttgart and Munich: Deutsche Verlags-Anstalt.

Jordan, Jennifer A. 2006 *Structures of Memory: Understanding Urban Change in Berlin and Beyond*, Stanford, CA: Stanford University Press.

Kansteiner, Wulf 2002 'Finding meaning in memory: a methodological critique of collective memory studies', *History and Theory* 41(May): 179–97.

Kansteiner, Wulf 2006a *In Pursuit of German Memory: History, Television, and Politics after Auschwitz*, Athens, OH: Ohio University Press.

Kansteiner, Wulf 2006b 'Losing the war, winning the memory battle: The legacy of Nazism, World War II, and the Holocaust in the Federal Republic of Germany', in R.N. Lewbow, W. Kansteiner and C. Fogu (eds) *The Politics of Memory in Postwar Europe*, Durham, NC: Duke University Press, pp. 102–46.

Kaplan, Flora E.S. 2006 'Making and remaking national identities', in Sharon Macdonald (ed.) *Companion to Museum Studies*, Oxford: Blackwell, pp. 152–69.

Karp, Ivan, Corinne A. Kratz, Lynn Szwaja and Tomás Ybarra-Frausto (eds) 2006 *Museum Frictions: Public Cultures/Global Transformations*, Durham, NC: Duke University Press.

Kaschuba, Wolfgang 2002 'Scars as tattoos', unpublished paper presented in New York.

Katriel, Tamar 1997 *Performing the Past: A Study of Israeli Settlement Museums*, Mahwah, NJ: Lawrence Erlaum Associates.

Kauders, Anthony D. 2003 'History as censure:"Repression" and "philo-Semitism" in postwar Germany', *History and Memory* 15(1): 97–122.

Kershaw, I. 1998 *Hitler: 1889–1936*, Harmondsworth: Penguin.

Kettenacker, Lothar 1997 *Germany since 1945*, Oxford: Oxford University Press.

King, Alex 1999 'Remembering and forgetting in the public memorials of the Great War', in A. Forty and S. Küchler (eds) *The Art of Forgetting*, pp. 147–69.

Kirshenblatt-Gimblett, Barbara 1998 *Destination Culture: Tourism, Museums, Heritage*, Berkeley, CA: University of California Press.

Kirshenblatt-Gimblett, Barbara 2006 'World heritage and cultural economics', in Ivan Karp, *et al.* (eds) *Museum Frictions*, Durham, NC: Duke University Press, pp. 161–202.

Knischewski, Gerd and Ulla Spittler 1997 'Memories of the Second World War and national identity in Germany', in M. Evans and K. Lunn (eds) *War and Memory in the Twentieth Century*, Oxford: Berg, pp. 239–54.

Koch, Christian 1995 'Bauen in Nürnberg 1933–45', in H. Beer *et al.* (eds) *Bauen in Nürnberg 1933–1945. Architektur und Bauformen im Nationalsozialismus*, Nuremberg: Tümmels Verlag, pp. 14–113.

König, Helmut 2003 *Die Zukunft der Vergangenheit. Der Nationalsozialismus im politischen Bewußtsein der Bundesrepublik*, Frankfurt: Fischer.

Köppen, Manuel and Klaus R. Scherpe (eds) 1997 *Bilder des Holocaust. Literatur – Film – Bildende Kunst*, Cologne: Böhlau.

Korrek, Norbert, Justus H. Ulbrecht and Christiane Wolf 2001 *Das Gauforum in Weimar. Ein Erbe des Dritten Reiches*, Weimar: Bauhaus University of Weimar University Press.

Koselleck, Reinhart 1999 'Stellen uns die Toten eine Termin?', in M. Jeismann (ed.) *Mahnmal Mitte. Eine Kontroverse*, Cologne: DuMont, pp. 44–53.

Kosfeld, Anne G. 2001 'Nürnberg', in E. François and H. Schulze (eds) *Deutsche Erinnerungsorte I*, Munich: C.H. Beck Verlag, pp. 68–85.

Koshar, Rudy 1998 *Germany's Transient Pasts: Preservation and National Memory in the Twentieth Century*, Chapel Hill, NC: University of North Carolina Press.

Koshar, Rudy 2000 *From Monuments to Traces: Artifacts of German Memory, 1870–1990*, Berkeley, CA: University of California Press.

Kress, Gunther and Theo van Leeuwen 2001 *Multimodal Discourse: The Modes and Media of Contemporary Communication*, London: Arnold.

Kress, Gunther and Theo van Leeuwen 2006 *Reading Images: The Grammar of Visual Design*, 2nd edition, London: Routledge.

Küchler, Susanne 1999 'The place of memory', in A. Forty and S. Küchler (eds) *The Art of Forgetting*, Oxford: Berg, pp. 53–72.

Kugelmass, Jack 1992 'The rites of the tribe: American Jewish tourism in Poland', in Ivan Karp, Christine Mullen Kreamer and Steven D. Lavine (eds) *Museums and Communities: The Politics of Public Culture*, Washington, DC WA: Smithsonian Institution Press, pp. 382–427.

Ladd, Brian 1997 *The Ghosts of Berlin: Confronting German History in the Urban Landscape*, Chicago, IL: Chicago University Press.

Landsberg, Alison 2004 *Prosthetic Memory: The Transformation of American Memory in the Age of Mass Culture*, New York: Columbia University Press.

Lang, Berel 1999 *The Future of the Holocaust: Between History and Memory*, Ithaca, NY: Cornell University Press.

Latour, Bruno 1993 *We Have Never Been Modern*, trans. C. Porter, Hemel Hempstead: Harvester Wheatsheaf.

Latour, Bruno 2005 *Reassembling the Social*, Oxford: Oxford University Press.

Laub, Peter and Konrad Scheurmann (eds) 1995 *Straße der Menschenrechte. Dani Karavan*, Bonn: Arbeitskreis selbständiger KulturInstitute e.V.

Law, John 1986 'On the methods of long distance control: vessels, navigation and the Portuguese route to India', in J. Law (ed.) *Power, Action and Belief: A New Sociology of Knowledge?*, London: Routledge and Kegan Paul.

Lefebvre, Henri 1991 *The Production of Space*, Oxford: Blackwell.

Lennon, John and Malcolm Foley 2000 *Dark Tourism: The Attraction of Death and Disaster*, London: Thomson.

Levy, Daniel and Nathan Sznaider 2001, *Erinnerung im globalen Zeitalter. Der Holocaust*, Frankfurt: Suhrkamp.

Levy, Daniel and Nathan Sznaider 2002 'Memory unbound: The Holocaust and the formation of cosmopolitan memory', *European Journal of Social Theory* 5(1): 87–106.

Levy, Daniel and Nathan Sznaider 2004 'The institutionalization of cosmopolitan morality: the Holocaust and human rights', *Journal of Human Rights* 3(2): 143–57.

Linenthal, Edward and Tom Engelhardt (eds) 1996 *History Wars: The Enola Gay and Other Battles for the American Past*, New York: Metropolitan.

Liss, Andrea 1998 *Trespassing through Shadows: Memory, Photography and the Holocaust*, Minneapolis, MN: University of Minnesota Press.

Littler, Jo 2005 'Introduction: British heritage and the legacies of "race"', in J. Littler and R. Naidoo (eds) *The Politics of Heritage: The Legacies of Race*, London: Routledge, pp. 1–19.

Littler, Jo and Roshi Naidoo (eds) 2005 *The Politics of Heritage: The Legacies of Race*, London: Routledge.

Lloyd, David W. 1998 *Battlefield Tourism: Pilgrimage and the Commemoration of the Great War in Britain, Australia and Canada, 1919–1939*, Oxford: Berg.

Lowenthal, David 1985 *The Past is a Foreign Country*, Cambridge: Cambridge University Press.

Lowenthal, David 1998 [1996] *Possessed by the Past: the Heritage Crusade and the Spoils of History*, New York: The Free Press.

Lübbeke, Wolfram 1987 'Denkmäler des Übertreffens. Das Reichsparteitagsgelände in Nürnberg als Denkmal und Gedenkstätte', *Jahrbuch der Bayerischen Denkmalpflege* 41: 210–22.

Lynch, Kevin 1976 *What Time is this Place?*, Cambridge, MA: MIT Press.

MacCannell, Dean 1989 [1976] *The Tourist: A New Theory of the Leisure Class*, 2nd edition, New York: Schocken Books.

Macdonald, Sharon 1997a *Reimagining Culture: Histories, Identities and the Gaelic Renaissance*, Oxford: Berg.

Macdonald, Sharon 1997b 'A people's story? Heritage, identity and authenticity', in C. Rojek and J. Urry (eds) *Touring Cultures: Transformations of Travel and Theory*, London: Routledge, pp. 155–75.

Macdonald, Sharon (ed.) 2000 *Approaches to European Historical Consciousness: Reflections and Provocations*, Hamburg: Körber.

219

Macdonald, Sharon 2002a 'Trafficking in history: multitemporal perspectives', in 'Shifting grounds: Experiments in doing Eethnography', special issue of *Anthropological Journal on European Cultures*, 11: 93–116.

Macdonald, Sharon 2002b *Behind the Scenes at the Science Museum*, Oxford: Berg.

Macdonald, Sharon 2002c 'Museums and identities: materializing German culture', in A. Phipps (ed.) *Contemporary German Cultural Studies*, London: Arnold, pp. 117–31.

Macdonald, Sharon 2005a 'Enchantment and its dilemmas: the museum as a ritual site', in M. Bouquet and N. Porto (eds) *Science, Magic and Religion: The Ritual Processes of Museum Magic*, Oxford: Berghahn, pp. 209–27.

Macdonald, Sharon 2005b 'Accessing audiences: visiting visitor books', *Museum and Society* 3(3): 119–36.

Macdonald, Sharon 2005c 'Commemorating the Holocaust: the ethics of national identity in the twenty-first century', in J. Littler and R. Naidoo (eds) *The Politics of Heritage: The Legacies of Race*, London: Routledge, pp. 49–68.

Macdonald, Sharon 2006a 'Undesirable heritage: Fascist material culture and historical consciousness in Nuremberg', *International Journal of Heritage Studies* 12(1): 9–28.

Macdonald, Sharon 2006b 'Mediating heritage: tour guides at the former Nazi Party Rally Grounds, Nuremberg', *Tourist Studies* 6(2): 119–38.

Macdonald, Sharon 2006c 'Words in stone? Agency and identity in a Nazi Landscape', *Journal of Material Culture* 11(1/2): 105–26.

Macdonald, Sharon 2007 'Schwierige Geschichte – Umstrittene Austellungen', *Museumskunde* 72(1–07): 75–84.

Macdonald, Sharon forthcoming 'Reassembling Nuremberg', *Culture and Economy*.

MacFarlane, Alan 2007 *Japan through the Looking Glass*, London: Profile.

Maier, Charles S. 1997 [1988] *The Unmasterable Past: History, Holocaust, and German National Identity*, Cambridge, MA: Harvard University Press.

Marcuse, Harald 2001 *Legacies of Dachau: The Uses and Abuses of a Concentration Camp, 1933–2001*, Cambridge: Cambridge University Press.

Markus, Thomas A. 1993 *Buildings and Power: Freedom and Control in the Origin of Modern Building Types*, London: Routledge.

Meethan, Kevin 2001 *Tourism in Global Society: Place, Culture, Consumption*, Basingstoke: Palgrave.

Michman, Dan (ed.) 2002 *Remembering the Holocaust in Germany, 1945–2000*, New York: Peter Lang.

Miller, Daniel 2005 'Materiality: an introduction', in D. Miller (ed.) *Materiality*, Durham, NC and London: Duke University Press, pp. 1–50.

Mistzal, Barbara A. 2003 *Theories of Social Remembering*, Maidenhead: Open University Press/ McGraw-Hill Education.

Mitscherlich, Alexander and Margarete Mitscherlich 1967 *Die Unfähigkeit zu trauern. Grundlagen kollektiven Verhaltens*, Munich: Piper.

Moeller, Robert G. 2001 *War Stories: The Search for a Usable Past in the Federal Republic of Germany*, Berkeley, CA: University of California Press.

Museen der Stadt Nürnberg 1999 *Projekt: Dokumentationszentrum Reichsparteitagsgelände*, Nuremberg: Museen der Stadt Nürnberg.

Museen der Stadt Nürnberg 2000 *Die Zukunft der Vergangenheit. Dokumentationszentrum Reichsparteitagsgelände*, Nuremberg: Museen der Stadt Nürnberg.

Nash, Douglas 1995 *The Politics of Space*, New York: Peter Lang.

Needham, Rodney (ed.) 1974 *Right and Left: Essays on Dual Symbolic Classification*, Chicago, IL: University of Chicago Press.

Nerdinger, Winfried 1995 'Bauen im Nationalsozialismus', in H. Beer *et al.* (eds) *Bauen in Nürnberg 1933–1945. Architektur und Bauformen im Nationalsozialismus*, Nuremberg: Tümmels Verlag, pp. 10–13.

Neumann, Klaus 2000 *Shifting Memories. The Nazi Past in the New Germany*, Ann Arbor, MI: The University of Michigan Press.

Niethammer, Lutz 1982 *Die Mitläuferfabrik. Die Entnazifizierung am Beispiel Bayerns*, Berlin and Bonn: Dietz Verlag.

Niven, Bill 2002 *Facing the Nazi Past: United Germany and the Legacy of the Third Reich*, London: Routledge.

Niven, Bill 2006a 'The GDR and memory of the bombing of Dresden', in Bill Niven (ed.) *Germans as Victims*, Basingstoke: Palgrave Macmillan, pp. 109–29.

Niven, Bill (ed.) 2006b *Germans as Victims*, Basingstoke: Palgrave Macmillan.

Nobles, Melissa 2003 'Official apologies and their effects on political membership in democracies', paper presented at American Political Science Association Meeting, Philadelphia.

Novick, Peter 1999 *The Holocaust and Collective Memory: The American Experience*, London: Bloomsbury.

Ogan, Bernd 1992 'Faszination und Gewalt – ein Überblick', in B. Ogan and W.W. Weiss (eds) *Faszination und Gewalt. Zur politischen Ästhetik des Nationalsozialismus*, Nuremberg: Tümmels Verlag, pp. 11–36.

Ogan, Bernd and Carlo Jahn 1996 *'Aber Hitler hat doch …'. Sieben Legenden über das Dritte Reich*, Nuremberg: Pädagogisches Institut.

Ogan, Bernd and Wolfgang W. Weiss (eds) 1992 *Faszination und Gewalt. Zur politischen Ästhetik des Nationalsozialismus*, Nuremberg: Tümmels Verlag.

Olick, Jeffrey K. 2003 'Introduction', in J.K. Olick (ed.) *States of memory: Continuities, Conflicts, and Transformations in National Retrospection*, Durham, NC: Duke University Press, pp. 1–16.

Olick, Jeffrey K. 2005 *In the House of the Hangman: The Agonies of German Defeat, 1943–1949*, Chicago. IL: Chicago University Press.

Olick, Jeffrey K. 2007 *The Politics of Regret: On Collective Memory and Historical Responsibility*, London: Routledge.

Parker Pearson, Mike and Colin Richards 1994 'Ordering the world: perceptions of architecture, space and time', in M. Parker Pearson and C. Richards (eds) *Architecture and Order: Approaches to Social Space*, London: Routledge, pp. 1–37.

Peters, Ursula 2000 'Dani Karavan: Weg der Menschenrechte', in U. Peters with A. Legde (eds) *Moderne Zeiten. Die Sammlungen zum 20. Jahrhundert*, Nuremberg: Germanic National Museum, pp. 275–80.

Petsch, Joachim 1992 'Architektur als Weltanschauung. Die Staats- und Parteiarchitektur im Nationalsozialismus', in B. Ogan and W.W. Weiss (eds) *Faszination und Gewalt. Zur politischen Ästhetik des Nationalsozialismus*, Nuremberg: Tümmels Verlag, pp. 197–204.

Pickard, Robert 2002 'A comparative review of policy for the protection of the architectural heritage of Europe', *International Journal of Heritage Studies* 8(4): 349–63.

Porombka, Stephan and Hilmar Schmundt (eds) 2006 *Böse Orte. Stätten nationalsozialistischer Selbstdarstellung – heute*, Berlin: List.

Puvogel, Ulrike and Martin Stanjowski, with Ursula Graf 1995 *Gedenkstätten für die Opfer des Nationalsozialismus. Eine Dokumentation*, volume 1, 2nd edition, Bonn: Bundeszentrale für politische Bildung.

Quinn, Malcolm 1994 *The Swastika: Constructing the Symbol*, London: Routledge.

Reichel, Peter 1992 ' "Volksgemeinschaft" und Führer-Mythos', in B. Ogan and W.W. Weiss (eds) *Faszination und Gewalt. Zur politischen Ästhetik des Nationalsozialismus*, Nuremberg: Tümmels Verlag, pp. 137–50.

Reichel, Peter 1999 [1995] *Politik mit der Erinnerung. Gedächtnisorte im Streit um die nationalsozialistische Vergangenheit*, Frankfurt: Fischer Verlag.

Reichel, Peter 2001 *Vergangenheitsbewältigung in Deutschland. Die Auseinandersetzung mit der NS-Diktatur von 1945 bis heute*, Munich: C.H. Beck.

Reither, Ingmar 1996 'Das ehemalige Reichsparteitagsgelände in Nürnberg als Excursionsziel: Methodische Ansätze einer schulklassenspezifischen Vermittlungstätigkeit', unpublished first state examination thesis, Friedrich-Alexander University, Erlangen-Nürnberg.

Reither, Ingmar 2000 *'Worte aus Stein' und die Sprache der Dichter. Das Reichsparteitagsgelände als poetische Landschaft*, Nuremberg: Sandberg Verlag.

Rittnar, Carol and John K. Roth 1991 *Memory Offended: The Auschwitz Convent Controversy*, New York: Greenwood.

Robertson, Roland 1995 'Glocalization: time-space and homogeneity-heterogeneity', in M. Featherstone, S. Lash and R. Robertson (eds) *Global Modernities*, London: Sage, pp. 25–44.

Roche, Maurice 2000 *Mega-Events and Modernity: Olympics and Expos in the Growth of Global Culture*, London: Routledge.

Rosenfeld, Gavriel D. 2000 *Munich and Memory: Architecture, Monuments, and the Legacy of the Third Reich*, Berkeley, CA: University of California Press.

Rowlands, Michael 1999 'Remembering to forget: sublimation as sacrifice in war memorials', in A. Forty and S. Küchler (eds) *The Art of Forgetting*, Oxford: Berg, pp. 129–45.

Rüsen, Jörn 1990 *Zeit und Sinn. Strategien historischen Denkens*, Frankfurt a.M.: Fischer.

Rüsen, Jörn 2001 *Geschichtsbewusstseins*, Vienna: Böhlau.

Rüsen, Jörn (ed.) 2002 *Western Historical Thinking: An Intercultural Debate*, Oxford: Berghahn.

Rüsen, Jörn 2005 *History: Narration, Interpretation, Orientation*, Oxford: Berghahn.

Saltzman, Lisa 1999 *Anselm Kiefer and Art after Auschwitz*, Cambridge: Cambridge University Press.

Sandell, Richard 2007 *Museums, Prejudice and the Reframing of Difference*, London: Routledge.

Schieber, Martin 2000 *Nürnberg. Eine illustrierte Geschichte der Stadt*, Munich: C.H. Beck.

Schlesinger, Philip and François Foret 2006 'Political roof and sacred canopy? Religion and the EU constitution', *European Journal of Social Theory* 9(1): 59–81.

Schmidt, Alexander 1995 'Saubere Altstadt', in H. Beer *et al.* (eds) *Bauen in Nürnberg 1933–1945. Architektur und Bauformen im Nationalsozialismus*, Nuremberg: Tümmels Verlag, pp. 130–51.

Schmidt, Alexander 2002 ' "Sind Sie der Führer?" Nationalsozialismus als Thema von Stadt-rundgängen (zum Beispiel in Nürnberg)', in S. Grillmeyer and Z. Ackermann (eds) *Erinnern für die Zukunft. Die nationalsozialistische Vergangenheit als Lernfeld der politischen Jugendbildung*, Schwalbach: Wochenschau Verlag.

Schneider, Ulrich 1993 'Mit dem Herzen sehen: Dani Karavans "Straße der Menschenrechte" ', in G. Bott and S. Randa (eds) *Aufbruch. Der Kartäuserbau und das Museumsforum des Germanischen Nationalmuseums 1993*, Nuremberg: Germanic National Museum, pp. 90–111.

Schöllgen, Gregor 2002 *Diehl. Ein Familienunternehmen in Deutschland, 1902–2002*, Berlin: Propyläen.

Schramm, Georg W. 1988 *Bomben auf Nürnberg. Luftangriffe 1940–1945*, Munich: Hugendubel.

Schramm, Georg W. 1993 'Nürnberg im Fadenkreuz. Bombardierung und Vernichtung', in *Centrum Industriekultur Unterm Hakenkreuz. Alltag in Nürnberg 1933–1945*, Munich: Hugendubel, pp. 194–205.

Scobie, Alex 1990 *Hitler's State Architecture: The Impact of Classical Antiquity*, University Park, PA: Pennsylvania State University Press.

Sebald, W.G. 2003 [orig. German 1999] *On the Natural History of Destruction*, trans. A. Bell, London: Hamish Hamilton.

Sereny, Gitta 1996 [orig. 1995] *Albert Speer: His Battle with Truth*, London: Picador.

Sereny, Gitta 2000 *The German Trauma: Experiences and Reflections 1938–2000*, London: Allen Lane.

Simons, Oliver 1997 'Gedächtnislandschaften, Erinnerungsbilder, Spurensicherung – Nachbilder des Holocaust', in M. Köppen and K.R. Scherpe (eds) *Bilder des Holocaust*, Cologne: Böhlau Verlag, pp. 191–213.

Smith, Laurajane 2006 *The Uses of Heritage*, London: Routledge.

Soane, John V.N. 2002 'Agreeing to differ? English and German conservation practices as alternative models for European notions of the built past', *International Journal of Heritage Studies* 8(3): 267–81.

Sonnenberger, Franz 1998 'Organized diversity: the Nuremberg municipal museums', *Museum International* 50(2): 55–9.

Sontag, Susan 1979 [orig. 1973] *On Photography*, Harmondsworth: Penguin.

Sontag, Susan 1990 [orig. 1974] 'Fascinating fascism', in B. Taylor and W. van der Will (eds) *The Nazification of Art: Art, Design, Music, Architecture and Film in the Third Reich*, Winchester: The Winchester Press, pp. 204–18.

Speer, Albert 1978 *Architektur*, Frankfurt, Berlin, Vienna: Verlag Ullstein GmbH.

Speer, Albert 1995 [1970 trans.] *Inside the Third Reich*, translated by R. and C. Winston, London: Phoenix.

Straub, Jürgen (ed.) 2005 *Narration, Identity and Historical Consciousness*, Oxford: Berghahn.

Sturken, Marita 1997 *Tangled Memories*, Berkeley, CA: University of California Press.

Sturken, Marita and Lisa Cartwright 2001 *Practices of Looking: An Introduction to Visual Culture*, Oxford: Oxford University Press.

Taylor, Charles 1989 *Sources of the Self: The Making of the Modern Identity*, Cambridge: Cambridge University Press.

Thiele, Hans-Günther (ed.) 1997 *Die Wehrmachtaustellung. Dokumentations einer Kontroverse*, Bremen: Edition Temmen.

Till, Karen E. 1999 'Staging the past: landscape design, cultural identity, and *Erinnerungspolitik* at Berlin's *Neue Wache*', *Ecumene* 6: 251–83.

Till, Karen E. 2005 *The New Berlin: Memory, Politics, Place*, Minneapolis, MN: University of Minnesota Press.

Tilley, Chris 2004 *The Materiality of Stone: Explorations in Landscape Phenomenology*, Oxford: Berg.

Tsing, Anna H. 2005 *Friction: An Ethnography of Global Connection*, Princeton, NJ: Princeton University Press.

Tunbridge, J.E. and G.J. Ashworth 1996 *Dissonant Heritage. The Management of the Past as a Resource in Conflict*, Chichester: John Wiley and Sons.

Turner, Victor 1967 *The Forest of Symbols: Aspects of Ndembu Ritual*, Ithaca, NY: Cornell University Press.

Urry, John 1990 *The Tourist Gaze: Leisure and Travel in Contemporary Societies*, London: Sage.

van Alphen, Ernst 1997 *Caught by History. Holocaust Effects in Contemporary Art, Literature and Theory*, Stanford, CA: Stanford University Press.

Virilio, Paul 1989 *War and Cinema: The Logistics of Perception*, trans. P. Camiller, London: Verso.

Wachter, Clemens 1999 *Kultur in Nürnberg 1945–1950. Kulturpolitik, kulturelles Leben und Bild der Stadt zwischen dem Ende der NS-Diktatur und der Prosperität der fünfziger Jahre*, Nuremberg: Stadtarchiv Nürnberg.

Weber, Jürgen 1990 'Vergangenheitsbewältigung', in Wolfgang Benz (ed.) *Legenden, Lügen, Vorurteile. Ein Lexicon zur Zeitgeschichte*, Munich: Saur K.G. Verlag, pp. 180–3.

Weiss, W.W. 1992 '"Ruinen-Werte": Das Nürnberger Reichsparteitagsgelände nach 1945', in B. Ogan and W.W. Weiss (eds) *Faszination und Gewalt. Zur politischen Ästhetik des Nationalsozialismus*, Nuremberg: Tümmels Verlag, pp. 225–40.

Welzer, Harald, Sabine Moller and Karoline Tschugnall 2002 *'Opa war kein Nazi' Nationalsozialismus und Holocaust im Familiengedächtnis*, Frankfurt am Main: Fischer.

Whyte, Iain Boyd 1998 'Modern German architecture', in E. Kolinsky and W. van der Will (eds) *The Cambridge Companion to Modern German Culture*, Cambridge: Cambridge University Press, pp. 282–301.

Williams, Paul 2007 *Memorial Museums: The Global Rush to Commemorate Atrocities*, Oxford: Berg.

Winckler, Lutz 1992 '"Die Meistersinger von Nürnberg". Eine Exilzeitung berichtet über die Nürnberger Parteitage', in B. Ogan and W.W. Weiss (eds) *Faszination und Gewalt. Zur politischen Ästhetik des Nationalsozialismus*, Nuremberg: Tümmels Verlag, pp. 127–34.

Winter, Jay 1995 *Sites of Memory, Sites of Mourning: The Great War in European Cultural History*, Cambridge: Cambridge University Press.

Winter, Jay and Emmanuel Sivan 2000 [1999] 'Setting the framework', in J. Winter and E. Sivan (eds) *War and Remembrance in the Twentieth Century*, Cambridge: Cambridge University Press, pp. 6–39.

Wood, Nancy 1999 *Vectors of Memory: Legacies of Trauma in Postwar Europe*, Oxford: Berg.

Wunder, Thomas 1984 *Das Reichsparteitagsgelände in Nürnberg. Entstehung, Kennzeichen, Wirkung*, Nuremberg: German National Museum.

Yoshida, Takashi 2006 *The Making of 'The Rape of Nanking': History and Memory in Japan, China and the United States*, Oxford: Oxford University Press.

Young, James E. 1993 *The Texture of Memory: Holocaust Memorials and Meaning*, New Haven, CT: Yale University Press.

Young, James E. 2000 *At Memory's Edge: After-Images of the Holocaust in Contemporary Art and Architecture*, New Haven, CT: Yale University Press.

Zeller, Joachim 1996 '"Deutschlands grösste Afrikaner" – Zur Geschichte der Denkmäler für Hermann von Wissmann', *Zeitschrift für Geschichtswissenschaft* 12: 1089–111.

Zelnhefer, Siegfried 1992 'Rituale und Bekenntnisse', in Centrum Industriekultur *Kulissen der Gewalt. Das Reichsparteitagsgelände in Nürnberg*, Munich: Hugendubel, pp. 89–98.

Zelnhefer, Siegfried 2002 *Die Reichsparteitage der NSDAP in Nürnberg*, Nuremberg: Verlag Nürnberger Press.

Zimmerer, Jürgen 2006 'Tony Blairs letzter Coup', *Frankfurter Allgemeine Zeitung*, 30 November, p. 40.

INDEX